THE HIGH PRIESTHOOD OF BEING GAY

THE HIGH PRIESTHOOD OF BEING GAY

JAMES HAGERTY

Library of Congress Control Number: 2012908812
ISBN: Hardcover   978-1-4771-1314-1
               Softcover   978-1-4771-1313-4
               Ebook   978-1-4771-1315-8

This book was printed in the United States of America.

To order additional copies of this book, contact:
Xlibris Corporation
1-888-795-4274
www.Xlibris.com
Orders@Xlibris.com
113300

I gratefully acknowledge Steven Spence
who shared the same journey

CONTENTS

———— ❦ ❧ ————

FORWARD

O Son of Being! With the hands of power I made thee and with the fingers of strength I created thee; and within thee have I placed the essence of My light. Be thou content with it and seek naught else, for my work is perfect and My command is binding.

—*Baha'u'llah*

Posed beside the highway, thumb out and overnight kit underarm, I thought *I'm close to hitting rock bottom.* I had on a Western hat, boots and snug Levi's, a not so subtle cruise getup. I'd left house and vehicle behind, unable to afford gas during a lean unemployed period. The gamble of braving the open highway might tell me something about the meaning of life, particularly my own recently outed one. Like the Prodigal Son, my destination was the family farm in the desert, which in summer could be hellishly hot or in winter harshly cold. A land of extremes.

Since I possessed a philosophic bent, it was also a chance to reflect on deeper meanings, in particular the three "trinities'" that had lately absorbed me. Their possible relation to each other, or lack thereof, formed a sort of Rubric's nine-faceted pyramid. On the primal body or glandular level was Freud's ego, id and superego. On the purely mental, Sartre's in itself, for itself and being for others. And at the lofty Christian apex, somewhat sacrilegiously, Father, Son and Holy Ghost. They overlapped, that was clear, and might well comprise conflicting and irreconcilable categories. How they applied to the gay condition was even foggier and likely insurmountable.

Then there was Oedipus Complex—other than a gay gene or undersized hypothalamus—as a cause of gayness. How did that relate to the fancifully constructed pyramid? I wanted it all to fit neatly into an ontology, the study of the nature of being. Heady stuff for a highwayside cowboy. I hated for my outward appearance to mirror an inner falsehood. But isn't all of life a hall-of-mirrors approximation or an *almost?* An exercise in contradiction?

While hoping my parents would accept, at least tolerate me in my fallen state, a late model Cadillac pulled over. The driver was a sharply dressed man in his late 40's with a quick, rather cunning smile. An unmistakable gleam danced in his eyes. I could tell my cowboy pose fit a fleeting fantasy of the moment.

"Need a ride, pal?"

That part was obvious. "Thanks. Sure could use one. I should tell you I'll be heading east toward the desert at the next interchange."

As I slid into the front seat, the driver leveled a challenging look bordering on lustful. "That can be negotiated," he said with a sly wink. A knee nudged covertly my direction.

I explained I'd fallen on temporary hard times and was trying to reach the family farm near a place called Indio. A nostalgic, take-stock reunion with the folks. Although grateful for the ride, I needed to disembark in less than ten miles.

That seemed to pose no obstacle. He owned a nightclub in Venice Beach and insisted I be his guest. I quickly computed that would involve heading west instead of east at the too-rapidly approaching interchange. The beach was nearly 100 miles in the wrong direction from my intended destination—a bait my wiser self warned me to leave alone. *Satan, or ego-body, stand behind me: Do not yield to temptation.*

The driver wasn't about to give up so easily. With the economy tanked and the Mid East about to blow up, we owed it to each other. Such an opportunity wouldn't come again. *Jump on it*, I told myself. "You're not dressed that way for a Christian Science reading room," he echoed my thoughts with self-important sarcasm.

I let go an uneasy chuckle. The man at the wheel was right. I was dressed for high adventure, not mystic meditation. As an abandoned Air Force base sped by under a shifting, slate-gray sky, I was locked in mortal combat. Could I throw caution to the four winds and take my rescuer up on his bold offer? Out of flattery or loneliness? The prospect of being a hot newcomer at a trendy nightclub?

Damp-palmed, near panic swept over me. I felt myself start to relent. Face it, I rationalized, my parents would be less than thrilled to see me in my financially strapped state. They'd expect a triumphant return, hair nicely combed, decked out in a coat and tie. The proffered temptation would postpone the fact I'd let everyone down, most of all myself, career-wise and about every other wise. I exactly fit the prodigal syndrome.

"Okay why not?" My voice sounded like an echo chamber in a cracked marble mausoleum of the lost and damned. A chauffeured ride to the beach could be exciting, a once in a lifetime opportunity, something I'd later regret not taking. *Jump on it.* "You talked me into it," I said with a constricted gulp in the throat.

"I like your attitude. We'll have a great time. I promise you won't regret it."

"I hope you're right. The beach is a long ways from the family farm. However, I do admit being something of a black sheep."

The arching interchange left inexorably behind, now powerless to claim me, we were soon speeding in the smooth-running, now flying at a near-90-mph Cadillac toward "land's end," beyond which I was certain the Pacific Ocean dropped off to oblivion. Knees nudging closer, then touching and scraping, we spoke little in anticipation of the expected romp in the hay that painted journey's end in lurid colors. In the gay cruise hierarchy that was a given, albeit a risky one. I'd never thought of myself a hustler.

The reckless choice accelerated by degrees through offhand looks and lustful side glances into a mounting premonition of danger. Multi-tiered interchanges increased in frequency at the city's too-rapid approach. What turned into the outer fringes and then downtown Los Angeles seemed a vast distance from the safe haven of the desert farm. In eerie, fading daylight, tall, pencil-thin palms lined the Pacific shoreline. Could Heidegger's Sea of Nothingness or Sartre's Tragic Finale be far behind? As protective armor, my thoughts sometimes turned morbidly sardonic in a nerve-sparing kind of joke.

We wound up at a beach apartment decorated with bamboo and woven mats. Muscle Beach and somehow fake, androgynous, cheesecake posters plastered the walls. With first casual banter and then calculated grunts, the preliminaries were quickly run through and dispensed with. A fallen pyramid of hastily chugged cans of beer, along with furtive then copious groping, accompanied unbuttoned and then dropped pants. The cruise world decreed that I owed my older rescuer-seducer his way with sex. I intuited he wasn't into anything timid or polite. We piled like charging broncos onto a slushy, heaving waterbed.

I tuned out what came next. I remember a painfully full bladder and a sense of shame at surrendering a last vestige of autonomous manhood. Worse, a sacrifice of my integrity of being. Kissing and faked humping, while exciting, somehow missed the mark. It lacked the compulsive passion of Oedipus. Or the rebellious intellect of Sartre. Let alone father/son/mirror-image, filtered down, forgive the blasphemy, from Father, Son and Holy Ghost. More like Sartre's anguish at betraying an innate, irrevocable freedom. Worse than "bad faith," we were guilty of being only partially fulfilled not-quites.

The ritual towel cleanup. Heavy silence pervaded the South Seas Paradise and unmade bed. More urgent than being drunk and feeling ravished, I was starving. An upscale restaurant with prime seafood or steak and lobster would make up for less than ideal sex.

Pants buckled back up, I was taken to—hardly the quaint charm of my mother's dining room—a Korean fast-food joint. Deep-fried chicken body parts came on greasy wax paper, French fries in a precarious paper boat, cokes watered down with too little syrup. Less reward than Seoul-style brute survival. Hardly the fine dining I envisioned from a man driving a flashy Cadillac. All the quick fling, I thought, on the flotilla waterbed was worth.

Undulating reality, like an imposed drug trip, soon careened into a nightmare. I was ushered, only to be abandoned, into a backstage primping area for a drag show. The excitement of theatric imposture was crammed into a claustrophic space. False eyelashes, caked on mascara, feather boas, grotesque high platform heels. Spotlights streaked past and zeroed in on stretched, mugging faces. My host and captor was a god to whom this giddy delegation paid reverent respect. He enabled the elaborate pantomime. My cowboy getup was for him just another faceless pose of a quick trick, a display of put-on butchness, to showcase the control prowess of a demagogue. More accurately, a piece of meat plucked from the ocean, sliced open and eviscerated to be thrown back overboard. Especially if the trick didn't synch with some Wyoming cowhand fantasy.

He particularly wasn't interested in a would-be philosopher searching for the Meaning of Life. Or a mystic soul dimension that underlies reality. Let alone a silver lining or golden shore. Instead, I'd descended into something akin to Sartre's "nausea." The otherness of brute matter alien and apart from my paltry *de trop* (too much, artificially excessive and therefore meaningless) existence.

My top priority swiftly morphed into a beer-blurred, stomach-burning fight for basic survival. In an insistent voice that seemed other than my own, I informed the Drag Queen Ring Master I felt out of place, on the verge of an anxiety attack that could spiral downward into panic. I'd made a big mistake that needed correcting. I must find my way or be taken to a bus depot. Obviously irked, as a first curtain call was imminent—particularly since it wasn't that great between us—he dug up enough spare dollars for a one-way ticket to points east with an inconvenienced promise to drop me off at a nearby onramp. It eventually connected with the downtown Greyhound. Unless I wanted to wind up drunk and freezing, guts and bladder screaming, sometime around dawn in the South Seas bamboo and grass mat apartment, it seemed my only option.

The impetuous, ill-advised and terminal fling unzipped—only to zip back up as fast as a drag queen's gown—like it never was in a blaze of color on a vanishing dark stage. I'd have preferred honest repartee, even heated recrimination, the raw sincerity of whips and chains! With scarcely a goodbye, I was back in chill, misting night air over a hundred miles—it seemed an infinite distance, the time span from hell to heaven—from the callously spurned family farm. If a gay god was anywhere present, I beseeched such Deity to deliver me from freezing or puking my guts on an alien side shoulder that even a burrowing rodent would find too barren and hostile to inhabit.

Head throbbing and chilled in a deep soul space, I had an under-five-minute stroke of luck. I hitched a ride with an aged Oriental driving a van with rubbed out side lettering, leaving only an undecipherable pagoda-like character. A pungent odor of cleaning fluid made me think him the proprietor of a Chinatown laundry. Through yellowed teeth and defiant watery eyes, he mumbled and muttered about the difficulty of earning a living in a high crime neighborhood. The constant danger was an aggravation an honest immigrant shouldn't have to live with, which I readily agreed with.

After an indeterminate time period, ghostly shapes whizzing chaotically past, I was ejected, rather than a portal to salvation, at the rock bottom of Purgatory. Betrayed by my bleach-reeking ride's pompous sincerity! With no marked roads in or out, I faced rows of train tracks at the foot of skyward interchanges that groaned and hummed far above with invisible traffic. The farm, which I'd forfeited in a spate of bad decisions, sat at a mythic and unattainable distance. Weighed in the Cosmic Balance and found wanting! Instead I'd plunged into a Sea of Nothingness beyond the saving reach of Higher Being . . . which I now wasn't sure even existed. Only raw, brute, mocking matter.

A several blocks-long, little used bridge with a narrow pedestrian sidewalk arched over spookily deserted tracks. I felt like a tiny ant stranded on a turning fist of industrial vastness. About a third of the way across, acrophobia set in. Might I leap onto the gleaming, sharklike tracks a mounting distance below? To quell sudden panic, I fell to my knees on a steel girder-turned-tightrope that could any moment crumble and shake to the laughter of diabolic angels.

Swimming in sweat, I found myself, incredibly, crawling on all fours to ward off an imminent leap onto serious maiming or death. Isolated and abandoned by greater L.A.'s 20 million unseen souls with little hope of reaching the far side! I had a foretaste of madness. Only a miracle could wrest me from some horrendous, ultimate horror.

Maybe it was the Western hat. The assumed swagger. A VW in bad need of a muffler belched out of nowhere and rattle-banged over to the crosswalk. A Latino in his late 20's threw me an odd look at seeing a fellow human crawling on all fours on a narrow strip of cement sidewalk, clutching a precarious, less than three-foot guardrail. Gay or not I couldn't tell. But I knew he wasn't part of the Venice Beach drag show.

I announced in a stammer that I was trying to reach the downtown Greyhound. "Thank God," I added in soaring hope. "You're my delivering angel. An undoubted saint."

He laughed with empathic, partial comprehension. "Comprendo. Hop in. I've been in worse jams."

In amazed shock and with his English halting next to nonexistent, not much was said as the exhaust-blasting escape vehicle surmounted the bridge's apex. A field of lights lifted into view that resembled an amphitheater filled with lit, praying candles, and then descended the far side into a farmers' market and industrial section of L.A. The stoically silent driver appeared to have no ulterior designs on my being or body. He was on the planet to help. He'd been in similar dire straits, perhaps illegally crossing the Mexican border, and was giving payback. Like hidden gold in tarry darkness, he was a luminous stepping stone to survival.

He skid-belched to a stop alongside the tawdry square block of downtown depot. A once respectable American institution, it might have been, with its unclean burnt odors, somewhere in India. Waiting, long suffering passengers, some in near rags, huddled against a bare wall, the few benches being taken. I apologized to the dusky-faced driver that if I had an extra dollar, which I didn't, I'd give it to him. With an understanding grin he waved off any need for monetary gain. He didn't realize, more than a good deed, he'd delivered me from near madness, even saved my life.

A Higher Power seemed to hover over the fast-fry, soot-aroma of an uprooted mankind. The universe hadn't turned its back after all! Maybe there *was* a God, even a special *gay* One. In an aura of distant light I made out, beyond my present fallen state, an extension or avatar of a similar yet higher self, one of the chosen elect, worthy of divine intervention and blessing . . . It was my first intimation of a priesthood I was to spend a good part of my life thinking and writing about.

I reached Indio shortly before dawn. Embarrassed, as neither of my parents was answering the phone, I had to call a neighboring farmer's wife I barely knew to please pick me up, I was stranded and in bad need of help. The sun was just emerging like a slippery egg on the horizon. The kindly, remembered churchgoer left me at the foot of a sand dune planted in grass beneath a Spanish-style house. My looming childhood home. And the heavy door with peep hole I must rap like a penitente to counteract a sinking wave of humiliation . . .

I must have been a grisly sight with depraved exhaustion lines around the eyes and rank need of a shower. My father had just come in from checking irrigation water in the fields. My mother, still in a bathrobe, was preparing a dessert she knew he liked. For several stymied moments they were a gaping blur, just as I was for them a gradually focusing ghost. Yet I was somehow reborn. The prodigal, although debased and beat up, wasn't defeated. My life was on the upswing. Their welcoming smiles, rather than *de trop*, told me I belonged. At least for the non-judgmental present.

There followed a day and night reunion—visits seldom exceed 24 hours—with my hard working, farm-scrubbed forebears. Despite initial well wishes, differences of belief soon cropped up. My gayness and the lack of a wife and children, as well as my foray into glandular psychiatry and atheistic existentialism, followed by a tangential but scandalous embrace of the Baha'i faith, was hard for them to confront head-on. Especially with a shovel propped outside the backdoor, a symbol of labor by the sweat of one's brow, and the authority of the outspread family bible.

They tried and I tried. Earnestly, even heroically. Nevertheless, an accumulated distance set in. Conversation steered clear of my sordid identity crisis in downtown L.A. It was either fiction or had happened to someone else. Catch-up centered around more promising, happier times. High school, college and beyond. Then, corn and grape harvests at risk from dust storms and other extremes of weather. Too bad there weren't more hands, mine implied, to help. I loved them as I believe they did me . . . from a cautious distance.

How explain the subtly widening chasm? My trajectory went beyond the claustrophobic space of the surreal drag show, as it did the prayer rug at the foot of the devotional table, crowded with family photos, I'd in younger years bowed beneath. Naively, unquestioningly. Sometimes rebelliously. Despite the comfort of their down-home presence, I felt more than ever on my own. Having come through the fires, I answered primarily only to myself. As they did to themselves. And their ancestors before them. So near and yet a vast distance apart. Not much had changed after all. Just a higher kind of *de trop*.

I somehow returned, after effusively thanking them for the "soul" rescue and hospitality, in a ride I don't remember—in retrospect it all seems like a fated time warp—to the proud reality of a house and vehicle that I owned outright near the less harsh coast that I shouldn't have left in a rash moment, but which nonetheless waited to welcome me. It told me my folly was forgiven. I was granted absolution from the impulsive detour in search of roots, of underlying Meaning and Belonging . . .

In the interest of this book, I propose contrasting and dissecting, along the lines of Sartre, the "Being and Nothingness" of the gay experience or dilemma—which I will take the liberty of changing to "Being and *Somethingness*." Fill in the ontologic gaps, as it were. At the same time, it seemed obvious a priesthood isn't attainable or even desirable for every out-of-the-closet gay man, maybe only a select shaman few. But it seemed worth the effort as well as my destiny to attempt.

Oh questing one, break through the veils, fear not, seek and ye shall find. Yet do so wisely. Though life's journey arc widely, yet you will return to your birthright as a child of the universe. Never be afraid to leave behind the sometimes gentle, sometimes tempestuous upheaval of the past. Don't disown even the most sordid moments. They, too, are part of the puzzle. It's your destiny to attain and delineate the mystic priesthood glimpsed dimly through the terror of a bridge of night . . .

—the Author

Finally:

O Son of Being! Thy paradise is My love; thy heavenly home, reunion with Me. Enter therein and tarry not. This is that which hath been destined for thee in Our kingdom above and Our exalted Dominion.

—Baha'u'llah

PREFACE

————— ⌘ —————

THE HIGH PRIESTHOOD OF BEING GAY

When I first conceived the idea for this book, I was, in retrospect, locked into a negative mind-set brought on by male menopause or some unpleasant equivalent. I'd succumbed to a sort of creeping despair. Not the best time to start. I still hadn't discovered the Spirit Guides—we all have them—who were to play a vital role in inspiring and shaping my thoughts. To them I say, Thanks, fellows—rather, gods—if I may be so bold. Welcome . . .

Having passed the big 5-0, I realized my gay life had been less than stellar. My longest affair lasted a little over three years. The usual was more like three months with numerous tricks sandwiched in. My ideal partner, Mister Right, was an unattainable mosaic. I feared my life was two-thirds over, youth forever gone. The specter of death loomed over a not too distant horizon. With such a gloomy outlook, I feared the book would turn into an exercise in angst with an absurd twist, after the French existentialist, Albert Camus. I nonetheless vowed to tell the truth as I saw it, no holds barred, no feelings spared.

In my late twenties and again in my early forties I read Jean Paul Sartre's mammoth but abstruse *Being and Nothingness*. In the same way, I had slogged through the entire Bible in mid-childhood and again in my early teens. Sartre, even more than holy scripture, in fact its polar opposite, left a lasting, arid and conflicting impression. Although an emotional residue remained from my Baptist upbringing, his barren atheism somehow fit my gay adaptation, or lack of one. To critique Being and Nothingness, as well as launch an investigation into the nature of homosexuality, insinuated itself. The idea was intellectually and perversely intriguing. If the project didn't overwhelm me, it would certainly be fraught with peril. The project was therefore repeatedly postponed. Particularly as I wanted it to succeed on the level of an ontology, that is, the study of the Nature of Being.

About the same time, I'd gone through the shock, while expected, of my father's death. This crucial event triggered my finally sitting down to a blank note pad. My relationship with this familiar yet alien being had been disastrous. From the dawn of memory he was a clot of darkness, a Rorschach blot maddeningly off center of vision. The struggle and travail of this earth life, interspersed with brief islets of joy, were insufficient to explain the distrust, even loathing, that arose between us. As if he'd been an ogre, at least someone extremely harmful or dangerous to my person in a past life.

Outwardly, he embodied the death throes of the Victorian era, just as I stood on the brink of a scarily undefined New World. I was ready to toss away the old, to annihilate like a mad Bolshevik, and start anew. Internal and external fragmentation in painting, music, and literature constituted for me the highest form of art. Picasso's cubism, Arnold Schoenberg's angst-filled dissonance, William Burroughs' literary nihilism. These were my idols. Call them high priests.

The bad vibes with my father, I contemplated, replayed the Greek tragedy of Oedipus Rex. Freud's Oedipus Complex was a still widely held theory of the cause and explanation of homosexuality. But even that had fallen into doubt, if not ill repute. In the deep subconscious hadn't I murdered my father many times over? More profoundly, willed his *nonexistence*? This went a step past murder. Murder, in a sense, confirms the victim's existence. The infantile pre-gay at one to five years old, or even while still in the womb, plots to do in this threatening colossus—only to regally and guiltily erase the primal murder from consciousness; cast it, in Biblical terms, into the Sea of God's Forgetfulness. As though patricide never happened.

This double nihilation formed a basis for my own version of Oedipus. Though my amended version contained kernels of truth, it turned out, not surprisingly, as dark and in some ways more cumbersome than the Greek original. Nonetheless, I decided to keep it as a working hypothesis until something better came along. That led me to ask how and why do a fixed percentage of the population turn out gay year after year, generation after generation? Had this steady production of miscreants gone on from the dawn of time? Would it continue into the indefinite future? The questions swirled wildly.

The borrowed, or pirated, Freudian and Sartrian models, along with my take on Oedipus, however, lacked something. In addition, more than genes or a vestigial or shrunken thalamus was needed. Something akin to heart and soul. Neither Freud nor Sartre said anything about a Higher Force that undergirds and animates human life. Although I'd delved into two organized religions, Christianity (mostly discarded) and Baha'i (accepted with caveats), I still believed in God as First Cause. At one point this ontology was ostentatiously titled "The Crisis of Being Gay." I'd not yet made the life-affirming discovery that to be gay isn't just a privilege, but a matchless gift.

In my quest for truth and spiritual cleansing (I inwardly worried that I'd somehow caused my father's actual physical death), I feared the investigation would career wildly between a sea of nothingness and heights of ecstasy without much in between. We gay men traverse an enormous distance in inventing ourselves from scratch. Simultaneously, we're asked to be the strongest beings on the Planet by virtue of the rejection and contradictions we face. Spurned by God, religion, country, the greater society and family. And for a man dying of AIDS, sometimes even his lover who can't take the cruel, emaciating sickness any longer. So he, too, bails. The courage needed to endure this multiple negation is immense. Whether in the work place, a church sanctuary, playground or a "tea room" raided by the police, we're called upon to be martyr/saints. Maybe "conscripted" applies. Better yet, "commissioned." No gay man I ever knew chose on at least a conscious level his gayness. It appears as a "given," imposed before the fact; decided and in place long before the Judaeo-Christian age of accountability.

A main purpose of this revised and hopefully enlightened version of the precursor Ontology is to proclaim as well as demonstrate (I didn't dare think it when I first faced the empty note pad) that gay men are the hidden founders and *fathers*—of civilization. From Socrates and Plato to Proust and Thomas Mann, from Vergil and Horace and the Apostle Paul to Tschaikovski and Van Gogh, it appears as undeniable fact. About time the world realized it, let go of blind prejudice and paid proper tribute!

Further reflection and soul-baring convinced me that heterosexual marriage—in primitive times, now, and in the future—is ideally performed by a gay high priest or shaman. This specialized being better comprehends the differences, much of it culturally determined and superficially imposed, between the sexes. Who better understands that androgyny is the hidden goal of physical union? In this respect, gay men are nearer to God. To be exclusively male or female expresses a Primal Lack. Combining both polarities within a single soul-existent more closely reflects the nature of God.

Is it just coincidence, I pondered, that man's idea of otherworldly beings like angels and elves is nearly always androgynous? This reflects man's nature as a spiritual being, which is to reach past temporal earth body toward timeless Spirit. The survival of Planet Earth, much less exploration of the stars, depends upon wide-scale androgynization. Otherwise, mankind is doomed to endlessly repeating the bloodbath of the last hundred or so centuries.

Not only are gays present and integral to the birth of religions (Jesus' love for the Disciple John, the homoerotic bond between Ramakrishna and his male devotees, Mullah Husayn's heroic attraction to the Bab in the early stages of the Baha'i faith), they are a leavening agent and safety valve for the survival and advancement of civilization. Though homosexuals don't reproduce genetically—without a little help from the opposite sex—I call this a mystic form of procreation.

In working out my psychoanalytic, ontologic and spiritual basis for homosexuality, there evolved with surprising swiftness a concept of Three Ordinations. Roughly: 1.) The infantile or Oedipal nihilation of the father, 2.) Coming-out-of-the-closet, i.e., self-acceptance and public acknowledgement, and 3.) Reconciliation with and return to Lost Father.

This impromptu schema I then tried to fit into a descending trinity of SPIRIT>Mind>body. Note the hierarchal progression of all caps to none. The arrows indicate downward or inward energy flow (God to man, Creator to created). Although this formula seemed fairly accurate, at least serviceable, I wondered if it subtly disrespected or downgraded body in a way that exposed my Victorian heritage. True, the body begins a slow decline in the late twenties or early thirties. It gets sick, stumbles and falters, turns frail and dies. The shed corpse winds up six feet under. Yet body is, or was, the intimate bearer of the Spirit-mind complex. Contrary to what fundamentalist religion crammed down my throat—original sin, the mortification of the flesh—gross body must be at least somewhat sacred as the carrier of Spirit.

I further sensed (with the inspired input of Those-Who-Have-Moved-On) that the body after death—an airy, improved and luminous version of this heavy matter one prone to sickness—continues to define and enshrine the ascended soul in the hereafter. No higher order being, even the most ethereal, is only Spirit. Any entity must have a form. Infinitely Diffuse Pure Spirit is surely reserved for the Primal Light Source—namely God. Some form of body, adapted and appropriate to the astral plane in which the soul spirit finds itself, remains. Truly body is here to stay. The poetry of Walt Whitman taught me the sacredness of the body, as did Michelangelo.

In my misguided attraction to a womblike, all-encompassing "vat of nothingness"—a consequence of my study of Sartre—I found that the much feared Void is maybe just that: illusion. Just as the transition of death is an illusion. Might the black hole or "coiled worm" at the core of Being, rather than an equal but opposite ontologic structure, be an illusory mindset that rises like swamp mist from a sense of being unwanted and unloved? I now believe that the Cosmos in which we move and have our being subsists on a foundation of Fullness; that is to say, Love. Furthermore, this plenitude isn't *de trop* but exactly right. Love indwells the human vessel according to its capacity to receive. I began to intuit, with the help of my hearty, ethereal cohorts, some with shades of the feminine, (as readily say spiritual guidance), that this ground-of-being is joy- and light-filled, not the vat of oblivion to which I had been so obsessively and morbidly drawn.

What a difference this made to my bleak view of life! Rather than an ink-black sea with mud pods of brute matter floating absurdly on top, the universe is a Fullness waiting to be tapped. Love repeals and annuls—rather, fills—the Void. Love's opposite, fear, arises from a hidden nostalgia for nonbeing (deathwish), most dramatically evidenced in suicide (passive) or murder (active). Love is ultimate Somethingness. As such, it possesses high spiritual "density." Fear, on the other hand, evanesces. Fear is *not*, just as sin and the Devil are not. Homosexuality, therefore, to the degree it manifests love possesses high spiritual density. Conversely, to the degree it is greedy, selfish, and cruel—that is, blights and blocks Higher Self—it spawns fear and veers toward Nothingness.

Love, whatever form it takes, I was certain, is a sign and reflection of a beneficent Creator; a bestowal from Source; an unlimited Somethingness. Life depends on what I shall call a Divine Substrate of Light. Without it, all life would vanish "faster than the twinkling of an eye." (Another Baptistism.) One could say Love is "truer than true." Homosexual love is therefore as timeless, eternal and sacred, as any other manifesting of love. To be gay is a unique bestowal that expresses an infinitely varied, primal Divine Love. It is the very face of God.

To this axiom I add a corollary: Homosexuals facilitate world progress by infusing it with a special wavelength of cosmic light. Without this unique frequency the planet would lapse into primitive darkness. Mankind would stagnate from drabness and boredom, its antidote being to liven things up with war and bloodshed. The arts would wither. Most significantly, man's spiritual growth would be stymied and stunted. This discovery transformed my arid vision of a meaningless universe into a rich oasis; from a black hole into an extravaganza of light! In a short time period I traversed a huge distance, galactic in scope, from a mindset of fear masquerading as resentment and gloom to that of love! That included no longer fearing, but accepting my gayness, unconditionally—the greatest gift from an inventive and caring Creator.

Despite this cheeriness, however, I couldn't simply toss onto the rubble heap what I'd written in the slough of male menopause. As part of the total spectrum, that, too, must bear some weight, have at least some validity. Neither could I, like Kierkegaard, oscillate or agonize in a halfway house of Either/Or (having to choose between hedonist and ethical imperatives, only to throw over both toward the dutifully religious). Sainthood is hardly my destiny. I must, rather, go for integration of the opposing positions I had taken, rightly or wrongly, morally or immorally, as a closeted and then outed gay man. All mental and emotional states, positive and negative, happy or rebellious, ecstatic or depressed, have something to add or contribute.

From this broader perspective, there is no absolute wrong or evil, only shades and degrees of distance from the Light. I had to fit my Baptist past and Baha'i present, Sartre, Freud, and my earthy, some might say, pornographic, experiences as a gay man into the equation. Stir them all, as it were, into the cosmic brew. I had to reconcile my idea of homosexuality arising from a double nihilation with my vision of Spiritual Fullness. A Herculean task.

Would anyone go along for such a bumpy ride? Would anyone care? I personally had to know, if "through a glass darkly." It seemed my special fate to live out, if need be in solitude, my penchant for hard questions as well as illusive answers. That's when I caught a glimpse, although obliquely, of a gay priesthood. A panoramic vision haloed in light. Decades, lifetimes, even centuries, of fear and anger flowed out of me like a noxious vapor. It was a cleansing moment. But didn't such a select calling involve multiple, even fatal contradictions? Wouldn't conflict be its very condition? Just as determinism is the condition or ground of free will; and, reciprocally, free will gels into determinism. Back and forth, an ever swinging pendulum. I had faith that from the lofty viewpoint of Spirit such wildly swinging contradictions would shrink and vanish. All would be made, if not perfectly, at least reasonably clear, depending on the sincerity and patience of the seeker.

Primitive man that inhabited the planet twenty thousand years ago (and isolated present day tribes) had an innate understanding of the uncommon vision and contribution of their homosexual members. This was expressed not only in improvements to everyday life, such as better ways to tan leather, make pottery or select colorful feathers for tribal ceremonies, but upreach toward a Creator. Homosexuals have a talent for celebrating rather than exploiting life. They have an inside view of the sacred. The modern-day denigration and criminalizing of these qualities into the forbidden and profane springs from the fear and distrust felt by the heterosexual majority at being ejected from its primal setting (i.e., the Garden of Eden) into ever more complex yet superficial societies. It may take decades, even centuries, for the shaman status of the gay man to again be understood and reintegrated. But so it shall.

In the last chapter, "Ghost Complex," I contrast Sartre's famous encounter with a chestnut tree to a personal experience of my own in Denver's Washington Park. Like his "nausea" at the indifferent upsurge of raw matter, I had a searing glimpse into the Void. It wasn't, however, something *out there*, something horrifyingly other than me. Rather it was something deep within that I create; a self-made fissure at the heart of being. The Void—the serpent of nothingness—rears its head *internally* through the blind misuse or abuse of freedom. That is, the denial of love. More tellingly, through the denial of my gayness!

I had refused to love this God-given part of my being. I still hadn't freed myself from the implanted notion that it's something shameful and unclean that must be played out in shadows. I was a homophobic homosexual. I had refused to see myself or my gay brothers as *just right*; as perfect creations of a loving God. In that moment of epiphany the faded, ghostly trees sprang back to life. Spring flowerbeds turned vivid with color. Silent birds resumed singing. For once I saw gay men in their infinite variety and beauty; as veritable gods dancing a sacred dance. It was like receiving the cosmic Wine and Host, with old musty vapors departing and golden light streaming in.

In the afterglow of this vision, I asked my spirit Guides (or Higher Self) if there is a gay heaven. Are gay men there *Cage a' Fole*? Do they band together like birds of a feather? Or is heaven integrated? If so, forcefully? I really had to know. It had great implications for the here and now, and certainly for this book. For a long frustrating, sometimes angry time no answer came. I meditated and prayed. I struggled to empty myself of preconceived ideas.

Finally in desperation, I decided to try to contact, through a quite expensive psychic, a gay man I'd known who died of AIDS. To somehow reach past the Great Divide. I suspected that the answer, apropos my incomplete state of spiritual growth, wouldn't be all sweetness and light. How right I was! The first vision was more than I bargained for! More like a descent into Purgatory.

A dark 1960's bar. The kind sometimes called a black toilet. Handcuffs and tattered T-shirts and jockstraps hang from the ceiling, bathed in eerie ultra-violet light. Huge underwater snakes writhe overhead as if at the top of an aquarium. Ghostly forms, some equi-spaced, others overlapping and fazing into each other, have been posing—"standing and modeling"—for timeless eons. Since eating and sleeping aren't necessary in this noncorporeal state, no one leaves for even a minute for fear of missing out on the perfect trick or male physique. A blink at the wrong moment can result in losing Mister Right forever. Finally overcome with exhaustion, the forms eventually drop, one by one, to the floor among their own urine and foul odors, to be reincarnated as an infant in an impoverished, third world country. This hellish vision left my palms wet, my whole body shaking.

In a sign of mercy, this changed into something entirely different. Higher order chills coursed through me. A vast congregation, assembled beneath an overarching (a Salvador Dali "ecumenical") sky, supported by celestial light beams, is singing in fervent unison. So powerful and multi-textured is the music that it creates its own mood and aura like a pulsing, psychedelic fountain. Something like canticle bells are being swung, stringed lyres strummed. The vast gathering has an unmistakable gay flavor. Then I saw the man I wanted to contact. Ordinary looking on earth, he's now radiant, as close to a hunk as an angel can be. Individual and collective joy shakes the cloud-formed rafters. Free of earthly limitation, these transfigured beings have returned to Source. Existence (loosely, for-itself) merges with essence (the given; timeless, unchanging in-itself) and conjoins with Spirit (being for others). Wishes and dreams are instantly realizable. These spiritual beings—not exactly lusty, but robust and vital—simply *are* in their primal innocence and glory.

My first thought was, "Wouldn't the atheist, Sartre, be surprised." The ontologic dilemma of the internal breach of self from Self and this tormented dyad from Being for Others (the third member of the triad), solved at last! Gone were all gaps, boundaries and warring factions. Bleak impossibilities were overruled and transcended, leaving only rich possibles. The most striking quality of this exultant gathering was that of Completion. Could there be any doubt that being gay—in a responsible, self-accepting, spiritual sense—is other than a divine visitation? The Creator is not, or never was a grim judge or vicious sadist without a sense of humor or love of variety. God—as Creator, Poet, Warrior, Magician, Mother Goddess, Benevolent Father—is a dance. Before this discovery, I was an artifact of a bygone era, sinking under the dead weight of religious piety and Void-questing (deathwish)—the very reasons for which I'd presumed to abhor, and murder, my father!

Thanks to my wondrous Guides (whether angels or fine-tuned intuition) I've learned to float and soar, rather than plod blindly across a barren landscape of embeddedness in Ego-Body that only results in more frustration and despair. In the process of uncovering gay soul, I discovered Universal Spirit. Spirit is all-embracing. It includes the gross matter vagaries of Oedipus Complex as well as the gay man's struggle to find himself. It pervades and informs the separate but overlapping Three Ordinations.

Birth and death, alienation and return: Spirit is the animus and final goal of gay and straight alike. Spirit catalyzes the reconciliation of in-itself, for-itself and being-for-others; of id, ego and super-ego. Or any other man-made schema. Even Father, Son and Holy Ghost.

Or more relevant to this book's purpose, the return of the gay man, after passing through a vast desert, to the oasis of true self which is a Divine Self. Homosexuality, at its fully self-accepted, most artful, aware and compassionate, is a giant leap toward Source.

CHAPTER ONE

THE THREE ORDINATIONS: CONFLICT AND RECONCILIATION

The original intent of this book, before the awakening mentioned in the added Forward, as well as in the Preface, was to discover what is positive and real in the gay experience in contrast to what is negative and illusory. Or more simply and comprehensively: to contrast Being and Nothingness.

That goal remains unchanged. But rather than the merely descriptive, logical or ontologic, my approach is now more multi-faceted and spiritual. Otherwise, I couldn't be true to anything approaching Ultimate Reality as I've experienced it. Now as then, I will attempt to weigh the Beingness of homosexuality against whatever about it veers toward Nothingness. That doesn't mean the good versus the bad, since this isn't a study in ethics, but rather, the real as opposed to a shadow world, the enduring in contrast to the ephemeral, the beneficial versus the deleterious.

The search will, moreover, juxtapose the sacred and the profane, the sacrosanct and the scurrilous. To separate out either pole might set the brave vessel of philosophic investigation foundering on a lopsided course or careening in a dizzying circle. No irreverent thought or untidy emotion will be excluded, to the point of sparing no one's feelings, gay or straight, including my own. I will strike at the heart of such loaded questions as: "Why are gays feared and shunned by the greater society?" Or: "Why is homosexuality not only a threat to religion but often to itself?"

A close examination of this "threat" should provide a key to the basic question, "*What* is homosexuality?" For credentials or specialized weaponry, I include a Baptist upbringing; an atheist period in which I read Sartre, Camus, Beckett, Burroughs and the theater of the absurd; a passing familiarity with Freud; two source books: Ken Wilber's *Up From Eden* and the anonymous *A Course in Miracles;* a tangential belief in the Baha'i faith; and my own experience as a gay man. From this diverse mixture hopefully will emerge a few light rays of truth. With faith and perseverance, a bold plunge into the unknown will lead, if not to the Emerald City, at least to a hopeful Eden.

Being is All-That-Is, utter plenitude, the undoubtedly true. Nothingness, on the other hand, is the absence of Being. It is characterized by what rings false or isn't fully there. It is all that is not. The "inside" of being, however, wouldn't have an "outside" without a certain infiltration or participation of nonbeing. The same is true of form and content, foreground and background, beginning and end, even joy and sorrow. These apparent opposites can't exist without a certain permeation of Being with Nothingness.

Simple negation, on the other hand, assumes a parasitic connection with reality through denial. Therefore, negation is to a degree an *is*. In this investigation—the quest for the nature of Being—I will employ the terminology and concepts of existentialism, even while questioning or refuting many of its underlying assumptions in much the same way that Sartre "fleeced" Hegel.

I will, however, retain much of Sartre, particularly in showing that the gay experience is, on one level, negation in response to a Central Lack. It's like a sailor aboard the Santa Maria with Columbus afraid of (negation) plunging off the edge of the world into oblivion (nothingness). I will also show that the project or "pre-choice" of gayness, beyond merely coming out of the closet, is *to be* the existential dilemma of father-severance (patricide) and self-invention across a chasm of nothingness. Homosexuality is a "no exit" dilemma. This double nihilation dates from early childhood, infancy, even the womb. Before that, to its origin in Primal Consciousness.

It would seem that the brave project of self-invention fails to enjoy—so the pre-gay later intuits—the sanction of God, country, the military, school, church and peers. Rather is it infused with such negative feelings as embarrassment and shame, even contempt. Why should this be? Is such a pariah state a cosmic given? A prior judgment from a stern, unyielding, even cruel Creator? Despite every effort at self-affirmation, the homosexual doesn't quite succeed in fully inventing or founding himself. That's because foundation is bestowed from without, from God, or so he's been taught to believe. But didn't that same

God reject him? He therefore fails, despite his urgent best efforts, at being his own foundation.

So what else is new? Does a heterosexual author his primal *raison d'etre*? Can the creature usurp the station of Creator? To be gay, like the sailor on the Santa Maria, is to be upended in the Void. To be contingent rather than absolute being. The hope of this book remains this: to weigh and bombard the somethingness against the nothingness of homosexuality, and to the degree that they are interpenetrable, to arrive at synthesis.

The American Psychology Association, together with the larger scientific community, affirms that homosexuality is generally established in embryonic form by age five, well before the Judaic/Christian idea of the age of accountability usually at about age twelve. We can therefore assume, without bogging down in a circular paradox, that *homosexuality precedes sexuality*.

If that be true, a homosexual isn't responsible at least as a reflective being or causal agent for his condition. Rather, it comes to him as a given; or in existential terms, as essence. He isn't gay as an act of will but in spite of himself. He doesn't choose it, it chooses him. It creeps up from behind. It appears to have always been there. As though God or a Higher Consciousness imprinted it from time immemorial on the core of his being.

This, however, doesn't rule out a "pre-cognitive" choice in the pre-gay infant/child. Nearly every case of homosexual development includes the sidelining or rejection of a father figure, often accompanied by the father's reciprocal rejection of the son. One denial produces the other. The pre-gay perceives the father as unsympathetic, hostile, even dangerous; someone who withholds affection and approval. This looming Cyclops, on its part, refuses to see the son as a proud extension of himself. On a subconscious level "it" refuses to claim him.

The son, especially if strong-willed, reacts further in kind. The result is mutual distaste, disapproval, censure; a negative judgment upon the other's worth of being. This reaches the point of the son daring to wish for the father's nonexistence. Denial is then carried a final, nihilating step into the realm of the Impossible: the willed nonbeing of another existent, in this case, one's forebear. Covert patricide, like a royal edict, is carried out, followed by bewilderment at the stubborn survival of the "corpse." The tragi-drama is secretly accomplished, sewed up, pigeonholed and stashed in a lockbox deep in the subconscious by the time the pre-gay enters school.

To deal with the buried conflict between the being of nonbeing (homosexuality) and the nonbeing of being (the father)—the "liberated" pre-gay strives to be as unlike this vanquished being as possible. If the father is a redneck tyrant who hunts wild game, the son may become a sissy, a bookworm, overly dramatic or a conscientious objector who hates guns. He conspires to be an "alter-boy," to be the non-being of his own heady and radical reinvention.

If no sympathetic older male is present to emulate in the father's stead, he may turn to females for role models, usually the mother because she's the most accessible. She's warm, supportive, unconditionally accepting. She gives affection. She touches. The touch confirms being. Withholding it confers a pariah state. An untouched child inwardly thinks himself an object to be shunned. Ego-reinforcement, prestige, comfort—in short, beingness—derive from her. Gradually he's absorbed into her milieu; becomes, as it were, an extension of the maternal skirts.

The curtailment of beingness as a boy child, while providing temporary comfort, confuses and retards development toward a concrete sexual identity. Concurrently with a subtle feminization taking place below the threshold of consciousness, he's thrown into an even more troubling dilemma. At the same time that he wills the father's nonexistence, he longs in a deep strata of the subconscious for union with this annihilated being. But the primal murder is irrevocable, the chasm unbridgeable. The pre-gay can't unite with a nonexistent. He can't call forth Lazarus from his tomb. Consequently, the double nihilation exists itself as an unrequited and unrequitable longing.

The school age pre-gay, then, enters a fantasy world that bears only a tangential resemblance to reality. The world appears as an unjust structure of male dominion. The nihilated father, as both absence and dogged surviving presence, epitomizes this unfair system. He represents the all-powerful male God. Government, the military, schools, corporations, sports, ministers, the postman—are all shot through with male domination. The undercover murder of the father, that oppressive cornerstone of a false society, has a domino effect: the *en bloc* toppling of God, government, the military, male school teachers, the works. All are neatly and inexorably swept away (like Pharaoh's army in the Red Sea), to be replaced by a more palatable and magical female alter-world.

The degree to which the pre-gay finds a niche in the male power structure may slow down, retard, even reverse this process. Token exposure or partial inclusion will determine the degree of acquisition of male attributes that will later enable him to play the game, hide his differentness, butch it up. It also depends upon the allure of the female "swamp"; how overwhelmingly the mother entices him into the Everglades of femininity. To the degree the male world is unaccepting and hostile, the boy is drawn toward greater feminization.

Since the covertly desired father is unavailable vis-a-vis his nonexistence (Mother likewise desires this nonbeing, a betrayal that must also be repressed), the pre-gay is forced to invent his sex life in limbo. Since it has no precedent or authorization "from the top," sexual experimentation is undercover, phantasmagoric, subversive and tinged with evil—since God, Who is unquestionably male, condemns all deviation from the norm.

The core sex drive—unrequitable desire for the nihilated father—thereby gets diverted into substitutes like a stagnant pond in a dammed stream. If father surrogates are censorious and hostile, the boy may enter the realm of masochism—the erotization of the impossible, or at least the very difficult. Though he face a brick wall of rejection, he (the masochist) doesn't entirely reject the rejecter (the sadist). He finds a perverse satisfaction in grasping at straws, in reaching for the unattainable. He becomes a martyr-saint.

The loss or overturn of God, that springs from father assassination, prompts the young murderer to fill the vacuum of the toppled deity with self. This is the origin of Ego-Body. This apotheosis has the virtue of enabling him to control, if only in fantasy, a succession of father or Lazarus surrogates. He can resurrect, manipulate and tear down at will. Ego-Body gradually evolves into Prime Ordainer. He creates a ritual, make-believe kingdom. He directs and presides over spectacular boudoir and battle scenes. The original murder becomes a theme and variations to be repeated over and over.

Simultaneously, however, he longs for love, approval and intimacy— universal drives he shares with the rest of mankind. Yet their attainment is increasingly vested in the realm of the unreal. The pre-gay stands outside any ordained line of succession. Religion regards separation from God as perdition, extreme loss. The wages of sin is death, eternal damnation in hell. He's a sinner before he knows the meaning of the word, condemned before the fact. Like Eve, he's a shameful vessel of original sin. He craves mercy and forgiveness. Oh to sink into the blissful marshlands of unconditional acceptance! To return to Eden! To the comfort of the womb!

Thus he's pulled farther into the female camp. Its judgments are less harsh and absolute. Mother Goddess is more inclined to bend, nurture and forgive. Like the womb, this softer, gentler world is so pleasant that he postpones forays into the male arena to a vague future when he'll have more spine, more bite, a bigger pile of stones for battle. The postponement inadvertently becomes permanent.

Just when he thinks he's safely ensconced in what I shall call Safe Court, there occurs another betrayal. It dawns that he's not biologically or psychologically suited to reflect its gentleness and grace, to mirror its curves. He's destined to remain an unwieldy imposter like an exhibit at a carnival sideshow. The City of Women equips him with only a caustic tongue and feminine wiles, the basic weapons of the queen-to-be. He hones his verbal skills (like the part man he is and can't escape being) the better to appease and tame the dangerous male camp. Unawares, he acquires the worst characteristics of women—sweet deceit, snide gossip, icy manipulation, but with a rougher edge—with few of the endearing qualities other than as camp or satire.

More deeply, he acquires that lethal weapon: betrayal. The universe betrayed him by pronouncing him unacceptable before the fact and then tripping him up in his attempt to compensate by impersonating or psychologically becoming a woman. He will now turn to multiple betrayal. He will mirror betrayal. He will become Betrayal (like the two J.C.'s, those consummate bitch icons, Crawford and Collins).

Not that the pre-gay set out to play either murderer or super bitch. The original patricide was a nonreflective act of survival. Only later did it evolve into a longing for reconciliation and acceptance, and when that failed, a mandate for control. Nor did he purposely sever the links of paternal continuity. That, too, was a subconscious grasp at survival. It seemed the only way out of a menacing, life-and-death situation. Now instead of a machine-tooled copy of Dad, he's a counterfeit, an odd duck, a sissy. Yet he bargained for none of this. The series of pre-cognitive events—father rejection, mother identification and the invention of an alter-image and alter-world—all preceded the age of accountability. The original diabolic nihilation took place before the life of the reflective consciousness ever kicked in. Thus the pre-gay starts school with an unspoken and unspeakable apologia. He's a guilty innocent or an innocent sinner, a walking contradiction.

By then the young traitor has come too far down the murderer/sorcerer's path, and too little down that of competing male, to turn back. He must fake it, cover up, improvise. The conflict, however, remains hidden, formless, maddeningly off-center. He's his own buried Greek tragedy. Society demands an at least token attempt at being a competing "scrapper boy." He must convince or con others as well as himself. He must speak the noxious word "Dad" easily and naturally, even though it curdles in his throat. The little actor learns to give lip service to the lie, even while tricking himself into believing it's the truth.

He thus begins life with a repressed, deeply ingrained schizophrenia. It's true/it isn't true; that's me/it's not me. He's fated to live out a wrenching paradox. The more rigorously he rejects the father and the male power structure, the more he craves union with a worthy and exciting stand-in for the Male. In the primal subconscious his heart truly "belongs to daddy." Thus is born in nebulous outline that future phantasm—Mister Right.

An uninhibited pre-gay may later in adolescence engage in such forbidden acts as fellating older boys to bridge the widening gap. Inhibited or religiously repressed types may wage a mortal struggle or go through a long period of denial. Internalized parental and social pressure (super-ego) may delay homosexual expression into the teens or early twenties; or as often happens, divert it into a passionless heterosexual marriage.

Consequently, buried guilt from the original patricide expresses itself in such anti-social behavior as too dramatic mannerisms, avoidance of peers, excessive masturbation or just feeling different and alone. In extreme cases it may result in self-incarceration, in shutting out the rest of the world as in a monastery. How relentlessly he plays his own judge and jury! But be done! Hasn't he agonized enough? The desire to be true to self finally demands a hearing. One must be what one innately is. Isn't all else a sham? More betrayal?

Embracing the truth of self burgeons into a compelling mandate. To hell with what society or its critics think! He can't deny the hotly flowing sap of his gay young manhood any longer! Inner and outer pressures combine to eject him from the closet. It's a watershed event, on the order of the willed nonexistence of the father. These opposite yet mirror image events I call the First and Second Ordinations. One is immediate or unreflective, the other mediate and reflective.

Although one occurs in infancy or early childhood and the other in adolescence or early adulthood, they are continuous in that each bears the stamp of full Beingness. Each is a brave attempt to come to terms with what appears inevitable and ordained. Both, as acts of survival, are basically moral and at least partly spiritual. The Second Ordination confers the Biblical Joseph's many-colored coat of salvation. For what is salvation, or deliverance, if not the letting go of an exhausting burden of conflict?

Upon this freed and jubilant landscape, however, there can occur a disillusioning setback. It comes from the fear-based hypocrisy of the larger society. The outed gay man must now confront or brush off such demeaning taunts as "queer," "pervert," "queen" and "faggot." In a rude awakening, he wonders, if rather than a "risen angel," he isn't a fallen Lucifer. Off-color remarks and cold stares express the scorn of the greater society toward "those immoral gays," to paraphrase the elder George Bush.

The specter of homophobia, if sufficiently aggressive and virulent, may send him fleeing back into the corridors of withdrawal, make him an activist or leave him somewhere in the middle as a frustrated fence sitter. Gay Pride, political rallies, AIDS fundraisers, gay friendly church events and socializing with other self-accepting gay men may provide temporary protection. It tells him his place on the planet and in the hereafter hasn't been forfeited just because a conspiracy of male elitist golfers, evangelists or generals say so. Giving and receiving support, cultivating friendships and taking responsibility for his actions in a committed subgroup—these provide real belonging. As such, they are positive and exhibit full Being. Yet somehow they aren't enough. Something is still missing, off kilter, as it were. Again that fearsome absence. Nothingness once more rears its head, or as Wilber puts it, "The skull grins in."

At this point one may ask: Why does gay banding together often exhibit a baffling lack of cohesion? Fail to add up to the sum of its parts? Why doesn't it, after Stonewall and Matthew Shepherd, possess the gravity and moral force of other freedom movements? Why, like Black or women's lib, doesn't it build into a universal mandate for social change?

Furthermore, why do religions—particularly that great espouser of Oneness, the Baha'i faith—while advocating other libs, turn their backs and refuse to sanction homosexuality? Instead sideline or outright condemn it? Why does gay lib, like abstract art, tend to fragment into a thousand pieces?

Might it be that homosexuality is so imbedded in the human psyche that outwardly voicing its right to exist or decrying its suppression is an oblique redundancy? So close as to be invisible, in the same way that one doesn't look directly at the sun? Like the illusive Creator, simultaneously allowing and condemning? The "scandalous" strikes closest to jungle danger in the collective memory of the race. Put another way, it expresses the growing pains and fright of "homo" sapiens in evolving forward.

Equally profoundly, rather than merely threaten, homosexuality *exposes* the tender, growing tips of the Tree of Life. It's a sign, the very face, of future Completion that sexual dichotomy and gender differentiation, which are mere fractions, can't attain unassisted . . . .

To the fear-based, closed-minded larger society, homosexuality, as we've seen, poses a threat to the sanctity of family, the set roles of male and female, the calling forth of armies and the exclusive maleness of God. Most terrifyingly, it offers a glimpse into the Void. It dares heterosexuals to take a long hard look at their own naked incompleteness. The fingers of the Sea of Nothingness infiltrate just as surely, maybe more so, into the ruling majority. The intolerance of heterosexual pundits and fundamentalist religion bear eloquent witness! Yet gay men, due to their vital, fluid, ever-changing place in the Great Wheel of Being, may be the most vulnerable to inroads into the Void by virtue of being *on the cutting edge of artistic, social and spiritual change.*

That helps explain, on the negative side of the ledger, the campiness, the lurking bitchiness and other not so pleasant qualities that seem to spring up everywhere like plumbing leaks in a Three Stooges movie; in a word, why gays are so menacing. For what subgroup of mankind better illustrates the truth of the following: The stage props for the human tragicomedy are constantly being put up and taken down. On the outside, gayness may appear all outrageous theatrics. But underneath, something far deeper is taking place, something on the order of a revolutionary sea change.

Such grand reflections, however, don't make the ostracism of the graduate of the Second Ordination any easier to stomach or bear. Gay liberation, which he thought sacred and true, now presents itself not as solidarity but as an absurd and ineffectual mixture of Castro clones, bearded nuns, leather-clad bikers, drag queens and other blatant stereotypes. Like the Biblical house on the sand, the desired stability erodes into camp. What went wrong? Deep inside, he knows he deserves better. Ideally everything should work out, add up. Yet he sees the dignity of gay life degenerating all around him into a farce. He feels himself the victim of an unseen conspiracy. He perceives a corrosive Absence that cuts through not just to the heart of homosexuality but Being itself.

Very well, so he's a walking, breathing contradiction, a sexual freak or outlaw—Isn't incompletion the nature of all contingent being? But why should he be singled out as its most glaring and vulnerable example; to be society's whipping boy? Hasn't he been taught his entire life to think of himself as flighty and insubstantial . . . even evil? That's what the social and religious systems that spawned and molded him, only to fling him aside, want him to believe about himself.

Finally, isn't the most pernicious kind of brainwashing to be maneuvered into thinking oneself genetically, politically and spiritually inferior? Into believing that homosexuality is a sickle- (or boa-) bearing grim reaper that should be "dragged" before a tribunal of the Grand Inquisition and burned at the stake in a final act of immolation?

This fear and hate theme has been hammered home by eons of tribal, military and religious rule. But now, at last, in the Twenty-First Century those so victimized aren't buying it. They know in a deep soul place it simply isn't true. It's the Great Lie. They're created from the same primal Edenic essence. They, too, are beautiful and right in the sight of God. Yet despite this redeeming discovery doubt lingers. Why so easily tricked over the eons into buying into such a glaring injustice! Might the accusers in some insidious way be right after all? Deprogramming millennia of brainwashing isn't easy!

Did he go through, he further ponders, all the soul-searching and emotional upheaval of the Second Ordination only to find that his quest for truth has led to a shadowy unreality? To yet more rejection and betrayal? Betrayal seems to be a leitmotif of his life, metaphysical estrangement his fate.

Unless, of course, he's fortunate enough to land in a relationship, one built on love and trust. Yet even that utopian state may depend on a suppression or amputation of maleness, moral integrity, spiritual fine tuning and true selfhood. Does being a partner in a gay marriage, like his straight counterparts, lull him into being a contented fraction? Into a pose that merely mimics heterosexual marriage? Relationship, as well as provide emotional support, is a status symbol, an outward sign the loved one is attractive enough to hold a lover. Both gay and straight share that in common.

Well and good. Even wonderful. Commitment to a partner has the appearance of the eternal. But can something still be missing? Don't artificial props likewise shore up heterosexual marriage? If it works for them, it should work for him. For a while this substitutes for divine sanction or missing father. The loved one feels himself a member of a privileged class, one of the elect, pumped up with Being. Yet underneath lurks the specter of nonbeing punctuated with off moments of fear and rage. The underlying Lack is foundation in Cosmic Continuity, in having an earth father who reflects Eternal Father.

But there's a flip side to the mystical coin. Can this Lack be nothing more substantial than the result or side effect of sexist brainwashing? A mainstay of male superiority is that homosexuality, as an abomination against God, is a grotesque and disgusting aberration, a freak show, and therefore fair game for suppression and persecution. Same-sex relationship or marriage can't possibly work or stand the test of time because a powerful Hunter God gives sexual deviation a death-worthy thumbs down. So would the dictatorship of the heterosexual majority like its *declasse* gay citizens to think down to the tips of their ballet slippers or engineer boots. The heterosexual manifesto requires that they fail as gays in the mode of being *who they are*. For what failure is more devastating than to fail at being one's self? To be unworthy of cosmic citizenship? To have one's essence vilified and condemned?

To carry this argument a further step into specious absurdity—What of gay men who fail at relationship? The has-beens who managed not to die of AIDS? Are they, in an ironic twist, forgiven and elevated by God by *dint of failure*? Religions place a high premium on patience, long-suffering and surrender to God's will, on sexual suppression and abstinence. In other words, on negation and nonbeing. Does the gay man-as-failure gain quicker or exclusive admittance to heaven through the crushing of his inmost desires; through his failure to find and latch onto Mister Right? Is his malcontent elevated into high order bliss through the glorifying of deprivation? By not being who he is and being what he is not? By being a martyr-saint?

For once I felt confident that the imposed strictures on being gay, rather than a solid ontologic structure or divine decree, are, rather, a gratuitous control device to make its victims feel bad about themselves, stupid and useless, lost and undone; irremediably Other. The tidewaters of Nothingness, rather than a separate but equal Anti-Force, are nothing more than a pirated tool, like borrowed blinders, to be utilized or inflicted. Rather, they're a fissure at the heart of Being that allows, justifies and incites, even glories in, the abuse of basic human rights. Like the mythic Satan, it facilitates evil. Isn't that the method and rationale previously used to make Blacks and women contrite, humble and easily controlled? By convincing them they have no soul or at least only a fraction of one?

Fast forward to mid or old age. With this passed-down stacked deck, small wonder the quest for gay self years later can lead to a quandary of cynical hedonism. The just rewards of a life well lived have been craftily edited out by the powers that be. What a shock to realize long after the decision to come out that he's still profoundly alone, a social and psychological misfit—even with a partner, career and the outward accouterments of a normal home life to parade in front of his peers. These are the touted golden years. Yet he's compulsively racking up a huge mileage on the odometer cruising a boulevard frequented by hustlers, while another part of him gesticulates and stagnates at smart brunches and elegant dinner parties. He loses on both counts: as hedonist and saint.

Just as he gave up the struggle to deny his gayness at the Second Ordination, now he's asked to relinquish not only the search for Mister Right, who doesn't exist, but what he thought was his own finest Self. Alas, he's an over-the-hill, unwanted troll. Betrayed again! Not by a young body bristling with hormones, but one that ages and dies! To hide the rude awakening, he may become an alcoholic habitué of a wrinkle room. A shored-up carcass waiting for the final toppling of death.

Such a grim prospect triggers the mid-life crisis or male menopause. The elder patriarch finds himself at the brink of a precipice of despair. God and church are powerless and irrelevant to his needs. From family and relatives he gets only token sympathy, little more than a superficial "I told you so."

But wait! Just when it seems there's nowhere to turn but to cocktails, drugs and more mindless cruising, he catches a glimpse of the Third Ordination. It's like the Emerald City. It proclaims both unconditional self-acceptance and cosmic surrender. This culminating milestone is simply this: the transcendence or highest use of his gayness (not its denial, which is impossible as well as a mutilation), along with giving up deep-seated anger left over from childhood. He is called upon to accept both the fatherhood of God and full belonging as a child of the Universe.

Voila! Instead of different and apart, he feels suddenly vital and connected. Solitude, which isn't loneliness but a foretaste of fullness, confers a sense of dignity and belonging. Born alone, you die alone; yet you *aren't* alone. He's supported by a caring Eternal Father and a mystic brotherhood. The miracle of the reforging of lost continuity takes place. His looking glass self, seen in a new light, is young, even younger and more vital than when he first stepped out of the closet. He views the image in the mirror as a new, unique and wondrous creation.

The full circle of the Three Ordinations—complete at last! Our mature hero survived a difficult, even impossible life. The long struggle bestows the crown of an unforeseen victory. True, the tyrannical Male Order he rebelled against and tried to overturn remains stubbornly intact (like the father). It's still there behind the counter-world he so artfully erected as a rebel pre-gay and then self-accepted gay man. But it's no longer a fire-snorting dragon. It's more manageable with shades of Safe Court. The old repression system was subtly altered by his presence. His soul efforts weren't in vain. In a small way, even a big way, he changed things. He transformed himself into a fully accepted human being and a *man* with full rights to be here.

Over time and against his awareness, his priorities subtly shifted. They became less self-centered, more universal. Oneness, to his surprise, is as important as gayness. To accept triumph and defeat, affirmation and surrender, priestly ordination and simultaneous "defrocking," while regarding neither terms of the seeming opposite couplets as overridingly important, is to conquer and transcend both.

The alumnus of the First and Second Ordination thereby returns to Source, to the place where he first severed the father-son cord for the heady perils of self-invention. By giving up the rage of lower self or Ego-Body (apart from which Mister Right never had much reality), he regains Cosmic Self. Which is an ordained gay self. The question isn't *whether* but *how* to best be gay. To be so triumphantly and transcendentally.

In conclusion, the Three Ordinations are courageous and motivated by a primal (divine) will to survive. Beyond that, by a desire to flourish and contribute to an ever-advancing world civilization; to participate in, even preside over, the colonizing of the stars. Hence all Three are inherently moral and deeply spiritual. The First is of the body, the Second of the Mind, the

Third of SPIRIT. All three are characterized by a progressive and cumulative Fullness of Being (high spiritual density).

These milestones, then, in the evolution of gay Beingness—despite their permeation with negation and nothingness—belong in the Somethingness column of the cosmic ledger.

CHAPTER TWO

LACK OF SPIRITUAL DENSITY: A DESCENT INTO NONBEING

Density of being, perhaps the most original and difficult concept in this book, can best be defined as a Concentration of Light. On the surface, this would appear to be the opposite of "density" as generally conceived on this earth plane of heavy matter. Lead or uranium, for instance, is heavier and more dense than hydrogen. Rocks are heavier than cumulus clouds. On the spiritual plane, however, I use density to refer to Meaning, that is, to a concentration of Meaningfulness.

In the same way that a blade of grass, sea anemone or human being is attracted to and strives toward the sun, all beings aspire consciously, subconsciously, as well as supraconsciously, to Purposefulness and Meaning. Meaning is the umbilical cord, the nourishment, the very lifeblood of the soul. It's a principle of physics that cold, static air carries more moisture (and the pollutants that make up smog) than hot, higher energy air. (This is one reason the worst smog blankets Denver in winter, where I first conceived this book.) The opposite is true of the spiritual plane. The highest energy is concentrated in what would seem the most diffuse and evanescent.

If Meaning is the ultimate and highest goal of human striving, having the most of it, a sort of enlightened hoarding, should bring the most joy and happiness. This is undoubtedly true. To be locked, as it were, into the space/time continuum (the human condition) is to "experience" a scarcity, a thinning out, a lessening of Light and Meaning. Density of being is an ontologic term that refers only tangentially and symbolically to the physical realm. Its inner meaning is only understood in regard to the life of the soul. Within this seeming paradox I will attempt to weigh the Being and Nothingness—the relative spiritual light and darkness—of the gay condition. I will do so both as I have experienced it and observed it in my fellow gay brothers.

Since spiritual density can't be demonstrated empirically, that is, through the five senses or by means of a scientific experiment, I will approach it indirectly. To further define terms, Density of Being refers to the degree of connection or harmony between the spiritual, mental and physical planes. A person or situation with high density beingness is one in which light from the spiritual realm flows unimpeded down into the mental and physical. Conversely, a person or situation of low density of being is one in which the spiritual light is obscured, resulting in a metaphysical or ontologic darkness.

A Southern Baptist minister might say "lost in sin." But since "sin" in the context of this investigation is a lack of Light or distance from Source—that is, evinces low spiritual density (sin and evil are parasitic in that they possess only illusory beingness)—"lost" is less a matter of theology or morals than a plea for education and enlightenment. Rather is it a longing of the incomplete for Completion or Wholeness.

Relative to this heavy matter earth life, it would appear to constitute an alter- or para-universe. Pure, highly concentrated Light has the greatest "weight" of beingness, while darkness, another name for the purely physical, is the illusory, the transitory, a symbol of loss and nonbeing—the portal to Nothingness. What appears the most dense (matter, body) is the most evanescent, while what seems the most diffuse (Spirit, light) is metaphysically the most dense and enduring. In this upside-down, topsy-turvy world a moonbeam can be said to be more substantial than a steel girder in a Manhattan skyscraper. Or a concept "whose time has time" is spiritually denser than a fistfight in a dark alley.

To help grasp this paradox, I offer the following: That which accumulates, adds up or points to benefits beyond itself has a greater density of being than that which is less than it appears, fails to build toward higher meaning or accrue lasting benefits. Sincerity, for instance, has a greater density of being than artifice; respect, a greater density than contempt.

This leads to the question relative to the purpose of this book: What or how much density of being is there in homosexuality? What meaning or meanings does it evince? Does it confer lasting happiness or benefits?

In addition, I'll further ask: Is gay density of being or its lack inwardly or outwardly imposed? Is it a prior "given" or learned at random from the environment? Is it woven into the nature of things or arbitrarily absorbed from the social milieu? I'll attempt tentative answers by briefly describing a trip to a gay bar. I trust the reader will understand that the leap from abstract theory to grit experience doesn't comprise a laundry list of complaints, but hopefully a window onto a deeper ontologic reality; or if such be possible, a quest for Being and Nothingness.

At the time of this writing, I'd moved to a ranch in the Southern California desert. The nearest gay bar was thirty miles away in a place called Cathedral City. Like Thoreau on Waldon Pond, I'd immersed myself in an austere regimen of physical and mystic self-improvement to the exclusion of my more adventurous, pleasure-seeking side. A visit to the bar, which I had variously placed off limits as being too superficial, a bad environment, a hangout for drunks, etc., was to be a reward for keeping my nose to the physical, mental and spiritual grindstones, so to speak. The deciding factor was a fierce sandstorm. It lashed a grape vineyard and new planting of alfalfa to shreds as well as reversed several days of housecleaning. I deserved a break, even if on the mildly vengeful, perverse, even kinky side.

It was Friday night. Late enough for a crowd to have gathered and justify the long drive. I donned cruising gear—Levi's, lace up boots and black leather vest (I was moderately into leather)—with the incongruous addition of an Ivy League shirt. I wasn't one to signal with hankies or keys. I preferred to remain ambiguous. (I hope, when all is said and done, that doesn't apply to the vagaries and wild turns of this ontology!)

I pulled into a familiar asphalt parking lot. "Here we go again," I warned myself, "—James' folly." It was maybe the two dozenth time I'd driven to this warehouse-like meeting place over a two year period. Yet I could count on one hand the times I'd struck up a meaningful conversation, let alone scored. More often than not, I would return home without speaking to anyone but the bartender. "Be friendly, enjoy yourself," I took myself firmly in tow. "This is the equivalent of a gay church, isn't it? A pagan Jungle Jim meant for romping.

Where else find a kindred soul in your hour of need?" I'd become somewhat of a cynic over the years, a mindset I found hard to shake.

A sign at the door read "$10 Cover." I'd forgotten it was the weekend. Problem is if you want to leave after a few minutes, you're stuck for the ten bucks.

"Ten dollars for what?" I bantered with the butched up doorman who had on a quite becoming hard hat. "This better be good."

He aloofly stamped my wrist. (Maybe I too came across as aloof: Only gorgeous young things have that right. Or maybe it was because I found him attractive and resented the fact that wrist-stamping was the only possible intimacy between us.) The inked "stigmata" meant I could come and go without repaying the door charge. Fair enough. Although it now felt as if the establishment owned me. Like I was an inmate in a psychedelic Gulag Archipelago.

I passed through the "vestibule" into the "main sanctuary." Disco music wasn't merely booming. The decibel level placed it beyond hearing range to the point of actual damage to the eardrums. It was meant not so much to be listened to as tactilely absorbed. The admission fee, I reflected, financed the technology needed for this overkill. Since I was a classical music and jazz fan, anything but a fine balance of instruments tended to darken my mood.

My flippant yet serious complaint to the bartender that the music might be just a wee bit loud, an aggravation akin to a cement mixer, was greeted with a boisterous, "Too bad. If you don't like it, get out."

That told me! Although he was camping it up—what, I assumed, he was being paid for—I still felt insulted. (I was a customer and he was providing a service.) Not to be outdone, I retorted in jest, "No. You get out." (I refrained from adding "Slut" or "Bitch.") My, the evening was off to a grand start!

Was I the one in need of a session on a psychiatrist's couch? A brain-altering frontal lobotomy? Was it me or the system? The majority of customers tolerated, even seemed to enjoy, the punishing noise level. A Beethoven or Bartok string quartet with the musicians in black tuxedos wouldn't sell many tickets. At least the din provided the opportunity to practically French kiss someone on the ear just to be heard.

Behind the macho pose, the bartender, known to be an after-hours drag queen, became almost deferential. "Hey, hot man. What'll it be?" He fairly oozed sweetness now that the butch preliminaries were over.

I forked over the required amount. "I'll take a beer. In a mug with a few ice slivers. I don't care what brand."

"Cough up another buck," he demanded with an abrupt thump on the counter in yet another personality reversal. That meant paying extra for the mug with ice.

It was his/her domain. He could act as outrageously as she/it liked, as long as the cash register kept ringing. Maybe he sensed that I belonged to no social clique, that I was a rustic from the hinterlands. Worse, maybe I came off as a crusty, standoffish grandfather (I'd soon crack 50). Oh well, he meant nothing to me either. Just doing his job. The brassy leather poseur had to be dealt with.

"Bitch," I nonetheless couldn't help imprecating under my breath.

I took my beer onto an outdoor patio. Distant stars twinkled in the inky dome of the desert night. It was a relief to be away from the pounding noise. Yet I had a feeling of somehow copping out, of running away from something. Other than the booming jungle din, what? An opportunity to mingle with diverse types? A chance to develop a more socialized gay image? By the same token, just by being there I felt compromised, as though something deep down inside, something of value, was in danger. I'd descended, if not into a soul-dead space, at least to a place of significantly reduced cosmic light.

When my vocal apparatus reeled off unbidden, "A graveyard of moribund scintillation," I knew I was in trouble. Such stream-of-consciousness psycho-babble is a sign of major discontent.

"Hey cool it," I coached myself. "Who d'you think you are, James Joyce?" I lustily added, "Come on, motherfucker. You're here for a good time. Relax."

The inner voice persisted: Nothing for you here. I recommend you leave.

"But I drove all this way!" my practical, hedonist side shot back. "I coughed up the bucks. I won't run like a scared rabbit!" The cruise world, I reflected, requires a monklike dedication, an almost superhuman stamina. "Hang in there awhile longer," I ordered myself. Church isn't dismissed until they say the benediction, the fat lady sings, or a soul mate or reasonable stand-in materializes out of the din and smoke.

As an endurance test, I circulated through the blaring disco area. I sidestepped the quasi-violent clicking noises of an in-use pool table. From there I climbed a short stairway to a secondary elevated bar. Since it was mostly deserted—it had the feel of invisible bats hanging in space under a dark eave—I descended back to the main action arena.

A concession stand sold "elbow grease" (for the red hankie crowd), amyl nitrate and assorted leather toys. Off to one side was a small clique in Hawaiian shirts, tennis shorts and sandals. Very Palm Springs. They were discussing condo decoration and a Caribbean cruise which they hilariously dubbed the Gay Flotilla. On the other side was an inbred circle from Metropolitan Community Church. Its members seemed guarded, as though protecting one another from some heathen threat. A short distance away were several "disco bunnies" with heavy eye shadow and spiked purple hair. Finally, complete with escort and entourage, a garishly made-up cross-dresser puffing a cigarette like Bette Davis. I quickly ordered another beer. A little euphoria in a barren land.

I sensed I probably wasn't going to speak to, let alone meet, anyone there. The stars and planets weren't cooperating. No one of interest, especially Mister Right, would enter this curiously dead zone. (In theory I sought a son, father, mirror image or some workable combination. No avatar of this ideal trinity was anywhere present.) The thought that I too was a non-entity, an inaccessible Absence for someone else, seemed terribly sad. All that remained was a glow from the beer and the honey-roasted peanuts I'd console myself with on the way home.

First, a quick detour into the men's room. The two beers had drained right through me. Planted in front of one of the stalls, an Elvis type was stroking his groin. With a neck jerk he flipped back a dark cowlick and half grinned. To be social, I pretended to stroke and grinned back. The pungent smell told me he'd been inhaling amyl. Probably high on other drugs as well. One step up from a figure in a wax museum, he was clearly inviting me to join him in the stall.

Rather than confront a sordid unknown and possible arrest for a lewd act in public, I beat a fast exit. Saved by the bell! An inner force I couldn't quite describe came to my aid. However the instant I left, up flared an impulse to sneak back inside. Somehow interact with the guy. That would at least be a quasi event.

I stood sweating in mortal indecision. Lower your standards: Get back in there. Justify the 30 odd miles, cruise outfit and squelched high hopes.

Several customers in the meantime sauntered in and out. Yet none stayed long enough to take Elvis up on his lurid invitation. What the hell: A shadow game was at least a "something." Battling a chorus of warning voices, I reentered what seemed a revolving door to the nether world.

To my consternation, the "bait" wasn't there. Or seemed not to be. Miffed at having my five senses played with, I boisterously swung open the stall door. Empty as a tomb. The toilet paper holder gleamed in isolated mockery. The poseur-in-wax had utterly vanished. Despite my search of urinals, ceiling, walls and the peed-on floor that displayed a discarded condom, he'd turned into a grinning "not" like the Cheshire cat. He either hadn't been there in the first place, I was hallucinating, or he'd surreptitiously slipped out behind a customer zipping up his pants.

I paused to regroup at the main bar. Ghostly forms came and went, but no sign anywhere of the disappeared Elvis. Like an upended bat, I felt tricked by the cosmos, robbed of a substantial slice of beingness.

After another round of "Should I?/Shouldn't I?" that intensified into "Go!—leave!," I beat a resolute exit past Mister Butch Hard Hot out onto the parking lot. I felt like Jonah vomited by the whale onto an alien beach. Compared to the restroom vanishing act, the "void" of the shredded vineyard, alfalfa field and sand-logged house that I'd been so anxious to leave were suddenly focal points of Fullness. Why, I cogitated, did I go to such lengths to come here? Sex, baby, another part of me retorted, you want sex. Wild lusty sex. Yeah right, but how hard to achieve at my age!

During the long drive home (while keeping a hawk eye on freeway offramps for a hitchhiker), I thought of the expression, *unconditional self-acceptance*. I'd seen it in an article in a monthly gay rag. Was I a failure in that department? The self-love principle was currently in vogue, a sort of collective coronation, almost a religious duty. As well as a requirement for coming totally out of the closet.

Was it arrogant hypocrisy to think that the gay world, of which I was an undeniable if somehow invisible part, secretly despises itself—while engaging in orgies of self-adoration? Like the sand storm, was I caught up in a swirling negation I couldn't see out of? Was such cynicism built into the order of things? Or did I invent it out of resentment at turning middle-aged, being alone and over the hill? Was it existence or essence?

To return to Density of Being, the fulcrum of this book—I was determined to look truth as I saw it squarely in the eye and not flinch or shy away. At the bar I had to admit I'd lost more than I'd gained. My efforts, rather than cumulative, were fragmentary. They added up to less than the sum of the parts. Nor did I feel like the recipient of any divine blessing. More like abandoned. I felt gripped by an inner paralysis, a stunting of Hegel's quest of spirit for Spirit.

On the practical side, there wasn't even any decent fantasy material present. To be even mildly attractive, Elvis had to cloak himself in shadows, before being sucked into an insulting, anonymous, all devouring night.

Which leads me to ask: Am I an impossible striving? A useless passion as Sartre would have one believe? Where was my personal Nirvana where all the threads of longing come together in a tapestry of golden fulfillment? How much of this lack was my doing? And how much, like a serpent coiled at the heart of being, built into the gay sub-system?

Since the 60's, the bar scene, I pondered, had thrown off any apology over its gayness (the beingness of self-acceptance) only to "progress" to a blatant cynicism (a drift back toward Nothingness). The gay subculture flaunts and costumes itself at the same time that it is haunted by a lack of continuance and foundation. What is more past tense than a former gay bar? The posturing and posing, the private tempests in a teapot, the brassy camping—all go unrecorded down the annals of time. Is such impermanence a sign of low spiritual density? A discomfiting veer toward the Sea of Nothingness?

A more fertile, less high-flown idea occurred to me. Had the greater society in league with an all-powerful deity (the last offramp came into view—alas, no hitchhiker), done this to me through centuries of oppression—in the same way that an abused child or slave is conditioned to think of himself as inherently worthless, even evil? Had I been brainwashed into thinking I was guilty before the fact, unclean and unacceptable before God? Did I go to the bar programmed to fail? Did a buried voice from my Baptist past whisper that abstinence would somehow endear me to the Creator, that through failure I'd earn His praise and avoid His wrath?

Original sin and brainwashing, I thought, are equally distasteful, as well as unacceptable. In the first case, I was a martyr and in the second, a robot. I adamantly rejected both. Neither struck to the metaphysical heart of the matter. It was as though the Deity, within and without, was withholding information. My soul self demanded deeper, more relevant and privileged, even celestial, answers.

With the evening a bust, where else was there to turn? The gay lovelorn or meat market ads? A video parlor or all-night baths? I'd been down those garden paths too often before. What about my need for intimacy with another man? The necessity of keeping hope alive? These drives, shared with the heterosexual majority, are too urgent to be ignored. Why is it, I agonized, that the need always exceeds the remedy, the disease the cure? You are what you cannot be/ you cannot be what you are. It was as though Sartre were describing not only the human condition, but the particular dilemma of being gay.

Emotional survival, just getting through the day (as any gay man will attest), I decided, depends upon at least the chance of finding Mister Right. I call this a livable error. One buys into the dream fantasy to compensate for a glaring lack in the Now. Or in fundamentalist Christian terms, to hide one's nakedness before God. Or simply, original sin. I'd dangled the carrot of Friday night at the bar in front of my nose to reward a self-imposed regimen of hard physical, mental and spiritual toil. Yet when I reached the "promised land," this "future" had already become a "past." The oasis evaporated into a Sahara of the soul.

Sartre asserts the present is "not." This is profoundly true when the present is vested purely in body-time. More precisely, when cut off from inmost soul, which has its being in timeless Spirit. The caboose of body time, like the clattering tracks racing by underneath, is a succession of nihilating instants. Each track nihilates and replaces the track that came before. To arrive is to have already left.

Is that why at the bar scant benefit accrues from reaching middle age, from acquiring wisdom—or density? To grow old is extreme loss, a death mask that mustn't be viewed head-on. Every public performance and private sex act is throwaway and terminal. Nothing outlives itself. Each moment one must start over again, reinvent oneself from the Original Nihilation, that is, from the Void. All this occurs in mutable body-time. The illusion of Eternal Body finds its magnificent yet unseeing, vacant symbol in Michelangelo's *David*.

In an attempt to integrate the gay experience and the broader human condition—and further contrast Being and Nothingness—I offer a simple schema. Despite infinite complexity, humankind can be defined but not reduced to SPIRIT>Mind>body. Body is at the base of a descending hierarchy.

It is energized by Mind, which is in turn illuminated by SPIRIT. Without Mind, body immediately starts to decompose. Similarly, without SPIRIT, Mind would vanish "quicker than the twinkling of an eye." An overused Baptist expression but useable.

The gay world, and the materialist society it emulates, I reflected, tends to be anti-intellectual or at least non-analytic, not due to any mental deficiency—on the contrary, the struggle to survive forces gays to exceed their straight peers in intellect and creativity—but because the perpetuation of gayness depends upon *not knowing itself.* It depends on not perceiving its roots in Negation. The component of nonbeing must be kept hidden. The gay man mustn't know that his inner discontent mirrors a longing for Nihilated Father.

But that's only the negative side of the coin. Desire for Lost Father is simultaneously a yearning for veiled Higher Self. Body-based Western society (and the gay subculture it spawns), as a consequence of suppressing Intellect or Mind, posits the irrelevance or nonexistence of Spirit. In other words, materialist society flirts with the Impossible. The riveting disco beat (the tribal repetition of brain-numbing catch mantras) is at once the blighting of mind and the denial of Spirit.

Can Spirit flourish in a din of flashing strobe lights and android-like cruising? (I suppose it can, but not terribly effectively.) The blatant body celebration of Mardi Gras (or the White Party held yearly in Palm Springs), I'm told, is a purging, even cleansing experience. But I doubt it ascends at any point into the rarified stratosphere of Pure Spirit.

At the same time, signs of Fullness (Density of Being)—unconditional and unselfish love, commitment to a partner, mutual enhancement of hopes and dreams, courage in the face of AIDS—manifest Spirit. Yet it would seem that Spirit shines brightest (for instance, Tchaikovsky and Van Gogh) when gayness is struggled against and transcended, in other words, not taken as a given, but rather something to be avoided under a stern cosmic law designed to trip up its beaten-down practitioners.

But self-acceptance (the holy writ of the gay rag) is at the core of the Second Ordination, which I have characterized as a Fullness, as possessing high spiritual density. This second great milestone is infused with Meaning in much the same way that a Christian takes holy communion. As a purifying groping in the dark toward a distant light.

As a basically religious person (and burgeoning mystic), I agree with Hegel that Spirit is omnipresent and all-embracing, a unifying substrate of the universe. Spirit, like Brahman, is All-That-Is. Why, then, is great achievement in art or mysticism so often founded on suffering? Why must the being-in-the-world of a gay man be a constant struggle? One fraught with contradiction and illusion, even leading to suicide? It's not because he is any less spiritual or stands in greater need of redemption. Rather the opposite. Gay men, by virtue of what they must endure, are quite possibly *the most spiritual beings on the planet.*

This soaring thought (all at once I didn't mind coming home from the bar trickless and alone) led to a dangling question from my Baptist past (and Baha'i present): Did the Apostle Paul's "enmity of the spirit and the flesh" refer to a secret gayness? My reading and rereading of the Bible strongly suggests that possibility. The tone of the Epistles is both heroic and deeply submissive with true believers composing the bride of Christ. If this hidden feminism be true, what part does such a psychic split play in a Universe of Oneness (a great Baha'i principle)? Isn't universal reconciliation and brotherhood the basis of all religions (before they turn into bloody Crusades)? Can the struggle against such an internal fissure (to be or not to be gay) be a requisite for salvation? Was the Apostle Paul trying to heal himself by saving the world? And vice versa? We will see that the result turns out quite different from the original intent.

The lack of spiritual light or connection, I believe, is what accounted for the low density, the transitory quality, the internal fragmentation—mine included—of the gay bar on that dark but pivotal Friday night. It was certainly a low point in my cruising career. Dimmed cosmic light reflected not only the tribal futility, but the empty, imperious materialism of Western civilization. The greater society imprints its lack, its collective twilight, on the gay subculture, which s(lavishly) assumes the burden in redoubled form. The last minority to remain acceptable to oppress, homosexuals are forced to act out civilization's dark side, a function previously filled by Blacks, Jews, Japs and Communists. Or more currently, evangelical Christians against radical Moslems. Gays, at the bottom of the totem pole, are conscripted to sacrifice, at least radically lower their Fullness of Being.

I herein re-define Density of Being as Oneness with Spirit. SPIRIT>Mind>body exists as an ideal unity. Without this unity man is a diaspora, a shower of fireworks against a night sky, a useless passion. Homosexuality, forced to shoulder the multiple denials of the heterosexual majority, elects in the interest of self- and soul-survival to act out the unjust sentence to the hilt. It will transform the oppressor's darkness into the glitter of Mardi Gras, turn imposed deprivation into celebration. If one truly thinks about it, what could be more justified, creative, generous and in this context, saintly?

To return to the Apostle to the Gentiles. How can a great spiritual reformer, afflicted with the thorn in the flesh of a repressed sexuality, advocate unity with universal Spirit? Can a physical, psychological and spiritual amputee be one with Oneness? Christianity has foundered on this quicksand for twenty centuries. In its great charity and claim of universal brotherhood, it singled out the gay man to bear the brunt of the conflict. In the process, Christianity and the heterosexual majority unwittingly bestowed sainthood upon a persecuted minority. The Apostle Paul may have gotten his secret wish after all!

To sum up: What makes life livable for the gay man is the *possibility* of loving and being loved by another man. The same was likely true for the great Apostle. For him, a light-haloed vision of the risen Lord. This was later diverted into an attraction to the ardent young men (Timothy and Titus) he chose to accompany him on his missionary journeys. A man of his stamina and charisma most probably lived out his passion in the form of a perpetually deferred consummation. Or since he was human, he may have slipped up on occasion, only to denounce or suppress his actions afterward. Whichever, perpetual postponement or the denial of homoerotic impulses altogether, helped produce one of the world's great religions.

This psychic split is very much with us today. It continues to act beneath the threshold of consciousness as a taboo against socially threatening behavior. "Thou shalt not," "all have fallen short of the glory of God," "the wages of sin is death," etc. How often does a gay man take an honest plunge into relationship only to find himself lusting after someone else or covertly scheming to be alone? He seeks relationship only to discover, once achieved, that he seeks its Absence (his heart really does belong to Daddy). It's as though he demands a fair shot at love, but the chance of winning mustn't be too great, under no circumstances be a sure bet. To maintain this tenuous balance or livable error, he must be what he is not and not be what he is. This multiple negation, like spokes leading to a central Nothingness (all roads lead to Rome), is the condition of the gay man's being-in-the-world as espoused by the love-inebriated but repressed Apostle.

Has the Creator, whether from indifference, perverse amusement or blood revenge at the least hint of blasphemy, allowed his gay creatures to flounder into a swirling contradiction? A diabolic dilemma? What about divine forgiveness and grace? Is salvation won only by overcoming a thorn in the flesh? How strange to be molded and formed by homosexuality in order not to be it! A curious salvation—achieved through the perpetuation of a psychic split!

Moreover, to resolve the dilemma by faking it with a woman only leads to greater alienation. What good is duty without passion? To engage in sanctioned intercourse just because God or holy writ says one must is contrary to the spirit of love, indeed does it violence. Love isn't forced, it flows. It flourishes in the fertile soil of human freedom and creativity. The gay man senses himself, if true to Higher Self and to Love, beyond any moral obligation to miraculously change into a heterosexual. To force oneself into an artificial, lock-jawed morality is itself immoral. Why launch an enterprise that involves even more sham and falsehood, that multiplies neurosis and negation in all concerned.

To know *who one is* (no religion will refute this; Socrates demands it) is a primary task on earth, even though it take a lifetime or lifetimes of soul-searching. To be true to oneself has a higher spiritual density than faking it with a woman, only to wind up on a psychiatrist's couch or the edge of suicide, just because it's the heaven-prescribed way. Life has already been too much of a charade or diabolic farce. The gay man, in order to survive and flourish, must be *the internal negation that he is*.

The quest for inner cohesion and integrity, flung into being at the First Ordination, demonstrates a watershed downflow (SPIRIT>Mind>body) of spiritual Light. The courage to choose and more than that, *will* the paradox that one is/isn't shows high density beingness, a leap of faith toward the divine. To be truly and authentically gay is a major step toward the Light. For such qualities as courage, honesty and joy directly manifest Spirit.

I here take the liberty of changing Sartre's famous "Man isn't free not to be free" into "Man isn't free not to be himself." This I further expand into "Man isn't free not to be Spirit." That changes "Existence precedes essence" into its polar opposite: Essence (Spirit) precedes existence (Ego-Body). After the First Ordination, the gay man hasn't the choice not to be gay. The course has been set, the dye cast. To embrace his gayness is to reclaim Essential Self. To deny this destiny is to fall back into body delusion, mental distress and soul fragmentation. The price of suppressing true self is neurosis leading to madness. Neurosis disrupts and reverses the SPIRIT>Mind>body continuum. Such mutilation is the epitome of immorality.

To leap forward in time— At the Third Ordination, the mature gay man gives Body Self greater rather than lesser credence—by placing it in a loftier perspective. He perceives body for what it is: a valued but dispensable vehicle that temporarily houses Spirit>Mind. Damming up the sexual juices and the creativity they produce for mankind can lead to personality disorder, nervous breakdown, ulcers, an enlarged prostate, not to mention irritability, stomach distress and depression—all of which can cause disease. Disease in turn dims the light of the soul. To be honestly and unapologetically gay is to dwell at the heart of Divine Will, to rest in the embrace of the Divine. For at stake is the highest form of *moral hence spiritual* Soul Survival.

If the Apostle Paul is taken in context or believed, the gay man can't "win" qua gay, that is, flourish in any way as a practicing homosexual. He can only alternate from one escape mode to another, from longing to denial and back again. Each pendulum swing makes the longing more intense, which must then be repressed and transcended with redoubled energy. What remains of sexual desire is a "being there" before and after the fact. Just as the past is to be *born in sin*, the Now of requited love is deferred to an indefinite future. As a member of the bride of Christ, the ascended (and repressed) gay believer is at the moment of death divested of the meddlesome, damming body. The thorn-in-the-flesh is mercifully extracted. The Now of sexual fulfillment never arrives. Or evanesces once it does.

Thus homosexuality in evangelical Christianity, and most major religions, mustn't be confronted head-on. Its beingness consists in its being elsewhere. On a deeper level—and here the Apostle was dead on—this perpetual deferment and denial points to a veiled desire (transcended deathwish) to escape this earthly prison of flesh and bone and return to the bliss of pure Spirit. Past and future disincarnate states (provided one believes in reincarnation) derive from and feed into a shared Memory of the Race. Homosexual desire is successively repressed (note the energy with which born-again's beat their children, White bigots burn Black churches and society bashes gays) and through the amnesia conferred at birth, blotted from everyday consciousness.

From a more comprehensive perspective, a taboo-, materialist- and conformity-based mentality results from being locked into the space-time continuum, while suppressing a common origin in Spirit. This was the Apostle's great contribution—that man is a spiritual being. That conviction, despite the fatality of allowable homosexual expression, placed him eons ahead of his time.

The gay man can take comfort that he's not alone. He shares the fate of all mankind. It's the human condition for Spirit to fall like a dark angel back into body (space-time) and then like a salmon fight its way back to spawning waters; to struggle for reunion with timeless Spirit. So it is in the Great Chain of Being. Life is a constant surpassing of self toward Self and of Self toward Oneness.

From a paramecium to an entire galaxy, all creation is in a constant state of flux. If it stopped evolving, it would revert to simple elements (entropy), compress into an infinitely heavy black hole or cease to exist as we know it. I intend to show that homosexuality is a vital and integral part of the evolutionary process. In Biblical terms, the salt of the earth, the leaven in the loaf, the Balm of Gilead.

Struggle, then, the nihilation and transcendence of the inertia-logged Given, is the stuff of evolution. This physically dense (and evanescent) clot of body, with its heavy matter resistance and fear of change, must be respected as a temporary carrier of the soul. When sick, a person should consult the best doctors. Or if financially and physically able, treat oneself to a wild and crazy vacation like a Caribbean cruise or Mardi Gras. Even the White Party. The endocrine glands must be heeded, ingrained sexuality respected. To sweep one's natural impulses under the rug of a religious taboo is immoral as well as anti-spiritual. It derails SPIRIT>Mind>body. Since sex releases and fulfills the organism, it follows that the responsible and reverent use of sex manifests Spirit. Similarly, gay sex is a privileged form of worship; in Hinduism, a tantric dance. A celebration of the limitless possibilities of a caring and wondrous Creator.

The mental landscape of a hardcore S&M addict, it might be objected, may include grossly unspiritual imagery for achieving release. Fantasies cut off from reality tend to become ever more embedded and depraved. Simple penetration no longer works so one goes on to fisting. At some point, a moral decision must be made in regard to the greater or lesser benefit or harm of erotically facilitating thoughts. One should stop short of inflicting or receiving serious injury. Or becoming a serial killer. However, if no lasting damage is done to oneself or others, "kinky" aids to sexual release are, in my opinion, morally neutral and indirectly spiritual. They reflect the mercy of a caring God Who Himself walked the earth, Who breathed its dust and felt its pain. They help a dispirited person find relief and a sense of autonomy in a violent world.

Is life worth living without an element of the forbidden? Or for a gay man, when prohibited from expressing God-given longings? The feeling of being illicit, naughty and extreme flavors most sex acts, male and female, heterosexual and homosexual. Sex is by nature rebellion; that is to say, it expresses incompletion. It's a momentary plunge into negation, connection through disconnection, a simultaneous building up and tearing down. It replays the eternal drama of separation and return. In short, it's a micro-replay of Original Creation, unless one limits oneself to the missionary position, to keeping one's eyes fixed rabbit-like on a puritanical far-off heaven.

All sexuality—hetero or homo, chaste or wildly creative—contains an element of conspiracy. An intolerant Creator would have to "look the other way" during even the most stainless coitus. Even the coupling of saints contains lusty elements. To create is to subvert, to inaugurate change. Homosexuals aren't alone in playing at subversion—or perversion. Nor is theirs the only sexual adaptation shot through with negation. All sexuality includes hostility and denial that finds temporary resolution in orgasm. (To be male is to deny being female, and vice versa. Both states are an estrangement from and denial of Oneness.)

A primary difference, if there be one, is that the homosexual goes a step beyond his heterosexual counterpart into the heady realm of Negation by willing the nonbeing of the father. In so doing, he bypasses the earthly "necessity" of Eve and severs a primary link with Cosmic Continuity. He stands alone in an odd company of angels.

Despite religious taboos, this radical bypass appears, and rightfully and inventively so, as an honor—until the Third Ordination. Suddenly everything, his gayness included, is again called into question. Although earned, widely accepted and wonderful, it's no longer enough. Something new is needed. That is the Rite of Reconciliation and Return.

To enter a mark, just barely and tentatively, on the debit or Nothingness side of the ledger: Homosexuality, as the projection of a collective negation (Nihilated Father), is what gave the bar (myself included) its lowered spiritual density and allure; like any vice, what made it both futile and exciting. The bar was a multiple Absence of Father, Son and Higher Self (Holy Ghost corporealized and brought down to earth); a sort of grainy, not-quite-there, sub-Christian trinity.

Or: *a graveyard of moribund scintillation.*

Those words simply rolled off my tongue, only to hang almost palpably in empty, soundless space. The disco blare ceased to exist. With it, the posturing and posing. Pax Elvis. A wax effigy slicking a jaunty shock of hair in a fading dream. The entire evening floated off into negation, evanesced. As though it never was.

That is why if I ever open a gay bar, which is unlikely, I will call it The Church of the Infamous (or Vanishing) Sacrament. Maybe Swimming with Sharks . . . or Ghosts. Or if that doesn't suffice, simply *Le Mirage.*

CHAPTER THREE

WHY I COULDN'T STAND MY FATHER OR HE, ME

The Origins of Sado-Masochism

During our time together, my father seemed like a clot of darkness, a spidery Rorschach blot, something ugly and unpleasant. A focal point of irritation and anger. These feelings are hard to confront without a great deal of guilt. Sons aren't supposed to have such an all-out, hostile response to their fathers. Its potency still surprises me. At least part of it had to do, I believe, with his refusal or inability to touch me. The touch confirms a child in his selfhood. More deeply, in his Soul Self.

A need for this withheld substantiation nudged me partway into the camp of women. If I was "boy," it was as an actor. What I fault my father for was forcing me into a life of posturing. Had I been allowed and not forbidden to play at being a little girl (not that I wanted to) without having to endure his scandalized and censorious silence, it would have been easier to slip naturally into the role of "little scrapper."

He tried to maneuver me into "boy" by forcing me to play softball. Endless games of catch, pitching and batting practice. How he tried! What energy was devoted to my masculinization! But too late: I already identified with Mother. Her softer world required less posturing. It flowed. The boy my father wanted me to be had to be externally imposed like a graft, a brand name or tattoo. I was a boy-girl masquerading as all boy.

Looking back, my father revealed his own incompletion by not being sufficiently a man to stand on his own male credentials. He needed reinforcement to prove himself an integral part of the male power structure. Unfortunately, the son was too sensitive and rebellious to play the game. My father was an imposter, which indirectly made me one. Just as he withheld love via the touch, I denied him the unqualified acceptance, the idolizing, little boys are expected to give their fathers.

Despite the battle raging inside him—"my girlish ways burned him up"—he was curiously aloof to the masquerade. The full burden of imposture was laid on me. When I showed a singular lack of talent or enthusiasm for softball, he transferred his interest—at Mother's urging, to take the pressure off me and the frustration off him—to the other little ball players. As a result, I got lost in the shuffle. That both relieved and infuriated me. The pariah hid in the most inconspicuous place he could find: right field. I longed not to be even there. Oh to be anywhere but the ball diamond! I wanted to disappear, to be invisible. Rather, to cease to exist altogether.

By thrusting me into the spotlight of the playing field, he pushed me farther into seclusion. I wanted to be beyond the bleachers, past the most distant chain link fence, a thousand miles from nowhere. Oh to transport myself to an alpine meadow of pristine beauty and escape the crude razzing! Father was determined to carve out the little warrior neither of us could be. We were each other's mutual shame.

Each denied the other's right to exist, then, only to be subtly confirmed in our reciprocal notness through the mediation of the female family members. That enabled us to play out a socially acceptable father-mother-son-daughter tableau: a tidy little unit. Thus life became a masquerade. Yet a vital biological link was missing. To atone for this glaring absence, we overemphasized our social/spiritual dimension. We donned community service and church attendance like an outer vestment to hide an inner shame. We prided ourselves on our humility and theological uprightness.

What an embarrassment to kneel in family devotions! Father rasped out stertorous prayers. Mother's buttocks protruded, her lips went slack and moist. Devotions seemed like a sex act. Ironically, in the body-transcendence of family prayer we came closest to regaining our lost biology. It was as though we had to sneak in through a back window or a trap door in the attic to find the forfeited biology of our missing physical selves. My parents seemed incapable of lust unless it entered through a missing roof shingle (more probably, the basement), or a stained glass window of God>procreation>divine-institution-of-marriage.

Sexuality for its own sake didn't exist, rather, was an immoral waste of time and energy. The lower animal nature was channeled into sweat-of-the-brow labor or sacrificed in Christian service.

Luckily, the penchant for sacrifice interfered with my father's efforts to forge a scrappy son. The feminine aspect of devotions (submission to God) exhorted him to be forgiving and kind, to seek God's will rather than just his own. His buried homosexuality wasn't allowed the open air it needed to breathe and grow. The only hope of expression was through a surrogate scrapper son, a partner in miniature, who would endure hardship and push to the limit for the sake of the team and for him; for the father and complete male he wasn't and couldn't be. This would graft back on a missing testicle.

Meanwhile, the poseur son was marooned in right field in secret terror that the next pitch would be knocked his direction. The pressure became too much. He refused to participate in the phony struggle. To secure his status as coach, Father transformed himself into an eight-year-old kid running energetically about. He became the apotheosis of the scrapper the universe demanded of little boys. Yet through it all he remained somehow too polite, kind and deferential.

These same qualities, however, endeared him to the community. He was known as a wonderful man. I didn't abhor him so much as I devoutly wanted him not to exist. Or rather, I willed him *not to be* (the First Ordination) to the same degree that I was forced into nonexistence. The judgment we placed on each other was harsh and irrevocable. The softball charade was the occasion of a permanent estrangement. Future rapprochement would consist of hollow gestures to please the womenfolk, as well as the greater community.

While Father transferred his stifled homosexuality onto the arena of little scrappers, Mother remained neglected and unsatisfied, hormones mal-secreting, on her side of the bed. Could a minister's daughter object to her husband devoting himself to church, community and little league? Her faith, undergirded by the writings of the Apostle Paul, exhorted her to play a subordinate role. She thereby made herself an unglamorous household servant, the bottom tier on the pyramid of earthly duty. Her saintliness fed on aridity; one produced the other.

To compensate for an uneasy puritanism—that is, the failure of sex—Father placed himself out of reach of romance. He spent sweat-soaked hours pruning grape vineyards and crawling about on all fours digging up nut grass, a noxious weed that he was determined to eradicate from the earth. It left little doubt he preferred fondling grape bunches to mammary glands. Instead, he kept voluminous ranch, softball and Sunday School records whose only long-term purpose, besides attracting dust and nesting insects, was to hold at arm's length the onerous duty of making love.

To compensate for the lack of a sex life, he and Mother alternated like musical chairs, more tellingly, beds, between the Baptist and Methodist churches. The first was too emotional, the second too formal; the former lacked social conscience, the latter was too theologically lax. They finally concentrated on the Migratory Camp and Rescue Mission, laboring class arenas of Christian service where the poverty of body found full expression.

Body denial had the further consequence of neglect of environment. Plumbing repairs were ignored. Clothing, medical check-ups, air-conditioning, comfort—all neglected as extensions of suppressed body. Father was fond of saying, "Today's youth are deprived of deprivation." Deprivation was raised to an absolute virtue, another way of making a virtue of failure. While physical needs went unheeded, the humble "smiled meekly through." We "turned the other cheek" in the best tradition of the Apostle's mortification of the flesh.

In elder years, the neglect of basic maintenance turned into dilapidation accompanied by hoarding. No provision was made for growing old, no money set aside for grave plots or funeral arrangements. Body denial gave rise to a myth of earthly immortality. "Senior citizen" was a dirty word. It was difficult or unthinkable to be old when one hadn't known the spontaneity of youth; when bliss in the Now is perpetually deferred to a distant future. Or when romance is the stingy bestowal of a God Who despite every effort to believe otherwise, can hardly be called bountiful. Making love isn't a spontaneous act in the now, but a Platonic duty. They lived out their preordained marriage second-hand; made themselves a living sacrifice, holy and acceptable unto God . . .

The belief that marriages are made in heaven further enabled them to escape the need for sexual improvisation and romantic renewal. All inadequacies and imperfections are left to God. But God is perfect and blameless. In His great mercy He puts his creatures through a meat grinder of frustration and conflict in order to test them. A condition of these tests is that they be seen as a mercy, punishment regarded as a privilege, denial misconstrued as love.

A resultant maxim: Sex, while designed to be enjoyed (but only minimally), must be repressed and transcended. Yet, at the same time, I must be a scrapper boy in order to uphold some cosmic formula of maleness. I must come up with a decent batting average—because they can't make it in the sack? Why is it a crime to be a sissy and not a crime for them to fail at making love? It fell upon me to take the bum wrap.

In my childish innocence I hazily computed the quandary thus: Because father, a closet homosexual, feels trapped or uneasy in his role as husband and father, I'm relegated to pariah status for not turning into an all-American boy. Their sexual failure enjoys eternal sanction; not so my sissyhood. I'm the unacceptable one who must be altered. They possess the diplomatic immunity of a marriage made in heaven that in turn rewards biological failure and denial.

Differently put, I'm to blame for being the maladjusted result of a belated mating of 30-year old virgins. Basic survival, abetted by a hidden perversity, made me rebel at being the cure-all of the breach. How nice could I have been a healing compress on the wound of their marriage! In retrospect, I could weep over all the misplaced striving and jockeying for love. Outwardly expressed emotion was a desert thunder storm that after a promising rumble and a few drops of rain evaporates into thin air, leaving only an arid and nostalgic memory.

I didn't choose to be a sissy so much as I withdrew like a turtle beneath a stoic shell. Father's attempted ego-extension in me propelled me into a twilight zone of social non-existence. The right field imposter took refuge in piano practice. Scales and arpeggios blotted out ball diamonds and the need to prove myself as a little scrapper. How I envied girls! They have it made, their actions flow. They don't have to prove anything. They simply *are*.

Boys, on the contrary, are this terrible claylike substance constantly being called into question, that needs painful altering through fistfights or the rough and tumble of the ball diamond. Whether from cowardice or a survival instinct, I thought fighting unreasonable. That was just it: Boys are expected to be unreasonable. They're forced to engage in the pointless competition of sports. One must act aggressively, razz one's opponent, knock the hell out of the ball; don the male world like a full metal jacket. The uniforms, the medals and pendants, along with all the posturing, amounted to a crushing load.

Boyhood wouldn't have been so bad had it been a simple expression of a tribal, father-son legacy. It might even have exhibited a Fullness. But as an outer fix on an inner lack it was intolerable. My features and behavior like the Pillsbury doughboy were too soft around the edges. That I needed altering due to an inherent deficiency perplexed and outraged me. An inner voice said it wasn't me but the world that was wrong. A child has a sense of belonging in the universe, of being all right *as is.*

Not that God rejected me. I suspected the Deity to be above such petty small-mindedness. Stern disapproval came from the male establishment: school principals, football coaches and other fully masculine boys—as well as from a glamorous type of female who got her endorphines flowing by supporting (in a Size D bra, falsies for all I knew) the male power structure whose raw aggressiveness would later deflower her, if it hadn't already, in the back seat of a sleek convertible. This predatory Lana Turner was seen posing at soda fountains and in the bleachers at ball diamonds. The sweater girl waited for the future wolves the little scrappers would become to hotly paw her panties and breasts. I was a scandal because I didn't buy into the rigged gyroscope of male-female tension. The Pillsbury doughboy with a receding chin had the audacity to question the sexual system.

A sense of being on the outside looking in may be one reason I didn't achieve orgasm until the late teens, and then by surprise while reading a shockingly sadistic passage from *The Brothers Karamazov.* Masturbation, while a private act, has a tribal dimension. Since I was fake, an ejected member of the team, I didn't produce semen. Not having to deal with sex was by compensation a blessed relief. The honeymoon night was an occasion of gross embarrassment. One threw the rice and looked the other way. Intercourse was certain to be a ghastly experience. The marriage victims pretended to enjoy the unspeakable. What was touted as a flight to heaven was really a descent into hell, a horror to be postponed as long as possible.

It was almost with a sigh of relief that I later embraced certain facets of sadomasochism. Anything, I thought, was better than the slaughterhouse of the wedding night. By the same token, not sparing the rod in child rearing or going to war was mild and inconsequential compared to the horror of burning forever in hell. At least a flogging comes to an end. S&M seemed tamer, more nostalgic and real than the terrible duty of intercourse laid down from a malevolent heaven.

This revised compulsion also served, paradoxically, as an escape route from the female camp to which I'd partly defected. Father should have been happy! Sadomasochism was a belated denial of the softly feminine, a backdoor return to the male camp; a kind of cosmic salvation.

For once I wanted to be as masculine as possible. S&M reinstated (in an altered, more malleable form) winner-loser, abuser-victim, dominate-submissive—indicators of social injustice I'd previously found odious. It made the big bully, and the oppressive society that produced him, both manageable and erotic. I transferred outrage over my father's rejection to the wider negation of sadism: gross body exploitation. And beyond that, forfeiture of any claim to a just universe. I'd found a devious way back at my oppressor as well as the Creator. I'd not only play the game, but exploit it to the hilt.

Sartre tells us that sadism is the failure of sex and masochism is the failure of love. I participated in both failures. To inflict pain is to deny pleasure as a moral value; to receive pain denies both pleasure and morality. For as we know, to inflict harm, first against oneself, is a primary immorality. This backdoor return to the male camp had the effect, however, of placing me farther outside the social system. I'd embraced a perversion within a perversion. That was a little scary. A network of interlocked negations held me precariously poised above the ink-black, annihilating waves of the Sea of Nothingness.

Let's examine sadomasochism more closely. For the masochist, pleasure, real or conjured, comes primarily before and after the pain. Masochism is a nihilating rejection of the Now. The sadist and masochist are estranged through union, joined through separation. A simultaneous coming together and falling apart; a whirling carousel of attraction-repulsion; a playing out of love-hate. Tension is held at fever pitch. The masochist secretly desires to turn the tables, but savors his failure to do so. He both resents and enjoys his helplessness. Can a male, who produces testosterone, accept a role that brings ego-loss, the curtailment of natural aggressiveness, even bruises—still be a man?

Simply this: by being forced against his will. Or hustling for money. The restraints he consents or even insists on wearing, or twenty dollar bills stashed in his pole dance briefs ("Honey, I also take Visa or Master Card"—better yet, a Mercedes or a house in the country), are symbols of a bartered freedom. For the masochist, coercion or the distancing intervention of money are the price of retaining masculinity.

No matter what a sadist may claim, it's difficult, without a mental sleight of hand, to love and honor a punching bag of abuse. If he respects the masochist, it's not only because the latter offers himself up as a sacrificial lamb, but because the victim inwardly rebels against his abasement. The fleshly object of abuse cries out, muscles bulge against the restraints. Sadism successively lowers the sadist's capacity to respect, let alone love, his victim. It depends, rather, for its perpetuation on a taut balance of anger, intolerance, a fascination with injustice and haste to pass judgment, combined with a talent for tuning out suffering.

In a word, it depends on indifference, which is a prelude to, or progressive numbing toward a final denouement of death. (Shown in the classic movie "The Night Porter.") To avenge and forget his own conflicted past, the sadist turns his victim into a helpless object. In some respects, the victim isn't even there. He might as well be a mannequin or voodoo doll. That is why the sadist and masochist often appear as an Absence to each other; why these separate Rorschach blots of darkness often disport themselves in black leather.

Despite this and against all odds, the masochist craves the sadist's love (anything but indifference), but with the following proviso: it must have the appearance of reality while remaining unattainable. He's already settled upon the impossibility of love in the Now. He conspires not to see or be the logical outcome of his futile striving. Rewards and success are systematically and cleverly sabotaged. How find love through blows whose underlying origin and purpose is the acting out or boiling off of a powerful Other's previous, anonymous and unresolved anger?

The masochist's love for his master is alternately slain and reborn in wild hope. The sadist, after all, is doing it *to him* and not to someone else. Great attention is being paid him. Such crumbs suffice to sustain him across the nihilating moments of Body-Time, from one flogging to the next.

The masochist wills himself a sacrifice because the unworthiness learned from never being touched as a child precludes his being simply pleasured. Rather than confirmed via the touch, his selfhood must be propped up through violence. It proves that he exists—in his vast incompletion. The blows, that simultaneously unravel and confirm him, perpetuate an indelible Lack he aspires to both remedy and stubbornly leave in place. The relationship remains an open wound, which of itself provides a covert excitement.

The masochist thus incarnates the Impossible. Sacrifice-atonement; I can't go on/I'll go on. What are these but hidden attempts to dethrone the Absolute, to replace God, Who by definition is Infinite Possibility? But hasn't the Deity proven to be unreliable by allowing, even fomenting, injustice against my striped body? But that's the only way I can find love—through the aegis of a God of Love Who glorifies sacrifice? Now I'm doing it full tilt to the core of my being—as a practicing leather freak. Thus commands the Apostle: "Offer up your body a living sacrifice, holy and acceptable unto God, which is your reasonable service . . ."

Herein lurks a contradiction. Body sacrifice, besides an act of love, is proclaimed to be *reasonable*. Innocently and in defiance of logic, sacrifice becomes sex-linked. (The tendrils of sexuality reach into unexpected places, the sanctified fortress of seminaries, church choirs, even the Eucharist.) What happens to become eroticized is an apparent toss of the dice. It depends on vulnerability, emotional readiness, hormone balance and present sperm count. With the theme of "Ye are unworthy" driven home from the pulpit, small wonder enticing aspects of body sacrifice are swept up into a brutal game. Sacrifice is reasonable and meritorious. Sacrifice buys worthiness. By the same token, no one is *ever* worthy. "All have sinned and come short of the glory of God." Enter sadomasochism.

More about the sadist. The last to admit the punishments he doles out are arbitrary and unjust, he stands on shaky moral ground. His iron will must be obeyed if the S&M couple, linked through violence, is to remain welded together and not dissolve into a mirage. Injustice and unworthiness are thereby elevated to absolute virtues. They reflect thrilling, diabolic Indifferent Body. This isn't surprising, since throughout childhood, puberty and young adulthood, God is seen as an unyielding Tyrant seated on a throne in the sky. He arbitrarily and perversely creates ten percent of His creatures gay, only to accuse them of being freaks and sinners and therefore fuel for hellfire. The eroticizing of sacrifice is thus the eroticization of the unjust and the unreasonable. But "Sacrifice is my reasonable service." A whirling contradiction that is at the heart of sadomasochism.

Most profoundly, masochism is the thrill of destruction. The masochist wants to topple his master, the system and ultimately God. He puts the Deity on trial as a fraud while touting his own saintliness. He triumphs by supplanting God with his bruised self as supreme judge. This auto-deification, however, is also true for homosexuality in general. And beyond that, all contingent being (gay or straight and in between) that attempts to usurp the station of the Absolute; that is, to impersonate and replace God.

Back to my father. I've tried to show the link between father-son enmity, body suppression and sado-masochism. S&M develops when revenge and hatred overflow the simple murder edict of the First Ordination. It spills over into a vendetta beyond mere nonbeing but rather to appear frighteningly center stage. My antipathy toward my father was so overwhelming it seems to have arisen simultaneously with conception. Or boiled over from a previous lifetime with sinister overtones. He was neither mean-spirited nor violent. It's hard to fault this dutiful community servant. He simply wasn't there. Rather, he was there as denial of himself and his shadow self in me. My irrational hatred was a spontaneous combustion that fed on a phantasm. It wasn't my genetic father that horrified and infuriated me so much as the mythic gorgon I erected in his stead, who, despite my every effort, to this day has the power to resurge and persist of his own volition and godlike timetable.

Might this primal enmity have arisen as readily from a hormone imbalance in my mother's emotionally charged chemistry? She nearly bled to death during menstruation. She was subject to irrational fears and depression. Did she secretly think the sex act an evil intrusion into the holy temple of her body? Did giving birth strike terror? She once described her own mother's screams (pain killers weren't yet invented) in the next room during the birth of her younger sister. During her own pregnancy did something basic yet unspoken about my father repel her?

This, together with hormonal imbalance, aggravated by a host of phobias and mood swings, got passed on to the fetus. It created a climate of sexual ambiguity and repugnance which provided a primordial stew for the evolution of a pre-gay. You're afraid/you're not afraid. You're a sinner/you're a saint. Making love is evil/making love is God's will. These inner dialogues, reflected in the blood chemistry, made the world beyond the snug harbor of the womb appear to the developing fetus as a dangerous storm at sea.

That fork-wielding Neptune, father, known from within the womb only by his voice and barbed effects, created the maelstrom. I came into the world abhorring him against all logic; logical for the womb, but not the infinitely vast world beyond. L'enfant terrible arrived pre-programmed and pre-prejudiced. The multiple nihilation (homosexuality) that would later mold, propel and define his life preexisted in embryonic form.

A final word about "Dad." The anarchy of children out of control threatened him. However, he didn't at all mind the noisy uproar of the little league; rather, gloried in it. His own family, on the other hand, he commandeered to talk in a tight little squadron down the sidewalk. Giggling and all spontaneity at the dinner table were forbidden. His mode of communication was pontification.

We developed eating and elimination disorders. My sister died of anorexia nervosa at age 43. Throughout grammar school, high school and college I nearly always ate alone. My right wrist trembled with other people present. I could scarcely hold a coffee cup or guide a soup spoon to my mouth. Or urinate with anyone watching. All a belated effort to escape his pontificating presence. He never admitted what was "eating him"—not that he or anyone else knew—beneath his solemn, rustic, preacher's pose.

Nor did we voice our exasperation at this gradual suffocation. The dark forces of the subconscious and the libido were never mentioned. Freud was a dirty word. The blind faith of fundamentalist Christianity required that such forces not exist. Enter neurosis. Something is wrong/nothing is wrong. We're God's sunny little unit happily engaged in dinner conversation. Doesn't saying "grace" prove it? A few forced formalities, then on to eating. A sense of shame pervaded the sharing of the divine bounty. But the Deity, like a devouring Gorgon fattened on our prayers, decrees that everything is perfectly fine. To imagine otherwise smacks of sinful ingratitude. Pass the butter please . . . .

The thought of being alone with Father at the dinner table still brings shudders. We sat in the jury box at each other's murder trial. We needed the calming presence of women. Mother served as mediator between warring camps. The combatants spoke a token two or three sentences that called for the shortest possible reply. A free-flowing conversation was unheard of. It would violate the long-standing pact of being each other's non-existence.

I here attempt, despite a backlog of pain and guilt, to list some of the reasons I abhorred my father. (As a caveat to be discussed later, bear in mind that hatred {Incompletion} contains in embryonic form a higher desire to merge with and transform itself into love {Completion}. This spiritual principle {the Return} is very much a part of, is written into the fabric, the priestly robes so to speak, of homosexuality.)

1. He forced me to live a masquerade.
2. He never revealed or admitted his own struggle, hence his humanity. He acted as though subconscious motivation doesn't exist.
3. Although he claimed to have a philosophic turn of mind, he slew intellect with pedantry. Pedantry is a direct gauge of biological embarrassment.

4. I was rejected as "son," only to be replaced by the surrogate "lovers" of the softball team.
5. Although he was a latent homosexual, I was the guilty one who required alteration, a psychological amputation, the equivalent of a frontal lobotomy.
6. He tuned out the libidinal needs of women. He expected to be nurtured without nurturing. He brought them the poverty of deprivation and then treated it as a virtue, the same as he did with me.
7. He catalyzed my homosexuality through denial of himself and his extension in me by withholding the warmth and touching that would have helped me succeed at relationship, gay or straight. He denied me the tools I needed to live a difficult and impossible life. The greatest gift is confidence, which springs from knowing oneself, that is, full acceptance of one's gayness.

Once in motion, homosexuality becomes causal, like the genetic code. The predilection or pattern is locked in concrete. I'll always desire the Male as Father, Son, Mirror Image or some combination thereof. Yet the consummation of this desire is blocked by the original father-son denial. The edict of mutual nonexistence precludes there being two winners, only the conqueror and the vanquished. Just as father-son reconciliation remains a buried impossibility—so with countless surrogates in the elusive form of Mister Right.

Not the most cheerful picture.

Even more bleakly, Sartre tells us that the attempt to capture the freedom or beingness of another human existent is doomed to failure. Like trying to pin down a drop of mercury with a sharp needle, the drop continuously escapes. Likewise, fellow humans. For Sartre, this holds for love in general. Homosexuality, like its hetero counterpart, exists by imposing limits and boundaries. Not so much male-female boundaries, that overlap and blur in gay relationships, but those that result from the derailing of body from SPIRIT>Mind; from splitting off Ego-Body from Cosmic Continuity.

In this alienated state, homosexuality appears not as a Fullness, but a fragmented mosaic against the background of an Absence. Yet this fragmentation totally shapes my being. My failure with my father and his with me is a microcosm not only of the failure of homosexuality, but of Being to be its own Foundation. From the first prototype of man onward, no one has ever succeeded at founding himself. In birth and death, mankind remains naked, unformed and incomplete. What is homosexuality if not an intensification of the human condition, a reach toward and merging with a self-fulfilling godness?

On a collective level, the multiple negations implicit in gay society are seen in the following: the more liberated, the seemingly more embedded and enslaved. The more it strives to be universal, the more it falls into particularity. Or: the more it flaunts itself, the more it vanishes. A gay parade with bearded men dressed as nuns and transvestites blowing kisses is both there and not there, at once surreal and ephemeral. The "success" of gay lib consists in its failure to reveal itself qua its true Self. Both unknown and unknowable, it never succeeds at even tentative cosmic foundation, only impersonation.

On the other hand, might not this evanescence, this not-thereness—a chasm across which freedom is made possible, thinks and acts—be the most tantalizing wine? What makes life exciting and worth living? I admit to being threatened by the frivolous, raw power of gay lib; consequently by the specter of my self-limited and limiting freedom—in the same way that giggling at the dinner table threatened my father. I, too (a chip off the old block, shudder!), fear the unregimented, the out of control. One must be careful what one hates, or rather, fears, for that is what one will come to resemble, if not *become*.

All beings fear failure; more profoundly, nonbeing. Fear is simultaneously a warning sign of Nonbeing and a prod back toward Fullness. By revoking my father's existence, I'm fated *to be* him in his primal incompletion. In the same way, through denial of himself and his extension in me, he condemns himself to face up to, beyond that, *to be* my more out-in-the-open, less repressed homosexuality.

To this I add a corollary: If I feel threatened by the outrageous campiness of some gay men, it's because I share their fate, because I risk becoming one of them, to being a party to the scandal of their outrageous possibilities; to be the fractured interplay of their Being and Nothingness.

I couldn't get over a bleak feeling. I tried to cheer myself with the maxim: There is no chasm that won't one day be bridged, no contradiction left unresolved. All hatred (including father-son) will be drawn into and melt into Love. All things return to Source, at last reveal their innate Oneness. The reasons for the scandalous outrage—and privilege—of homosexuality won't be fully revealed prior to the shedding of earth-body, for therein lies its underlying amnesia.

And ultimate triumph.

To conclude: There is nothing immoral or evil about one man desiring another man and consummating that desire. A primal miscalculation perhaps, or livable error, starting with the breach of paternal continuity at the First Ordination—but what is life if not a cumulative and exciting chain of errors? A rocket ship or homing pigeon zeroes in on its target by constantly correcting deviations away from course.

However, first realize in this context that "miscalculation" and "error" are terms not of sin and immorality but behavioral psychology and objective ontology. A sea anemone opens and closes in response to the interplay of tides and light. A baby cries to be fed. A soldier avoids a stray bullet or roadside IED. The First Ordination, in the same way, arises from the basic morality of a rage to survive. Sin first appears in the vacuum of human freedom with the merging in of the reflective consciousness. Sin is a "not," the opposite of Fullness. Like shadows that shift with the sun's position in the sky, evil (or sin) is an ever-present but fleeting possibility. It cowers like a jackal in a cemetery, terrified of the sun, which due to its dazzling brilliance, it mistakes for a malevolent deity.

Homosexuality—after allowing for secondary physical factors like hormone imbalance, a smaller brain stem or a gay gene—is an ordained playing out of pre-cognitive father-son denial. A reciprocal will to nonexistence, a flirting with shadows. But nonetheless a compelling flirtation. For it is precisely this tilt toward Nothingness that serves as a compulsion, a springboard, to higher destiny, even greatness.

Finally, all physical phenomena are subject to: "This too shall pass away." Only love and its effects endure. To the degree that homosexuality evinces love, loyalty, unselfishness and other divine attributes, it contains high spiritual density. It endures as a transcendence. That is to say, it endures in its essence, not in the brief flicker of Ego-Body. Matter-based, ego-fueled love—of which homosexuality is but one of many faces—must remain a hazy outline, an unfulfilled hunger, a mere potential for Love. Ultimate consummation only takes place in the spiritual realm. Committed gay relationship, then, manifests—despite multiple welts and scars on this battered earth plane—timeless Spirit.

In conclusion, homosexuality yearns beyond the incompletion it has made of itself for the Fullness it is not yet. All physical yearning involves a Lack, an incursion from the Void. To the brave graduate of the Second Ordination, sexual orientation has a primeval sense of urgency, appears as the realest of the real. And rightly so—even though, in and of itself (apart from Spirit) it has no enduring reality. Self-foundation is temporarily sought in the Other, in Mister Right. The acting out of sex roles, male and female, gay or straight, like the obliterating flow of tides, exists as denial and resurgence, as a constant disappearing and reappearance, against a roiling, ever shifting firmament.

By the same token, to the degree that sexuality strives for a value beyond itself—union with the Eternal—it mirrors the Divine. This bestows cohesion, purpose and nobility on man's lower animal nature. Thereby is sexual bent or persuasion elevated through eons of struggle to a final conjoining with Spirit. Even while locked in Ego Body, it's no surprise that sexuality retains a sacred flavor and dimension owing to its unlimited potential to evolve toward greatness and godness.

Despite its origin and roots in negation, homosexuality, then, is an ecstatic forward cresting on a tide of human freedom. Whether S&M or vanilla, whether founded on father absence or rage, it's a resounding *IS*. Through this saving knowledge, gained from experience, intuition and mental sweat, I heaved a sigh of relief. I didn't hesitate to inscribe another positive entry on the cosmic ledger.

An added note. Negation and transcendence, conflict and resolution, are the condition of life. I've shown the deleterious effects of body-denial. To suppress homosexuality, once established in the psyche through pre-cognitive choice and primal destiny, is itself immoral. Suppression unlooses fear and guilt, inflames and perpetuates prejudice. The survival and health of the planet require that the homosexual child, teenager and adult be given full expression. From the First Ordination, homosexuality, even while suppressed, appears as a *given,* as essence, as a manifesting of Primal Will. It is only collective Ego-Body, the body politic, that distorts and fails to perceive homosexuality as the gift that it is to mankind.

The nihilation of the First Ordination—refusal to be a mindless replica of the father—in turn catalyzes the corrective course of the Second Ordination. This serves the gay man well until the "menopause" of middle age. The Third

Ordination looms on a stormy horizon. A final correction of the ship of selfhood is needed.

This brings us full circle, to a summons to be whole. This spiritual mandate repositions disconnected Ego-body in its proper place in the SPIRIT>Mind>body continuum. The gay man redirects his flight toward Primal Source. The Creator designed him exactly as he is—to be gay. Once again all is well, as it always was, in the heavens.

Just as the goal of death, which is an illusion, is to bid this earth body a fond and reverent farewell and move on to a higher plane—even so the final goal of his preordained, earth-embedded journey is to manifest while here his highest, most transcendent and luminous *gay* Self.

CHAPTER FOUR

ALIENATION AND RETURN

The AIDS Victim as Martyr-Hero

Like accelerated protons in the Hadron Collider (it spans a border between Switzerland and France), I will continue to bombard Somethingness and Nothingness with the intention of arriving at a higher synthesis. The illusive Higgs boson or "God particle" may actually exceed the speed of light by a whopping 60 billionths of a second! In similar audacious hope of gaining insight and flying higher into the heavens, I turn to a sociological approach to later return to ontology.

One of the worst threats to the quality of life on Planet Earth is over-population. "Gays don't procreate," quipped a famous Las Vegas entertainer with macho sarcasm, much to the outrage of the gay community. He didn't realize he was voicing one of their major contributions. Planet Earth at present plays host to over six billion (and rapidly climbing) human beings. Nearly half are malnourished. Over-population accelerates crime, pollution (chemical, visual, aural), depletion of Earth's resources and creates a widespread learning disability. It's proven that children raised in the crowd of a large family without their own space don't think or learn properly.

Gays don't overburden the planet with genetic replicas of themselves. Rather than take space, they give it. They contribute creativity, a flair for style, are non-combative, seek a safe and sane world, maintain and improve property (case in point: restored Victorian houses in most major cities), show racial tolerance, advocate women's rights as well as their own and stimulate the advancement of the arts from window display to opera.

Gayness holds up to the straight world a mirror image of itself that it doesn't want to see. A Wall Street-dominated, White male culture that denigrates its feminine component by yanking funding for family planning and outlawing abortion. Telling examples—The rampant greed (multi-million dollar bonuses) of the corporate world. The artlessness of the suburban middle class. Good ole boy hunters and Klansmen. Gays call into question the straight world's arrogant project of self-aggrandizement. They understand the contingent, shifting-sand nature of life. They are an Alice in Wonderland looking-glass in which their straight peers are made to behold their cracked flaws.

AIDS, with the suffering that accompanies slow death, made the afflicted gay men of the 1980's and 90's society's ultimate martyr. Thankfully, things have improved. Due to a drug cocktail, AIDS is no longer a death sentence. However, for the purpose of this book, I will focus on the pre-cocktail two decades of horror.

Consider what was stacked against him. Ignored and rejected by God and religion. Shunted aside by government and centers of medical research. Increased gay bashing. AIDS victims, wasting away in bleak hospital rooms across the U.S. and Europe, and by the millions in Third World countries, the worst in Africa, watched in shocked disbelief as desperately needed medicines and treatment techniques were swept under a mountain of bureaucratic red tape.

Not until non-gay families and children became infected—the "real" or "deserving" human beings—did urgent publicity aimed at prevention and a cure gain significant impetus. So long as the epidemic was confined to gays, drug users and prostitutes (a "just" retribution from God) the government turned a bigoted, cold shoulder. In spite of the cocktail, protease inhibitors and the promise of a vaccine, gay men continue to die in stigmatized anonymity. These undervalued and expendable contributors to world culture were shown, and in many ways still are, about the same compassion as a leper colony in Bangladesh.

The martyrdom of the 80s through the 90s was made the more devastating by the fact it had to be borne against a groundlessness of being. Condemned by God, politicians, top brass in the Pentagon (before the repeal of Don't Ask,

Don't Tell) and the Evangelical Right, the gay man was coerced into assuming the heroism of an ignominious martyrdom. That gay-bashing should increase in direct ratio to gay suffering is a sad commentary on humankind.

In the late 1960's Mayor Davis of Los Angeles sniped, "Gays have their own germs," as though they were a mutant variant of Homo sapiens. Anita Bryant called them "cannibals who drink each other's sperm," it being "the purest form of blood" (whatever that means). When asked about gay pride, Nancy Reagan snippily replied, "Pride for what?"

A man afflicted with AIDS, just by being gay—so goes the cocky judgment of the greater society—is the moral equivalent of a prostitute or drug user. These social pariahs deserve their fate. The AIDS victim bears multiple rejection by God, society and family, often avoidance by peers, even a lover. The ultimate martyrdom is to suffer without glory or hope of appeal.

The early Christians, driven by lead-tipped whips into the slaughter of the Roman Coliseum as bloodthirsty entertainment, had the promise of an eternal reward in heaven. Blacks before Martin Luther King had a vision of universal justice and full membership in the human race. Women, of equal partnership with men. Since to be gay is to break the chain of tribal continuity, the AIDS sufferer—after enduring the ravishing of body, sometimes the brain, even the loss of a will to live—dies with no certainty that God, the Final Appeal, forgives or even cares.

To die a shameful death, then, with the only sense of integrity coming from within, requires superhuman courage and strength. Even at the lowest ebb of sickness, the AIDS sufferer perceives a dignity and sense of belonging in the universe. An innate divinity precedes his gayness. A spiritual resource he didn't know was there connects him with Higher Being. AIDS, terrible though it be, hastens the deliverance and salvation of the Third Ordination.

Suffering rends the veil of Ego-Body. The AIDS patient finds himself free of lust-addiction in a way he never dreamed possible. He finds Spirit—or It finds him—apart from any religious or moral code. The alumnus of a self-invented life, he comes unencumbered to the portal of Higher Self. The Third Ordination facilitates the uncovering of true Selfhood (the goal of all religions), patience (the acceptance of "death" is the great patience-bringer) and genuine self-love (from embracing the All). Through the purification of suffering, the particularity of gayness leads not to separation but to Oneness.

Witness the AIDS patchwork quilt. This decidedly feminine symbol points to reforged male solidarity. Diversity is knitted into unity, femininity woven into masculinity. (Androgyny is a requisite step of spiritual growth.) The gay man, rather than lost and alone in the outer darkness of social exile, finds a skylight to Spirit. To his surprise, its warming light nurtured and enveloped him all along!

To trigger bombardment into a higher truth (the Hadron Collider may threaten the sanctity of Einstein's relativity), I interject an urgent, perhaps the most insidious, negation (portal of nothingness) presently on the Planet. That is machismo. Once vital for survival, colonization, industrial expansion and warfare, it has become the opposite, a lead weight on the back of world civilization. It bears responsibility for the scourge of overpopulation. It reveals itself in the belittling of women, over-breeding, shooting-from-the-hip warfare, vigilante squads, torture and rape if need be and the vanquishing and extermination of rivals. A grim example is the ethnic cleansing practiced by the Serbs against the Bosnian and Kosovo Muslims. Now in the Arab spring, most horrifically, Syria's assault on its own people. Machismo stands in mortal and suicidal dread of anything that isn't a genetic, social or religious replica of itself, that doesn't square with the tribe.

Sadomasochism (dare I speak its forbidden name?) remains entrenched in the war-ravaged Twentieth and Twenty First Century psyches. Primitive tribes not only enslaved or wiped out the opponent, but imagined themselves thereby empowered. Child-beating is a cause and consequence of machismo. Differently stated, sadomasochism, a basic ingredient of machismo, is a belated attempt by the victim or child to even the score later in adulthood. Without the institution of child-beating and other abuse, there probably wouldn't be, since violence begets violence, a Marine Corps as we know it.

Assembly line production of the fearless ground troop operates on the same principle. The macho man is whipped into shape (taught death by incremental degrees) and so he beats his wife, child or pet. Or slaughters wild game for sport. More significantly to society, he blindly consents to offer up his life on the battlefield. So the abuse cycle goes on. The effects are felt for centuries.

Since the perpetuation of machismo requires a hate object, it elevates the opposite poles of superiority-inferiority, winner-loser, vanquisher-victim, sinning-atoning into absolute virtues. The Book of Revelation and later Dante's vision of flaming Hades, besides instilling fear in the masses, glorify violence, reward the suppression of the weak by the strong and subtly foster, justify and even gloat over (while tuning out) suffering. It makes the short-lived "discomfort" of pillage, rape and war seem mild compared to eternal torment in hell. Machismo doesn't stop to consider that hell, rather than the invention of a sacrifice-hungry God, is a projection of man's viciousness towards man.

While fomenting violence, squelching equality and denying compassion, machismo decorates itself with medals while labeling itself a pillar of society and keeper of the peace. The gay leatherman plays at machismo in order to come to terms with a primal force that dogged him from childhood. However, once the fantasy is played out and expended, he returns to the comforts of job and apartment. Few have the desire or endurance to play round-the-clock warrior. By dabbling with hunting or war fantasies, the gay man, unlike his straight counterpart, largely defuses his need to subjugate others.

Although machismo infiltrates the gay leather scene and gives it a tough look, heterosexual machismo tends to target for gay bashing butch bars in rougher neighborhoods. Like recognizes like in the falsity of their masquerade. Each side sees the other as a poseur or enemy (as well as secret shadow self). Fluff bars are usually located in a more uptown setting with better, at least cursory, police protection. However, with their swishy, bizarre-looking patrons, they are by no means free from harassment, even though prejudice tends to be less virulent in affluent neighborhoods.

Back to metaphysics and/or ontology. Machismo, as the perpetrator, has lower spiritual density than its victim. Even-the-score machismo is a glaring *not*. By targeting homosexuals, it makes itself a double, triple- and so on to infinity, regression into nonbeing. Through mindless, shooting-from-the-hip attack, it places itself a rung lower on the descending ladder into Nothingness.

In a collision course back into Somethingness, happily, we can conclude—besides contributing to the arts, helping check the population explosion, holding up a mirror image to society, advancing mysticism through attraction to the inner life and defusing the cycle of revenge by consenting to take on a vicarious martyrdom—the gay man breaks the iron grip of machismo. This is no small achievement. Brute survival depends upon a similar awakening of the entire planet.

However, in a veer back toward Nothingness, one can contrast with a certain bewilderment the fragmenting anomaly of bitchiness. One wishes it weren't so, that this bad family secret would just go away. It robs the Second Ordination of gravitas and infuses it with a secret shame. It rears its caustic head in the incongruity of a vengeful, Medea-like female persona inhabiting a male body. Originally a defense learned in the female camp against the male oppressor (both spurned and ardently desired), bitchiness downgrades into combat between gays themselves.

Since the tools of the trade—sarcastic carping and gesticulating, the icy put-down—are usually learned from maladjusted female family members, these come off as ineffectual and silly in the competitive male work arena. Consequently, the combat skirmishes take place in the faux-elegant safety of gay bars, smart brunches and drag shows where the enemy isn't present. The downtrodden vent their rage upon each other. This is vividly portrayed in the Genet plays, *The Maids* and *Deathwatch*.

Gay society, as shown, is by no means exempt from internal conflict and fracture, just as wider, straight machismo disports itself in outward competition and combat. Bitchiness (in-turned warfare) infects the spectrum of gay society. This, together with aped machismo, replays the original father-son warfare. And beyond that, futile foundation in the illusive, off-center "not-quite" of Nothingness. Bitchiness haunts collective gay beingness like the Phantom of the Opera lurking ominously in the wings.

Let us return to the noonday sunlight of unclouded Somethingness. Spirit manifests as tolerance, trust, equality, dignity and unconditional love. Rather than copied from straight society, these attributes are inborn. It may take years, if not a lifetime, for a gay man to attain self-love on all strata of the subconscious, when society, religion and his own family proclaim him an outcast.

Yet even if self-love is achieved, contrarily, he has the daunting task of accepting his freak sisters: the misfits, queens and spiteful gossipers. At first he'll have nothing to do with them. They exhibit a flagrant nihilism—a need to shock, to get high and stay high, to mimic eccentric aunts and show biz idols—rather than reveal their inner selves; in other words, be the sons of their slain fathers. Rather have they chosen themselves as daughters. They carry the comfort of regression to the womb a final step. The tension of murder is exchanged for the scandalous relaxation of auto-castration.

The freak show doesn't mesh well, as seen, with universal brotherhood. Assimilation into the larger society depends upon internal acceptance and integration of the "home scene" or bar. For most gay men, across-the-board acceptance of the gamut of fellow gays—from drag queen to leatherman (a gay stock broker in a Brooks Brothers suit may reject both)—is hard to achieve. Collective gay society, more than individual members, accelerates the (proton-bombardment) plunge into fragmentation (Higg's boson and other infinitely tiny particles); to totaling less than the sum of its parts. It fractures into mutually repellent cliques. Once again, low spiritual density—until awakened by a Stonewall, AIDS or Matthew Shepherd. Only then does it rally its forces into the solidarity of genuine brotherhood.

Does gay society, one may argue, attain nobility and divine sanction only through debasement and suffering? Through fear of meaninglessness or extinction? Integrity, a precursor of nobility, instills an awareness of inner worth. It unites the seeming opposites of confidence and humility. These contradictory states, like double ship's figureheads pulling in different directions, revolve faster and faster until they blur and merge into one—the confidence of true humility and the humility of genuine confidence. Nobility has no need to flaunt itself. It *is* in the serene knowledge of its credentials of fullness.

Homosexuality, leading up to the Third Ordination, is a relentless calling into question of itself, a truth that must remain an enigma; or a perpetual refusal to confront the suppressed ghost of its origins. Gayness appears on the scene without a past. The First Ordination throws up boundaries. These exclude Father and consequently other males (or the Male Principle) from the inner sanctum of Self. Homosexuality catches a first glimpse of fullness by leaving itself behind and pulling down self-erected walls; by transcending the double nihilation (father-self) at the core of its being.

The tendency to internally fragment is further shown in the following: the more liberated, the more enslaved to Ego-Body, with the resulting self-contempt and satirization. This is because gay lib hasn't freed itself from borrowing its actions, attitudes and self-image from the oppressing society. In times of crisis the gay man will often turn to his genetic family. He never loses a secret nostalgia for the breach of continuity in the First Ordination. Conversely, his genetic family needs him, for they *are* he. If the larger society wishes to solve the "gay problem" and heal itself—the two are inextricably bound—it must integrate gays and Lesbians into the fabric of its beingness, just as it has begun in stages to do with women, racial minorities and followers of other religions.

The ideal is a generous blend, then, in which gays and straights through free interaction accept and empower each other. Besides a healing tonic, such blending adds bouquet to the wine, zest to the salad, flavor to the main entrée and delight to the dessert. Gays must be more than in our midst, they must be "in our mix." They must be appreciated for enriching the culture; for upgrading property and preserving the heritage of the past; for reducing hypocrisy and fanaticism; for providing special insights as teachers and counselors; and for making devoted parents.

To ignore these special talents is to keep the larger society primitive, deprive it of richness and prevent its reaching maturity. The extraction of the double cancers of machismo and homophobia, the same with corrosive bitchiness, will bring about a less neurotic, healthier and more livable world. The sexually unpressured child doesn't need to escape into schizoid role-playing. The demise of aggressor-victim, superiority-inferiority myths make him an unapologetic, contributing and eloquent world citizen with nothing to hide.

Since homosexuality is ever with us, the redneck Las Vegas entertainer was wrong—psychologically, sociologically and ontologically—in claiming that gays don't procreate. Spawned in a secret underbelly of the parent society, they in turn recreate themselves in the image of their neurotic and fanatic heterosexual progenitors. Society is guilty of casting away its most treasured children. Society can't advance to the next evolutionary phase (from Wilber's Mental Egoic to the Psychic Intuitional) until it reclaims and assimilates its lost children. The mental health of the heterosexual parent is precisely reflected in the happiness and well-being of its homosexual offspring.

I now leave sociology—with my wild bombardment toy, my own cerebral Collider, clutched excitedly underarm—to return to metaphysics and ontology. From the lofty vantage point of Spirit, commitment to a gay relationship is morally superior to the bitter isolation of a lonely single. Yet relationship, with its tenuous balance of physical pleasure and ethical commitment, remains permeated with Ego-Body and poised for the final transition ("This too shall pass away") of death into the Beyond.

The gay man, brought by a gnawing sense of lack to the threshold of the Third Ordination, realizes that his true relationship isn't with a lover (even if picture perfect, a veiled quest of Self) but with the Cosmos. At last, a ground of being! But with the proviso that, unlike the Second Ordination, this undergirding leaves no clearly defined, heaven-sent sex role to play. That's a little frightening. Rather than loss, he's being prepared to be an Androgyne Lover of the Cosmos.

Is divine sanction as a homosexual, it seems, only possible in the *past tense*? As a vanishing act? Is he made complete only by leaving his pleasure-seeking self behind? Acceptable only as a sexual cadaver? This gives rise to a fear that his freed hedonist side at the Second Ordination was a mirage, a trick to make him feel even guiltier. Was the all-seeing God looking the other way? Was the body that carried him from childhood and that he later came to accept, enjoy and revere in the service of a lie? His liberation a miscalculation? A bad Polish or Irish joke?

Betrayed by God and man . . . yet somehow not by Being itself. It comes as a bolt from the blue. He heaves an immense sigh of relief. All is well in the heavens after all! Aren't God and Beingness one and the same? An inner voice refuses to accept this artificial split. Life itself (Mother Goddess, if one prefers) tells him that the body as part of the SPIRIT>Mind>body complex is sacred and must be respected. His limbs and organs, blood and sweat are undeniably real, just as orgasm is designed to feel wonderful. Otherwise there wouldn't be 6,000,000,000 plus humans on the planet. Or gay men willing to spend countless hours and a small fortune cruising for a partner.

Undeniably real are the neural pathways in the brain that trigger sexual response. The playing out of sexual desire projected on a blank screen (millions of nerve impulses leaping across chasm-like synapses of Nothingness) gains greater physical and psychological reality through repetition and interaction with the outside world. The response exhibits the concrete reality of a distinct mental and physical event. Once set in motion, repeated and ritualized, sexual identity shows forth a hint of full Beingness.

The infant-king, however, who broke the Chain of Paternity in the First Ordination, must still be unearthed and dealt with. He still rules a large portion of the subconscious. This hidden tyrant casts a pall of unreality over the neural circuitry the way an octopus clouds its immediate environment with black ink. Since the primal murder occurred before the age of accountability, *l'enfant terrible* stands morally clear of his impulsive act. Yet he still must face the consequences of the pre-cognitive choice of himself.

By age five or six the basic neural pathways of desire are in place. Sexually he is a large part of what he will become. To try in adolescence or adulthood to root out the embedded aberration as though it never happened is destructive and immoral as well as impossible. The blueprint for becoming an olive tree can't be changed into that of an oak. The primal project of self as *denial of being the father's son* (of being irremediably Other), serves, as concretely as the genetic code inscribed in the chromosomes, as a template for sexual response. Whether socially approved or aberrant, it simply is. He "decided" what he would become long before he knew what deciding was.

Back to ethics. Survival and growth depend on basic integrity. All life exhibits and is guided by this moral/biologic force. The pre-gay develops in every way, including libidinally, because it feels both right and inevitable. The simplest algae strives toward the more complex. A tortoise longs to be a freely soaring bird.

For the pre-gay, however, something goes awry, deviates from the allowable norm. The reach for higher growth stalls at an early childhood or pre-adolescent stage. The evolutionary flow gets diverted into brackish side eddies and pools. The result isn't accretion into a higher unity (a grasp at completion), but a troubling detour. Confused and angry, he's further assaulted with irrational guilt. He's both too simple and too complex, too blind and openly intelligent, too mired in Ego-Body while soaring too high in the stratosphere.

The reader may ask, amidst this host of contradictions, what gives society or religion the right to say a gay man isn't perfectly all right as is, in both his simplicity and unfathomable complexity? What kind of a universe is it, with its huge appetite for waste, that can't stomach an iota of sexual variety? The pre-gay and later outed gay man is like an exotic plant that, although altered and reshaped through pruning, continues to exhibit a highly individual or eccentric growth pattern with unique bio-rhythms and destiny. He is what he is—queer, freak or prodigy. The integrity of growth demands that artificial grafting stop and acceptance begin. Forced re-engineering only results in more stunting and misery for all concerned.

This brings us to a related maxim: Love is a requisite of survival. Like mother-love, it's based on *being*. Whereas conditional father-love is based on *doing*, on proving oneself. It is the latter, paradoxically, that the gay man yearns for most deeply. Doing is being projected outside itself onto the blank screen of becoming. This perpetual nihilation/transcendence creates a forward momentum that provides a glimpse of the continuity forfeited at the First Ordination. He needs Mother love to preserve balance and a sense of well-being. This, however, doesn't free him from warrior darts of regret over a vexing sense of incompletion, of betraying the team. For deep inside he's still a radical split with Male Continuity and Eternal Self.

Absolute (in contrast to *unconditional)* self-love is, however, unattainable. It doesn't exist any more than total freedom, which is neither possible nor desirable. Such freedom is a brushfire that leaves nothing standing in its scorched forward march. Similarly, total self-love would freeze the organism in a false perfection, ossify it into a statue like the too-perfect *David.* To truly love, one must leave self behind; rather, love beyond oneself. Separation (Ego-Body) from Source is a millstone around the neck of higher growth. Conscience, a bestowal of Spirit upon mind (just as moderation is an imposition of mind upon body), is a guidance system of cosmic checks and balances. If all behavior were permitted, if there were no error, popularly known as sin, the moral struggle needed for spiritual advancement couldn't take place.

Can't one achieve a tentative perfection, one may ask, as a "becoming" if not as an "arrived?" The gay man's struggle hastens the "sainthood factor," a longing for higher attainment and growth. He has more to overcome, struggle against, anguish over than his straight peer. He is both more "stuck" in a primitive state and more highly evolved. Yet for all his brave striving—different but loosely analogous for straights—the work of becoming is never finished or quite arrives. Ultimate completion can't occur on the physical plane because earth body must ever remain a "not," a solar eclipse of the full shining of SPIRIT>Mind. Sexual particularity is a gnat's shadow compared to the full shining of Spirit.

In his biography, *Saint Genet, Actor & Martyr,* Sartre asserts that Genet possesses grandeur even though the incorrigible thief glorifies the vilest thugs and murderers. A world of brute male beauty arises from what enchants, what turns him on and gets him off in the moment. Orgasm is a definitive cosmic event. It alone determines morality.

A terrible beauty (I'm reminded of Baudelaire's *Flowers of Evil)* permeates Genet's writing. With a sorcerer's wand he makes religion a farce, reduces the establishment to a cardboard caricature, turns excrement into flowers. Without peer in his arsenal of literary shocks, he is also without appeal. He self-exists through the power of onanistic improvisation. His glory is the degree of his perdition, his perdition the measure of his glory. He founds himself in the brilliance of the magnitude of his error. He is the audacious crystallization of his own nothingness. That is why the heterosexual Sartre found him so fascinating; as an archetype of existential Twentieth Century man.

Sartre and Edmund White in a later biography tell how the aging Genet attaches himself to surrogate, mostly Arab families as a sort of uncle figure. The worshipper of handsome murderers feels a stirring of the ethical. He has a belated need to reconnect the broken chain of continuity.

Sartre, even more than Genet, was blinded by his own brilliance. Although he erects a vast literary and philosophic edifice (like the empty scaffolding in Fellini's *Eight and a Half*), he fails to find the skylight to Spirit. At the end of *The Words*, he admits to making errors that could undermine the entire superstructure. Similarly, in later life Genet turns for support to an ordinary family free of the thugs and murderers that populate his fiction.

No surprise that Sartre never got around to writing the ethical discussion he promised at the end of *Being and Nothingness*. It wasn't home territory. The ethical is linked by conscience to the domain of Spirit. Sartrian existentialism denies a supernal realm altogether. No higher power motivates, justifies and energizes physical matter. No noumenon underlies the phenomenon. Being is simply *there* to glandular and nauseous excess. Sartre floundered on the rocks of a simplistic Marxism. This led to further inconsistencies. He is Logos carried to the limit short of Spirit. Just as Genet is Eros taken to the limit short of Ethos.

We now return, with our fanciful, all-powerful collider underarm, to ethics and morality. Built-in integrity sustains the ongoing pageant of life. For the gay man, the discovery of an inner divinity catalyzes the transcendence of the double negation (father/self) that he both made of himself (existence) and is (essence). Integrity enables him in the fiery furnace of the AIDS epidemic to go on believing in himself. It tells him he has an honored place in the universe, that he belongs. As he speeds toward the Third Ordination, innate dignity flowers exponentially. He is inwardly more magnificent than a thousand *Davids*.

A gay man with full-blown AIDS, whom I shall call "D," is invited to a Baha'i fireside. A mainstay of the Baha'i faith is the oneness of mankind. A video is presented. It shows a radiant mixture of humanity—Indians, Blacks, Whites, Persians, Orientals, rich, poor, learned, primitive—giving their impressions of the magnificent Baha'i shrines and gardens at Haifa, Israel.

During group discussion D asks, "What about the gays of San Francisco's Castro Street?" (He once lived in this epicenter of gay-pride, blatantly open, in-your-face sexual expression.)

The group leader, thrown off guard by such impromptu boldness, is reluctant to add to a dying man's burden by pointing out that the holy book of Baha'i law disapproves, even forbids homosexuality. The question hangs in the air like an invisible black hole. The leader replies woodenly, "Baha'u'llah is like Christ. He has little or nothing to say on the subject. Not that the Founder-Prophet condones homosexuality. That's made clear in the book of law. It's just that sins like back-biting are much worse."

Another way of saying homosexuality doesn't quite exist. There's no polite, religious language in which to couch the uneasy topic. Unsuitable for a public airing, it's accorded the status of a taboo; swept under the rug as a *non-existent*. No reason is given for its exclusion from the spectrum of divinely sanctioned behavior. Or why it should pose a threat to a New World Order.

Yet sexually transmitted AIDS is the single, most overriding factor in D's life. He lives with its multi-pronged reality in the form of a disease that saps his energy by day, leaves red patches on his face, sores inside his mouth and brings cold sweats at night.

He ruminates over which gay encounter was the fatal one. Whether it happened at a bathhouse or was transmitted by a quick trick or lover. But instead of guilt and recrimination, he's determined to dwell on the positive. He'll never forget coming out of the closet, a quasi-religious experience in which he stopped fighting himself and came to terms with who he was. For once he felt fully alive.

Nor will he forget great times with other gay men. He doesn't deny the amyl nitrate and drugs (he's way too honest), memories of boating and sunsets, he and a lover's plans to go fishing and camping—before the news hit like a bludgeon blow. Still a young man, he's propelled into the Third Ordination long before his time. The heady validation of the Second Ordination is precipitously called into question to be replaced by the grim specter of a devastating illness, premature aging and almost certain death.

In his fight to survive, D leaves the Baha'i fireside inwardly stirred, yet empty-handed. "Why are gays excluded from the Prophet's vision of planetary renewal and redemption?" The question is left unanswered as if by both tribal and civilized unspoken agreement. Is homophobia so different from racial prejudice? Is extra-normal use of the penis a category completely alien from skin color? Why is homosexuality off limits to religious enquiry? Like toilet habits, something one doesn't mention in polite company? The Baha'is, busily throwing off the yoke of the Old World Order, ignore homosexuality as a tainted distraction, a redundancy, something without a past, present or future. It floats rootless, groundless, hopeless. Even the Prophet won't look it in the eye.

D senses a glaring contradiction, even an insult. The yoke that is being shed (the Old World Order) excludes him and his kind. He's permanently linked to a defective and obsolete system without hope of joining the New. Out of the closet for ten years and a believer in self-acceptance almost as a mantra, D is now too weak to even think about sex. Homosexuality, he realizes, goes beyond the grossly physical. Even if he never engaged in a single sex act in his life, he'd still be gay. Total sexlessness doesn't exist. Even saints and angels retain some sort of gender identity. Now he's told that sexual abstinence, which he's been reduced to, and which, ironically, no longer matters, is the only path into God's good graces. Spiritually speaking, he's a day late and a dollar short.

Amidst the confusion and outrage, a minor miracle occurs. A flood of light stands his neck and arm hairs on end. Maybe all isn't lost after all! He feels on the brink of an encounter with the Infinite; intuits the outline of a Divine Groom. Quickened awareness replaces his anger over gay persecution, hate campaigns by TV evangelists, the thinly veiled homophobia of politicians . . . and his failing body. Eternal love shimmers on a nearby horizon. Not left behind after all, even included! But a final, rocky distance must still be traversed for him to fully believe it.

A world religion is presented, he reflects between hot flashes, yet nothing has changed. Homosexuality for which he is dying, is a no-no; brands him a sexual outlaw. The only consistent support comes from his mother (his latest lover abandoned him), who nonetheless has a hard time understanding his sexual predilections. But at least she tries; her love doesn't falter. More importantly and surprisingly, real support comes from an awakened sense of being a vessel of Eternal Spirit.

Organized religion, touted as a great comforter, he agonizes with a mingling of ecstasy, will accept him—how wrongly, he's not buying it!—only as a sexual amputee. What can those radiant multiracial faces mean to him? To join them, he must prefer female breasts to hairy chests. His neural pathways must be rewired, his endocrine glands ordered not to respond as they invariably do.

The universe once more, in a new dispensation, espouses denial and nonbeing. He won't buy that either.

It's not so much that he's unclean, unworthy, out of step, a sinner. Unlike the sticks and stones of physical abuse, mere words can't hurt him. It's something more profound. Simply this: Despite the struggle and pain, an outside conspiracy wants to make him believe he doesn't fully exist. Yet he never felt his existence so keenly! To be told otherwise is an affront to his integrity as a human being. His mission, he decides then and there, is to prove down to his boot soles that this shadowy non-existence foisted on him from without is false and untrue!

He sets out driving alone from California to Atlanta, Georgia, in the hope of receiving hemothermia treatment. According to hearsay and newspaper accounts, several AIDS patients showed dramatic improvement after having their blood pumped out, heated and returned to the body. D has tried everything: AZT, aerobics, hot and cold packs, a vegetarian diet, endless salves, lotions, vitamins and herbs. In desperation he believes hemothermia to be his last chance for survival.

Three thousand miles later and drugged on coffee, he arrives in this Southern city only to find the touted treatment banned by local officials. After long waits in hospital corridors that reek of vomiting and death, he encounters outside the hotel where he's staying not only picketing against the sluggish medical establishment, but a backlash of name-calling and hate crimes against gays.

He sees a young man with eye shadow and a pendulous earring in the shape of a cross beaten unconscious by a baton-wielding skinhead. Queers are to blame for AIDS and the other ills of society. In their darkest hour, they are America's last approved target for violence. D is turned away. The innovative doctor, labeled a quack, can't buck the establishment either. He escapes with his practice and revolutionary technique to Mexico City. D's last hope—whisked off like an elusive lost ark to a foreign land.

He's put on a waiting list to see an approved doctor who when he's finally seen, lectures him about his lifestyle, that it's his fault for not using a condom, worse, for not exercising abstinence. To actually be treated in any meaningful way, let alone cured, D realizes, is largely fantasy. Every avenue of hope . . . met with clinical indifference and religiously implanted shame. The long journey of faith was to no avail. No choice, if flagging energy holds out, but to return to California.

He again sets out cross-country, physically and morally exhausted. The rigors of the long drive further weaken lungs, liver and heart. Skin blotches, diarrhea and vomiting worsen. Yet, crossing state lines in a twilight of despair, he clings more than ever to the fading flicker of life, which has a sacred cast, that still remains.

At a drive-in restaurant in Oklahoma, where carhops on roller-skates deliver hamburgers in an art deco recreation of the 1950's, he has a perfect cup of coffee. In New Mexico he savors majestic saguaros against a flaming sunset. He plans, once home, to take his waiting dogs to a rock house in the eastern Sierra foothills where the air is clear and dry. He'll find time to visit an elderly shut-in before he too is confined to a hospital bed.

It isn't just the solidarity of a shared martyrdom that he learned from the gay men of Atlanta. It goes far deeper. Despite the endless sickness, medication and his wasting body, he's the most complete and resplendent being he's ever been! Although he doesn't see it directly, he's attained the Third Ordination thirty years early!

How irrelevant sexual persuasion and play all at once seem! This brief sojourn of dust is soon rolled up and forgotten, body particularity caught up into Timeless Spirit. He did nothing to deserve punishment in hell. How tedious, feeble-minded and vicious of any minister, priest or religion to think so! An extraordinary realization for a once bar owner that included a porn shop equipped with sex toys! Mere childish trivia; none of that any longer matters. Rescued not through some rigid blueprint of religious penitence, but a common humanity!

How, he wonders, does he know that unjust suffering in the face of bigotry will one day be rewarded many times over? That justice is a *necessity* of the stars spinning in their courses? Otherwise, he inhabits a flawed universe. The Designer of such a faulty system can't help him or anyone else!

The flame of gay soul, he concludes, burns just as brightly, if not more brightly, as that of his straight brothers in the Niche of Being. No one, gay or straight, Christian or heathen, bursting with health or feeble, is created without integrity and the capacity to love. Otherwise, Creation is botched and imperfect and will self-destruct. All are heir to a birthright of justice, just as all have the right to love as they choose. If not, the Oneness taught by the Baha'is is fraudulent, farcical and in serious error.

I leave D to the tender mercy of the universe. Once, while standing on a dark terrace, I perceived the vast compassion that underlies the stars. That compassion knew no boundaries or favorites. Total and complete, it engaged in no exclusions. The quilt of Being is a seamless continuum. Apartness is an illusion. The pre-gay who naively severs the father-son bond at the First Ordination is not thereby condemned for his "murderous" past. Rather he's granted his most ardent soul wish: joyful reunion with timeless Spirit.

To be gay, therefore, isn't a choice of the existential moment, but a heaven-sent destiny. Free will is the ground of predestination and predestination is the ground of free will. Can this eternal, seemingly colliding couplet be otherwise? One doesn't exist without the other. A gay man is gay "through-and-through." This is the ground of his godness.

D's spirit, radiant and free, knows that his patch on the quilt is made more colorful, distinctive and magnificent by his gayness. (He died a few days ago.) His contribution to the Planet is indeed rare. Faith and courage were forged in the fires of this brief earth span (like the God particle surpassing by nanoseconds the speed of light) into a highly-polished gem—a confessedly feeble analogy for the soul. He's a valued member of the Cosmos. Welcome home, Eternal Spirit tells him. You never left.

CHAPTER FIVE

THE ATTEMPT AT FOUNDATION

The Sought-After and the Ardent Suitor

In Chapter Four I gathered up and reassembled a broken mosaic of Somethingness in order to end on a happy, near ecstatic note of self-realization. I now challenge the reader to take a perilous and terrifying look into the Void. I evoke the Abyss, or the absence of God, in order to show Being in glowing bas relief. This is no simple task. To stand back and look one's faults (or Lack) squarely in the face takes persistence and fortitude. I again attempt to do this with homosexuality. It's my hope that confronting gayness as a collectivity will correspond at least in part with personal examination and experience.

Why does the brave affirmation of the Second Ordination, one asks, in later years often backfire into disillusionment? Is it the loss of youth? A romance gone wrong? The prospect of one's life rolled up and thrown on the rubbish heap of nearing death . . . ? Is gayness then a gauge of nonbeing? If so, am I close to unearthing and delineating the negation that underlies homosexuality? And beyond that, Nothingness that permeates and afflicts all life?

As in Chapter Two, I return to the cruise bar as a metaphor for a shadow alter-world. With the aid of the ontologic "3-D glasses" that I will provide, an obscuring haze of negation like Los Angeles smog will be perceived not as a property of Being, but as vaporous fingers of Nonexistence.

On a typical night at the bar, a young, recently outed gay man is struck by how dark everything is. He knows he looks great. He's one of the hottest numbers there. The "new kid on the block" laughs and jokes easily. He thrives on being the center of attention. He feels a lover close at hand beyond the next pool game or turn on the dance floor. This mystery man is practically breathing down his neck. Yet everything has been arranged to obscure or defeat this central goal: to show himself in the best possible light for meeting Mister Right.

He suddenly feels the chill whisper of a lurking Grim Reaper. The dark area between the bar and prison-like walls appears as a posing ground of equi-spaced statues. Rather than invite camaraderie, each "statue" is a closed space that discourages or prohibits intrusion. It's as though the hard-won coming out of the Second Ordination included buying into an invisible system of forbidden zones.

"Don't bother me, I won't bother you." Or: "This is my space, beat it, buddy."

Hardly a friendly, back-slapping fraternity of sky-is-the-limit possibilities! Rather does an unspoken apologia, a hidden shame, permeate—despite the pulse-pounding disco beat—a blaring silence. It seems he's entered a world of boundaries in which the light of Oneness is progressively dimmed.

Yet he perceives little of this. Nor does he realize that behind the frozen poses is a collective paranoia caused by fear of rejection. The bar goers subconsciously ape or interiorize the greater society by imposing on each other the same rejection it inflicts on them. The zone of inaccessibility around each bar customer reflects the collective denial of self *as a real being*. The attempt to present a Primal Negation (the First Ordination) as solid reality—fantasy-self-as-real-self—risks appearing phony.

Every bar goer wants his self-presentation to bear the stamp of authenticity. That's not to say the Second Ordination was phony or inauthentic. It exhibited high spiritual density. Now (fast forward thirty years) it reveals in retrospect a mounting, unreal, nihilist underside, which must remain hidden. This forbidden zone comes wrapped in camouflage netting that now (at the threshold of the Third Ordination) is misread as shaky but solid beingness, which the aging bar goer fights to authenticate as the "real deal."

Can he have come into his own, he wonders, into what he thought was a universe of solid values—only to find he's embraced a chimera? Nothing is what it seems. Rather, it isn't there at all. Everything flies away like meteorites in space, leaving him spookily alone. His dilemma can be thus expressed: He's joined a fraternity with no legacy of self-foundation. Or: the beingness of the fraternity is a flight away from itself. Instead of an ivy-covered edifice with hallowed, built-in traditions, he's party to a decreasing fraction (Sartre would say a detotalized totality) that has lost its connection, across the chasm of the First and Second Ordinations, with primal Wholeness.

A socially well-adapted, mid-aged alumnus of the Second Ordination, rather than yield to such gloomy thoughts, may launch a last ditch effort to bring back the good times. This buys time to anesthetize or excise threatening intrusions of SPIRIT>Mind. This mode of escape, however, soon catches up with him. The honest baptism of the Second ordination backfires into betrayal. He's left with no way of knowing "what hit him." Or how utterly his attempts at foundation-in-the-Other have failed. The SPIRIT>Mind apparatus for understanding his metaphysical dilemma has been successively whittled away. No moral or religious safety net exists to catch his fall.

Whether party animal or shy introvert, our subject is forced to come to terms with a long arduous journey—only to discover that a criterion of success is that he not take himself seriously. Rather, to regard himself as a quasi-existent. For mental and emotional survival, he must further bury his Oedipal origins. The first commandment of hedonism: Thou shalt have a good time. The success of body is thus the suppression of SPIRIT>Mind. He dons a mask of vacuity in order to immerse himself in a glittering Mardi Gras of group non-existence. At the same time, he catches a fleeting glimpse into the Void. A skull with sunken eye sockets and roots of missing teeth grins in. To insure that this frightening vision not be seen again, he plunges into the unholy trinity of cocktails, camp and promiscuity.

However, try as he might, he fights off a haunting feeling that beyond layers of illusion there's "nothing there." God, founding fathers, country, church, Boy Scouts and apple pie, with a gay tinge wrapped in rainbow colors—all fake. Those values long since flew the coop. The integrity of coming out is nonetheless still there, albeit diminished. No diplomas were handed out, no homilies voiced. Yet it was a rite of passage that couldn't be postponed. He obeyed an urgent, glandular, even spiritual summons.

Did he follow the demands of his vigorous young body, he cogitates, only to find years later that body qua body is illusion? Was he tricked into trusting a mirage? Yet it was Mind>body, he hazily intuits, from the necessity of its inner structures, that triggered the Second Ordination. Was SPIRIT looking the other way? Did his Higher Self trick him into embracing a false Fullness only to abandon him, in a peal of mocking laughter, to ghostly incompletion?

A closer look through our 3-D glasses (a symbolic step outside the space-time continuum) reveals the cruise bar enveloped in a negative force field. The posing statues are "what they are not and not what they are." They are misrepresentations. Rather, they're a ploy to deflect potential admirers from the internal rupture of the First Ordination. That's why the space around each statue forbids entry. Our young initiate failed to perceive that as a defense against rejection he, too, would develop an inner/outer disparity that ossifies into yet another statue on display. The brave idealism of the Second Ordination erodes into deception; high spiritual density reduces to a fog of obfuscating gross matter.

To fight off the chill of this invisible nether world, although eager to make friends and find Mr. Right, he takes refuge in an inviolable statue existence. He plays at rejecting and being rejected the way suns, planets and moons repel and attract in space. But the game isn't quite so simple. Besides the solidity of a statue or heavenly body orbiting in space, he must also be an inane vanity, a laughing clown mask. The contradictions that must now be borne are even more daunting than the trauma of coming-out. To be a clown on the surface and a stony absence underneath is more than he bargained for. He can't help feeling shipwrecked, manipulated . . . and betrayed.

With luck, on a brighter note, he may forestall skirmishes with Nonbeing by ringing up the coveted jackpot of landing in a relationship. The arms of a lover—though not Mister Right (this mythic being exists only in the past and the future)—provides solace and protection from the chill otherness of the bar. In this case, the Second Ordination leads not to disillusionment but a pieced together salvation. He and his lover are among the elect. They seek out and socialize with other similarly blessed couples. They throw smart dinner parties, collect valuable antiques, join gay political movements. All that was forfeited—independence, freedom to pursue mindless cruising, plus the trappings of a patently false hetero society, religion, the world—returned a hundredfold!

This imprinted happiness, bubbling like champagne from wellsprings of mutual pleasure and prestige, may last for years. If this be a livable error, it's a pleasant one. The dragon of loneliness is kept chained in a background, off-center dungeon. But how often is enduring happiness in a superficial, cyber, meat market world the exception rather than the rule! Most gay men at some point, many for long stretches of time, lead lives of quiet desperation.

"Something is wrong/nothing is wrong." Or: "I'm depressed/I'm happy as a lark."

Conjugal bliss based on physical attraction and prowess, which lasts only as long as the body holds out, depends on an illusion of foundation-in-the-Other. The unspoken contract of relationship (this often requires a symbolic amputation, even castration) survives the ravages of time to the degree that it reflects the primary relationship—the Fatherhood of the Universe. This, however, often fails, for more often than not it exists *contra* this paternity.

Let us reexamine the search for a mate. This universal drive reflects a longing for Original Wholeness. But we'll see how fleeting and off center this quest can become for even the sincerest gay man. That is due to its genesis in a double nihilation. I showed the attempt to present inward negation as outward authenticity. Under these conditions, the cruising urge is a quest for an Absence. For the object of the soul's longing, Lost Father, has been banished into nonexistence. Thus the cruise bar remains a graveyard of shadowy ghosts . . . or statues.

This quest for the unsearchable and unfindable can be further refracted into component parts—

The average gay man secretly wants a more masculine mate. At the same time he wants to control, if only because even the most effeminate man produces testosterone. A gay man who opts to play bottom may be frustrated by a lack of success. He doesn't realize how stoic, self-contained and inapproachable his bar pose makes him appear. Bottom man receptivity is lost in the darkness; he comes across as solidly male, even butch. An unintended display of maleness—he wasn't, after all, born a woman—eclipses the projected image of eager bottom. Thus, in searching for a dominant mate, he, too, gives off a signal of inapproachable top. This is due to the fact that although he's willing to sacrifice maleness for a submissive role, he has no intention of giving up control. Rather, he seeks to amass control by attracting a more butch number into his orbit—that is, by making him fall in love with him.

On the other hand, a masculine but socially unskilled top may put off making the first move. He doesn't want to risk the compromise of his masculinity which he regards as an absolute value. He reins in innate aggressiveness in order to avoid a reflex rejection response from a naïve or reticent bottom. The latter's youthful desirability makes him appear opaquely Other. In truth, this ambiguous passivity arises from sex role uncertainty, underscored by a sense of incompletion (a resultant fear of rejection) hidden beneath a put-on decorum, despite the fact that the last thing this "lady in waiting" wants is to be ignored.

Thus: "Sweep me off my feet/leave me alone."

By the same token, masculinity, its own expression of artificial wholeness, requires confirmation by a willing and enthusiastic bottom. The condition of its inmost being is that it be admired. (If this fails, then it must subjugate). In other words, masculinity demands a response; it won't wait forever.

The one force strong enough to overcome fear of rejection, loss of control, surrender of masculinity or all of these, is a search for intimacy. This can result in bumbled exploratory remarks that either break the ice or make each party wish the other never opened his mouth! In the first instance, such chance-taking may bring about an exciting introduction to a surrogate Mister Right. If the encounter is botched, it is quickly repressed (consigned to nonexistence), a mental sleight-of-hand for which both parties have considerable experience; that is, from infancy, even the womb. For it mustn't be allowed to dawn that the object-fled is the nihilated Father's "detested barking voice."

The top man, on his part, expects from the bottom a friendly, respectful and obedient facade (Little Red Riding Hood meets the Wolf) that synchs with his own carefully edited self-image. To complement and confirm this trumped up aggressiveness, he looks for a high sincerity factor (call this boyishness) in the Other, the better to exert control.

This is especially true of daddy-son relationships. The goal of "experience" is to capture the "innocence" of the Other against his will or awareness. The top man hides his devious designs under the guise of a Daddy Warbucks-style "generosity of the aggressor." All poses exact a price for their unveiling. Yet this posturing hopes, in the search for intimacy, that this very unveiling take place. The opposite goals of secrecy and self-revelation do a balancing act on the high wire of desire. Transparent and opaque, known and not-known (alternate faces of Control), are negotiable trade-offs between aggressor and aggressed.

The "sought-after," furthermore, expects the top man to be everything the nihilated Father wasn't. Not only must he be generous and adapt to shifting moods and poses, he must serve as stud. He must provide financial and emotional support. He must look great in public as well as be a sexual virtuoso. The bottom expects to be treated with the deference and respect which that hazy nonentity, the Father-Fraud, failed to give the Mother before the violence-enshrouded amnesia of the First Ordination.

Consequently, the top man—I'll call him the ardent suitor—is asked to desire only the sought-after in the way that heroic knights of old were dedicated to and defined by loyalty to the queen or some mythical goddess figure. The ardent suitor's grandiosity is funneled into a difficult, if impossible, constriction. He's expected to be everything and *nothing*, since he is, after all, mere fantasy.

To further obscure the masquerade, the ardent suitor seldom thinks of the sought-after as a "loved one," but as another "lover." An aggressive top rarely identifies with the role of ardent suitor, with which he soon grows uneasy, bored or even insulted, but rather of himself as a likewise coveted sought-after. An entrenched narcissism pervades both parties. The gay world, it would seem, is populated only with lovers (not loved ones). One can say the lover/loved-one dyad lacks concrete existence, since gay men are ontologically facing the same direction—away from each other.

To further elaborate— A habitual bottom may postpone playing ardent suitor until he's over the hill, after a lifetime of expending himself as a cuddly Cupid, teddy bear or lady in waiting. He must now hustle against the grain to pull in tricks. He becomes a top too late (already an unwanted troll!). In this regard, the gay world is the opposite of women's lib. Gay men want to be sex objects, to be pursued for their hot, toned body, to be considered cheese or beef cake, *in addition* to being an object of fantasy and intrigue. Even to be raped. These attentions effect a metamorphosis into Eternal Body.

The majority, however, no matter how many hours spent at a gym, fall short as an adonis. The body inflates and sags in the wrong places; organs fail. Since the aging sought-after-turned-ardent-suitor must use every possible stratagem to snare a younger or more virile male, he schools himself in devious tactics. One of these is the Jewish mother mouth: control via the caustic tongue. Another is the fashion plate: being the more stylish and trendy. Still another is the aristocrat: better educated, from a better family, more cultured and socially positioned.

Despite all the jockeying for control, the fact remains that males aren't sufficiently different from each other, no matter how creative and diverse the role playing, to form eternal complements. Both parties produce testosterone and at the same time have a feminine component founded on the nihilation of the Male (starting with Oedipal Father). Both top and bottom fantasize being pursued by a more masculine suitor. Yet in the existential Now, male secondary sex characteristics, the initial basis of attraction, get in the way. They subvert differentness into sameness, allure into disillusionment, romance into boredom, no matter what premium one party may place on his partner having broad shoulders and an impressive control tool.

The simultaneous quest for a mirror image and an opposite sets in motion a perpetual conflict. Same-different, smooth-hairy. I dominate, I give in. I resist, I obey. I want you to be the male, but at my permission. The Male-Satisfier-of-the-Inner-Female is my creation . . .

The great hermaphroditic God cajoles, manipulates and in effect thumbs His/Her nose at the male-female charade or comedy—in order to control. The ultimate goal of this imperious deity, even more than landing a lover, is to stand alone as queen-for-a-day in uncontested glory.

Thus the demigod (that I am) casts himself as male (or male impersonator) in order to capture a more authentic male who is male without needing altering or foundation. This authentic Other didn't start as a boy/girl, but rather, comes pre-made as male through-and-through. The ardent suitor mustn't arise from a miasma of sexual ambiguity. Rather he must possess solid credentials of prior masculinity.

What the sought-after contrives not to see is that the ardent suitor seeks to lay his own burden of nihilated and reinvented maleness on a worthy Other. The ardent suitor's preeminent position as top requires that he hide all evidence of weakness or lack and present himself as Total Male. He is expected to be the Rock of Gibraltar.

The ardent suitor's apotheosis into a demigod, however, doesn't stop there. The sought-after wants this Gibraltar to dissolve like a genie the better to piece him back together in fantasy. However a convincing apotheosis requires physical intimacy. The goal of intimacy is the breaking up of solidity into vulnerability. This is accomplished by the embrace. Here, the opposites of ardent suitor and sought-after blend and melt away. Rigid sex roles dissolve like ocean waves one moment to be reformed the next. By embracing, one contains or controls. Conversely, by being embraced, one is contained and controlled. A contradiction both thrilling and inwardly disquieting.

But there's another side of the coin. By yielding to an embrace, one surrenders self-sufficiency and *admits need.* The one embraced receives (or hoards) Beingness and thereby lays at least partial claim to Completion. Because the embrace simultaneously seeks to dominate (to capture the Other's freedom) and submit (foundation in the Other), it is never what it seems. Nor does it gain what it sets out to accomplish. It perpetually ceases to be what it was the moment before.

That is to say, it harbors a nostalgia for the Impossible. Be a rock/be putty in my hands. Be your opaque self/be my transparent invention. Every emotion is its own opposite, every image its own unraveling. The thrill of the embrace lies in just this circular trap.

A further dissection. By being controlled, I'm looked out for and protected. But I lose autonomy, become a transparency, with all my greed, betrayal and bad faith painfully visible. This includes my desire to be all-in-all; in a word, God. My deification must remain hidden, most of all to myself, because I know full well it's imposture. The usurpation of divinity disallows the mortal weakness of being known, of being held and fondled. Thus am I fated to remain an unrevealed vulnerability.

Still more audaciously, I insist that my oceanic lack be viewed as Completion. Otherwise, how am I a treasure? You must fathom my depths without opening the lid. I'm your adored mystery, big boy. Trust me, the jewels are fabulous, but you mustn't gaze at them. Assume an attitude of worship for only then will I lift the lid on my glittering array . . . .

As noted, the ardent suitor has *his own* jewels and guarded mysteries. Beneath the outer shell of manliness, he desires to reveal to the same degree that he's determined to conceal. This is a basic dynamic of not only gay relationships but in an analogous way for straights. Intimacy is based on knowing each other. Founding oneself on the Other is based on not knowing. The conflict between self-revelation and concealment sets up a perpetual and ultimately exhausting masquerade.

A final flight of fancy. An interior dialogue somewhat as follows reverberates through the echo chamber of the sought-after's sacrosanct cranium—

My fickleness makes me exciting. You'd be bored if I was only what I seem. What a sparkler! These sequins are for show. They conceal my inner volcano. My man has the muscle to shoulder (like Atlas) the universe. He may be a simpleton, but he's steady, while Miss Glitter lives in dreams. Enchanting the night sky with a burst of fireworks isn't a man's job. The Rock is content to watch the dazzling display from a solid footing on Terra Firma.

Or if you will— The classic mafioso in the nightclub audience transfixed by the blonde torch singer: He aims both his prick and gun at the object of desire, who is both coolly out of reach and trashily accessible.

This jaded scenario suggests that gay relationship requires on the part of at least one partner the equivalent of a mental, emotional or ontologic frontal lobotomy. This is seen in a further paradox—

Besides "masculinity-femininity versus control," one partner may be called upon to sacrifice intellect; that is, play a daddy version of the dumb blonde. Traditionally, to intellectualize means to exercise White male political control. Such rigid paternalism, however, is anathema to a True Romances-addicted sought-after. For her hunk to read the editorial page, even worse than the sports section, while ignoring her is a no-no.

He mustn't lay claim to godhead through omnipotent reasoning; that is, by taking a rigid, judgmental view of life (which we all know, my dear, is a party). That would resurrect the stiff upper-lipped father she so cleverly disposed of and blotted from existence. He can be anything and everything—overgrown boy, ruffian, gangster, beer-guzzling sports fan—but he mustn't play god through aloof intellectualizing. That might give the clue to the fraudulence of her being. If he must be intellectual, let it be to make him wealthy in order to support the lifestyle to which she's grown accustomed.

Finally— The sought-after declines or refuses to transcend "her" endocrine glands and emotions in order to join in soaring in the stratosphere of abstract thought. Politics and philosophy threaten the theatrics of her shrunken feminine universe. Icarus must be shot wounded from the sky and delivered in bondage to the boudoir, the better to cherish the Mystery Queen who, despite her magic powers, remains maddeningly earthbound. Icarus must be content with his station as Rock of Gibraltar. Anyway, he's more endearing as a simpleton. She'll take a drunk over a thinker any day. The former is less likely to see her as the sham she is, while placing her on an unquestioned pedestal.

This version of relationship, then, as well as the others described, survives and flourishes in the mode of non-analysis. So viewed, the gay world is anti-intellectual. It stops short of both understanding and undermining itself, which amount to the same thing. True knowing leads to the awareness of body mortality and the primacy of SPIRIT>Mind. Spirit summons Ego-Body to the place of sacrifice, to soul cleansing; decrees an end to diabolic artifice. Body, on the other hand, seeks to prolong delusion through a network of alibis. Its ultimate expression are the blankly staring, equi-spaced statues of the cruise bar. These enticingly represent—while disporting themselves as immortal—separation, alienation and the descending curtain of physical death.

Spirit beckons steadily and inexorably in the Third Ordination to the transcendence not of being gay—which is not only undesirable but impossible—but from indenture to Ego-Body. It offers to free our naive young and later (fast forward 30 years) older, jaded bar goer from addiction to heavy matter (consequently evanescent) delusion. Spirit beams a penetrating light onto what gayness, in order to maintain and perpetuate itself, schemes to keep hidden: its origin in the nihilation of earthly and therefore Cosmic Father.

To recapitulate: Each partner in a gay relationship wants to be thought masculine while retaining a private region labeled "unisex"—all the while hoping that the Other doesn't see or possess this aberration. The sought-after paints him/herself as unique, as a glorious (and secretly manipulating) live mannequin. This region of nothingness is the control center, the Seat of the Hermaphrodite. Its arrogance must be kept hidden, for it possesses Olympian ambition.

It is also utterly unsure of itself; it thrashes in a limbo of self-doubt. To hide its vast insecurity—permeation with nonbeing—the control center demands that the Male be kept in bondage. Yet, paradoxically, this stud captive must be allowed a limited range of expression or "supervision by mommy" in order to found the would-be captor's existence. As is readily apparent, this is a furious whirligig that has its roots in the diabolic; which is to say, the Impossible.

I've gone to great, confessedly exaggerated, lengths to expose Nothingness in its subtle, sometimes glaring, invasion of being. Otherwise, how extol the glory of full Beingness? A foretaste of Completion rises phoenix-like from the ashes. For what is the Seat of the Hermaphrodite but a temporarily vacated Dwelling Place of the Soul?—which in turn holds concourse with Spirit. In the twinkling of an eye or through the labors of a lifetime, depending upon the speed and efficiency of the Third Ordination, the Void is transmuted into an oasis of homecoming.

Despite the Absence at its core, the homosexual quest for relationship replays the spiritual journey of all mankind. The male/female, controller/controlled, intellectual/airhead "traps" are evolutionary artifacts, an outgrown clinging to a primitive stage of human development. These games of one-upmanship bespeak, more like howl at, incompletion, which is still a *something*, in that all such games are a roundabout path to Completion. They strive for what they presently reject—already are what they are not yet—by unconsciously trying to repeal and reverse the Denial at the core of their being.

The gay man is infiltrated by the vaporous fingers of Nothingness, but only if the ontologic glasses given out at this exploratory session are fixated on Ego-Body. No living existent—eternal soul—can fall into total Nonbeing, any more than there is a powerful Devil capable of dragging all of mankind down into ruin. One can only approach this ink-dark Sea, sense its chill Otherness and recoil in horror back toward the Cosmic All.

The metaphor of the cruise bar, then, besides an outward search for Mister Right and an inner quest for forfeited Earth Father, veils a deeper yearning for Eternal Father. By daring to venture onto this pockmarked, bloodied and at last silent battlefield, the gay warrior (or priest), without realizing it, lifts himself through self-expenditure and sacrifice, and therefore all mankind as he would his own children or congregation, into the transforming light of Eternal Reunion.

CHAPTER SIX

TRANSCENDENCE TOWARD ATMAN

The project of union with the Male, as we've seen, has wiped out its primal roots in the desire for union with Lost Father. These two projects, one conscious and the other subconscious, while interrelated, are in direct opposition. The deep-seated contradiction, like all unresolved conflict, gives rise to disturbed or deviant behavior, which can be defined as behavior out of step with the effectiveness and best interests of the organism. On the conscious level, anything that resembles the rejected father must be shunned, gives the shudders, produces anger and is zealously repressed. In the deep subconscious, however, reunion with the father or an ideal surrogate is actively and fervently sought.

On a transcendent plane, the conflict is none other than timeless Spirit via individual soul trying to break through to the reversed and distorted body>mind liaison. The soul is Spirit incarnate, its individual content. It seeks conciliation and transcendence toward Higher Self (in Hinduism called Atman), union not just with Father but the entire world process. The lower self or Ego-Body, on the other hand, leads to separation and death. Spirit is both the great All (Brahman in Hinduism) and the process of individual soul attaining and joining with its highest purpose (Atman).

As a subtext, only through Spirit can Sartre's atheistic in-itself and for-itself hope to come together and unite, since only in Spirit is foundation-of-being possible. Likewise, Freud's ego/super-ego/id. His triad exhibits a clinical, glandular and lonely lack of Spirit. All three modes fail to attain the seat of the soul. Sartre's roughly analogous in-itself/for-itself/for-others is even bleaker.

His superstructure, like airy scaffolding, depicts modes of acrophobic even terrifying isolation. Similarly but more down to earth, the ego is infantile, in-turned, monarchical. Id is a dark jungle of man's tribal, spear-wielding past. Superego is a fastidious but unexamined repository of parental, societal and civilized demands on the infant, child and later adult.

To return to Sartre. In-itself is brute, self-absorbed, opaque beingness with no need or belief of God. For-itself is a jealous and estranged consciousness that both reflects on and tries to join (impossibly) the in-itself. It is "doing" attempting to merge by its own powers and under its own auspices with "being." To complete the triad, being-for-others, like the super-ego, is a structure of isolation in which the hapless existent is haunted and fixed by the corrosive "gaze" of the Other. Tyranny and betrayal, enslavement and appeasement are the primary modes of expression.

As is apparent, neither the Freudian nor Sartrian system admits to or holds concourse with Spirit, the Source of all Being. Both operate in arid isolation. The individual has little more than a superficial or glancing association with his fellow man. As such, these are "static dynamics" or "dynamic stases." They spin furiously in a closed circle that can never break free from its centripetal, inward-spinning force field.

From an ontologic overview, homosexuality begins as a prior yearning, hunger or "malaise" that soon spreads to Mind>body. It then reveals itself under societal pressure (super-ego) as a physical and social aberration. It has already passed from Cause into Effect, gone from *a priori* to *a posteriori*. However, in the infinite chain of cause-and-effect no link is just one or the other.

On a conscious level, the "aberration" appears unwilled, preordained, parachuted in out of the blue. Freedom of choice devolves into predestination. That's because on this earth plane of heavy matter and boundaries, freedom and determinism appear to be contradictory and mutually exclusive. In the realm of Spirit, however, they are reciprocal images, opposite yet transcendentally consonant, if not the same.

Homosexuality, as previously claimed, precedes sexuality. It precedes the awareness of having a penis, or of the father having one and the mother not. Sexual response is a network of secondarily forged neural pathways stranded in the no-man's-land of Effect. These pathways are carved out as spontaneous acts (Cause), only to later settle into routine performance (Effect). Sexual performance is like show horses going around a circus ring. The more "set" the original creative act through repetition, the greater the differentiation from, desire for and even mistrust of fellow humans, who are likewise conditioned through diverse circumstances, individual preference, culturally approved modes of behavior and genetic predisposition, to express sexuality differently. The thrill of radical action (the origin of sexual arousal) settles into reactionary ritual as sex becomes channeled and locked into established neural pathways—rather like social and political institutions. (Aristocracy at its inception or some point in its origins is based on piracy.)

The radical father/son or Creator/created split therefore occurs at a pre-reflective and sexually undifferentiated stage before accountability and penis awareness. It takes place in the primordial dawn of Spirit. We shouldn't, however, discount the determinative role of the mother's body chemistry. Hormone imbalance, fear of childbirth, secret revulsion of her sex role, along with genetic factors, can trigger a fetal or infantile shift toward homosexuality. Along with the murdered father, the mother is a prime sex role facilitator.

Yet a priori to physiological and psychological factors is the pre-reflective and crucial feeling that the father doesn't "ring true." He's an imposter, a fake. He's not in the mother's best interests. He upsets her balances. He doesn't love her; he's therefore incapable of loving her offspring. He's a threat not only to the eternal Mother-son duo as in Michelangelo's *Pieta*, but to Love itself. The infantile mind, a tiny spark of Spirit, perceives the father—the way an oyster protects itself from a foreign grain of sand by secreting a protective pearl around it—as a conspiracy to rob him of nurturing and love. For love is the all-surrounding amniotic fluid of Life.

The alarm signal that the father is an imposter or predator is apt to be distorted or erroneous since it goes off at stressed, highly impressionable moments. Furthermore, an overly sensitive, individualistic fetus or infant is more likely to draw such a dramatic conclusion and act on it. Against the matrix of an unbalanced maternal hormonal-emotional mix, primal (soul) rejection of the father is "kicked downstairs." It lands, like the fall of Lucifer, in more fertile territory. It gets implanted in the domain of heavy matter. Once it settles into Earth-Body, the aberration has come home. It goes crazy like bacteria in a petri dish. It exhibits a primal "rage" not only to survive, but to flourish and feverishly reproduce.

The first several orgasms, especially those consciously directed (as opposed to wet dreams), are usually determinative. Once established, as heterosexual or homosexual, aggressive or passive, oral or anal, the neural network leaves only the possibility of variations on a theme. Obviously there are cases in which the first response(s) is unsatisfying or incomplete and new pathways are forged. Such an individual has a high versatility or "Don Juan quotient." This virtuoso sexual range can overflow in new directions, any of which may be a watershed of change. But that's the exception rather than the rule. Once established, sexual identity and response tend to remain set. Just as political and social institutions as well as religions are "set."

In *Up From Eden* Ken Wilber formulates a theory of Atman and Atman Project. Atman is the attainment and state of cosmic Oneness. It is union with Primal Essence (God or Brahman). Atman Project, what I take the liberty of renaming False Atman, is a lower order attempt to avoid evolution into a higher form along with the various "deaths" that growth entails. The positive and negative aspects of Atman Project Wilber calls Eros and Thanatos. They can be called "Lust" and "Fear of the Loss of Lust."

Eros is a "positive" clinging to lower order pleasure. Thanatos is a "negative" abhorrence and fear of what brings about its dissolution and rebirth onto a higher plane. While both Atman and False Atman operate in the subconscious, they are in constant combat. Atman is pure Spirit. False Atman is body immortality in league with denial of Spirit. A negation at the heart of Being, False Atman is extremely clever at inventing alibis and in its capacity for mimicry.

Back to Freud and Sartre. Both of their invented trinities, besides being too pat and artificially all-inclusive, subordinate SPIRIT>Mind to brute body. They are systems for describing Ego-Body. Both deny transcendent Spirit. For Sartre, Being is simply the endless succession of its appearances. Beyond brute matter—nothing. Furthermore, both systems are inadequate to explain the phenomenon, let alone the origin, of homosexuality.

The pre-choice to be gay, despite its primal innocence, unleashes a scandal in the "hallowed halls of heaven." It causes simultaneous weeping and hand clapping among the angels. To be homosexual entails cosmic risk. It's the essence of audacity. For it dares to subvert the downflow of SPIRIT>Mind>body into unnatural upflow. Like trying to reach the sky with a spurt of a garden hose or build a stone Tower of Babel.

Can such a bold experiment succeed? (I've known gay men who describe themselves as an "experiment.") With fear and trembling, willfulness and wild joy, it (homosexuality) plunges into Ego-Body. It forgets its divine origin in order to fully *be* in the particularity of the flesh. But isn't it the human condition, one asks, to fall from grace, followed by a long struggle, like a salmon to spawning waters, back to Source? The difference is that the homosexual takes the greater risk. He sets out on his journey unaided and alone, without a map, compass or father. He reinvents the train, paints the clouds scudding past, pencils in the costumes and towns. (Like David Hockney designing a stage set for a Stravinsky ballet.)

The aberration is now seated in body. It looms like an opaque mass at the center of the universe that obscures the life-giving sun. It daringly commandeers SPIRIT>Mind from below; it preempts and impersonates God. The essential is thereby eclipsed by the particular, eternal values swallowed up in transient pleasures. This helps explain both the excesses and clone-like conformity of a West Hollywood or Castro. The whole show is directed from the perspective of Ego-Body cut off from Eternal Continuity. Outrageousness replaces celestial grace. Surface glitter, getting high and promiscuity mask an underlying dis-ease. Life is a faux elegant royal court threatened by plebes.

Is the gay man, singly or collectively, to blame for this imbalance? Does he go out of his way to create a scandal in the heavens? Or does he simply mirror a basic ontology? I'll here attempt a tentative answer. He's as innocent of the "malaise" that afflicts him as he is of the homophobia it engenders in the larger society. In a universe of Oneness, the evanescence of homosexuality is, paradoxically, the "bedrock," the mutually causal other face, of heterosexuality. One produces the other, is the other's illusory foundation. One isn't guilty and the other innocent. No matter how outwardly hostile, *they are unwitting bedfellows.*

Just as homosexuality precedes sexuality, so does homosexuality precede "sin." Sin can be defined as the choice of short- over long-term survival, futility over fullness, vice over virtue, darkness over light. The homosexual is fated to live out the unforeseen consequences of his primal soul choice that precedes the age of accountability and the kicking in of the reflective consciousness. In the existential here and now of raw matter, predestination appears to rule the roost. No one chooses to be gay; it comes down as a Given. How was he to know that as an initiation rite he'd be allied with False Atman? That his earth idols would be Eros and Thanatos? That he'd go to war hoisting the banner of Lust like an absolute value worth dying for?

Transcendentally, how could he remember that being gay was a *primal soul choice*? Most profoundly and incredibly, that he's on the planet to be prepped and trained as a high priest?

Accepting oneself as gay comes after the fact of a prior destiny to "go it alone." The Second Ordination reinforces the dictum to be oneself no matter how dangerous or dire the consequences. That's not to say he doesn't feel estranged and lonely. In the great unfolding of life, to be fatherless is also to be motherless. Just as heterosexuality and homosexuality rise and fall together, so with male and female. One doesn't exist without the other. God the Father has no lasting dominion or credibility without a Divine Mother. The attempt to ground oneself on an exclusive Patriarchy or Matriarchy is like a sand castle about to be washed away by an obliterating tide.

I'll now attempt to equate Sartre's concept of the for-itself to the appearance of homosexuality on the evolutionary landscape. The reflective consciousness (an infinite regression of images in a house of mirrors) comprises both the beingness and function of the for-itself. The for-itself "creates" the world—that is, makes the in-itself *be*—by viewing it across a chasm of separation. Differently put, through the heady nothingness of freedom. Or again: the for-itself is the nothingness it makes itself be in order to fix and hold in place, in a kind of envy (like the penis variety), the opaque self-sufficiency of the in-itself.

Besides "creating" Being, the for-itself refracts time into past, present and future. It flees the past, which it still is but can't hold onto across a fleeting present towards a future that is not yet but which still defines its being. The for-itself has the daunting task of not only severing ties with the past and skidding blindly across the buckling ice of a precarious present (intended by Spirit as the Eternal Now), but clinging to an arbitrarily invented future—not only as a goal but as *constitutive* being.

This starts to sound like the multiple denial at the heart of being gay. Or more cogently, the veiled quest of the pre-gay and later outed gay man for Lost Father. If the gay man is simply the pre-choice of himself as denial-of-father, he can never come to rest in the beneficent downflow of Spirit. He's an unrelieved and unrelievable tension. Unnatural upflow "stands one's hairs on end," whereas downflow lays them smoothly at rest. A spiritually aligned for-itself/in-itself/being-for-others becomes Self-Aligned-with-Cosmic-Father-and-Eternal-Continuity. A confident and serene merging with Brahman.

Sartre's *Being and Nothingness* is hounded at every turn by man's inability to found himself. For-itself (symbolized by the gay man) can't found itself on the in-itself (Lost Father) because it has made itself the negation of the object of its longing. The same is true of the heterosexual's inability, by rejecting "those disgusting gays," to come to rest without a weighted burden of guilt in the combat zone of being-for-others. Afflicted with boundaries, the human existent can never see himself as the Other sees him. Separation freezes both parties into combatants. The piercing "look," which can never be understood or appropriated, comprises an ongoing Purgatory. These unspannable chasms, which crack into countless secondary fissures, describe not only the gay psyche, but the schizophrenia of the oppressing larger society.

Inner and outer fragmenting is a gauge of man's inability to achieve foundation in isolation. Wholeness isn't attained through a buffed body, but a tuned-in Soul Self. False Atman makes man (witness the ardent-suitor/sought-after at the cruise bar) a diaspora of fireworks against an icy night sky. Existence is then (correctly) characterized by anguish (the inability to escape the chilling responsibility of freedom), nausea (being a lone body surrounded by other bodies that offer neither comfort nor solidarity) and Thanatos (fear of a future with no guarantee of success).

This self-immolating triad arises from the false perception of self as a body-in-isolation and the Other as enemy. Foundation is impossible so long as meaning comes only in the past or from an evanescent future. Or so long as existence precedes essence. Man only attains foundation by rending the veil of Ego-Body and embracing his intrinsic nature as a spiritual being with the Other-as-Brother.

Why, one asks, can't man found himself qua man, that is, qua self? The answer lies in the nothingness of freedom. Freedom is a *not*, the space or Void across which projected action takes place. Lower body freedom refracts the eternal Now into a series of disjointed instants. Each denies the one that came just before and the one that comes immediately after. Estrangement from Spirit renders impossible a contented dwelling in the Now. It leaves "no exit" from the lust and greed of earthbound maya (in Hinduism, earthbound pleasure-seeking, the equivalent of hedonism). With body domination all-determinative (made into a god), the burden of inventing oneself anew is reimposed at every instant. Only by coming to rest in the eternal Now is the peace of solid foundation possible. Otherwise, the cornerstone and bricks go flying into space. The project of installing oneself as another statue in the cruise bar is seen for the mirage that it is.

A typical Sartrian sophism: Freedom isn't free not to be free. Two negatives creep into the equation that can be thus rearranged: Man isn't what he schemes (in bad faith) to be: unfree. This points to the fact that all negatives are self-immolating. Sin is employed to "punish" sin. Similarly, homosexuality is "used" to explode the myth that heterosexuality possesses any moral or spiritual superiority. It is the nature of negatives to sink and vanish like a mutual suicide pact into the Sea of Nothingness that underlies and threatens Being, leaving only the Great All of Brahman.

Human history, from the forming of families and tribes to the inception of religions, shows that the desire for foundation is as strong or stronger than the urge to be free. They are opposite faces of the age-old dilemma: whether to stay where one is (False Atman) or advance to a higher plane (Atman). Man's nature as a *becoming*, caught in a space-time cocoon, makes these two forces appear at loggerheads. The roadblock dissolves in the timeless realm of Spirit. There, freedom is a reflection of sure foundation, while foundation enables a full expression of freedom. This, however, is only possible by transcending Ego-Body through merging with Divine Will. The great surprise is that the heart's deepest longing exactly corresponds to the will of God.

To attain true understanding and self-realization, then, one must strip the for-itself of its pretense of being an absolute value (both a nothingness and God) and accord it a subordinate status as team player; to change it from a demi-god into a contingent yet vitally contributing member of the Cosmos. For the for-itself, as a purveyor of freedom, to be artificially elevated to a fearsome nothingness that can only do and never be, that can never in its wildest dreams achieve the peace of foundation, borders on Dante's description of hell.

It suddenly dawns that the for-itself, as a function of mind, can be transformed from a corrosive "not" into a luminous "something" by virtue of being a *Harbinger of the Light,* that is, as a receptacle and channel of Spirit. Is a camera a negation because it takes pictures that only simulate reality? Is rereading a paragraph one has just written an annihilating act? Is looking in the mirror—the reflection-reflected (the image referred back to the decoding brain)—a mere phantasm? If one conceives the mirror, camera and written page as organic appendages of Being, rather than grafted on . . . must one *still* regard the for-itself as an agent of estrangement and negation . . . ?

If so, the result is an endless duality, a limbo of diabolic Otherness. But wait, there is hope, a flicker of light penetrates the darkness. By pushing free from the trap, one sees that this self-inflicted hell need not be. It's all illusion. All things operate as part of a greater, ordaining Whole. By a similar logic, homosexuality isn't a multiple negation, a vanishing at the heart of Being, an ontologic suicide, but an alter-face of the Divine—a priesthood for the plurality of mankind.

The darkness gives way to a burst of light when one conceives the for-itself, its internal and external negations not taken as constitutive but as spiritual enablers—as a means of *differentiation*. The ability to differentiate is fundamental to the unity in diversity at the core of Oneness. The true goal of the for-itself (rather then marooned in isolation) is to conjoin and serve indwelling Spirit.

Similarly, the hidden destiny (First Ordination) of the gay man is to express (Second Ordination) and transcend (Third Ordination) his gayness in order to unite with Cosmic Father. But he must first live out the differentiation of selfhood, that is, fully manifest his gayness, since its final goal in all its lack and longing, joy and sorrow is to regain the dignity of Wholeness and merge with all-embracing Spirit.

In a meaningful hence spiritual universe, the direction of evolution is toward ever greater complexity. Differentiation is a basic ingredient of Oneness. Only the complex can comprehend the innate unity of its being. "Diaspora" (it applies to both members of the suitor/sought-after dyad) is complexity squandered in radical separation. Differentiation, however, in service of Spirit has a goal of oneness leading to Oneness merging with ONENESS (Brahman).

Lust (Eros) and fear of its loss (Thanatos) are positive and negative poles of the project to remain separate and alone. Separation is illusion, whereas diversification into a higher unity exponentially increases spiritual density (meaningfulness) leading to Atman. A necessary step toward finding Lost Father, then, is for the gay man to recognize his fellow gays, not as isolated Ego-Bodies or sides of beef at a meat rack, but as soul brothers.

To return to the existential subtext— Can the gay man (and mankind whom he reflects) flourish in any sense of the term as a struggle between the for-itself and in-itself? As an unrelieved tension between what he is no longer across the void of the present toward what he is not yet? Or as an unrequited longing for Lost Father?

The conflict arises from clogged or reversed energy flow. With artificial upflow, the universe fragments into bits and pieces. The extremes of separation are the boring and the grotesque, about the way straights view gays. Body idolatry casts dark boundaries in which one's fellow man stands out in bas relief like heavy metal cartoons. In separation, human relations oscillate between distrust and attack. Little surprise that Sartre characterizes the mode of being-for-others as conflict.

Or: hell is other people.

Addicted to separation, man is cut off from the possibility of true fraternity. But when the veils of Ego-Body are rent, letting in the spiritual light, separateness is seen for the illusion that it is. Spirit fills in the interstices of nothingness with the flowing gold of brotherhood under the paternity (and maternity) of God. That's the great achievement and blessing of the Third Ordination.

But before leaping head over heels with unbridled joy, a further dissection of the for-itself (Ego-Body) as an agent of alienation clamors for expression. The gay psyche is haunted by the original split from Father and then fated to a life of separation in which union with a surrogate male is, if not impossible, fraught with difficulty. I call this the "unworkability factor."

The illusion of Ego-Body is based on disruption in time, on discontinuity. It is always "elsewhere." "How it was" and "how it will be" are greater enticements to cruising than the hairy chest on blatant display in the next cubicle at the baths. The image of "hairy chest" is plucked from the past and hustled into the future. Its preeminence is a vanishing act, a chance configuration of fickle matter. The for-itself strives to make past scenes more vivid and exciting, while devising hot future scenarios. It edits, amplifies and distorts over and beyond the pallid present. Reality is in perpetual need of "fleshing out." The reason is that gay sex is hounded by a malcontent that no progress is being made toward reunion with estranged father or spiritual advancement toward Atman.

A gay man may cling, for instance, to a persona of "leatherman." It is he, an image arisen from compulsion and reinforced with repetition. He earned it and he won't let it go. Millions of nerve endings hold the image in place. Yet underneath, "leatherman" is a phantasm to be put on and shed at will. "Resting in the character" is in reality the maintenance of tension. Deep inside he knows the central Lack (earthly and Cosmic Father) can't be filled and cured with mortal self. The phantasm remains an outline, an uneasy caricature, of a core Absence incapable of uniting with Higher Self or fellow man, while chained to False Atman.

If, contrarily, someone in the street yells "fag," it can trigger an anger response. He fought for his leather image and no redneck punk is going to deprive him of it! But should the voice turn out to be a burly basher intent on shattering his cheek bones, he may as readily beat a fast retreat as stand up and fight. The chiseled face beneath the pose mustn't be bruised or damaged. It's the face of royalty, the face of a revolving king-queen, not a plebe private subservient to a Male Warrior God. The leatherman flees to the sanctuary of his elegant foyer. He is the being of nonbeing and the nonbeing of being of the edifice he's spent so much time erecting in airy space. He's a future-past and a past-future that, due to a primal rupture at the core of his being, never comes to rest in the NOW.

That's not to say the leatherman is cowardly or wrong for shedding a "butch" facade in order to avoid a fight. Nor is the basher the least bit admirable for trying to wipe out the heresy of what he sees as male impersonation and betrayal. The gay victim shows the greater pliability, intelligence and humanity. The gut impulse to wipe out anything different from oneself is the desperate howl of Ego-Body. The wartime plunder of foreign cultures, racial intolerance, killing wild animals for blood sport, suppression of modern art and gay-bashing—all despicable. It's the unreflective freedom of willed slavery whose ultimate aim is isolation and death. Maintaining boundaries is an attribute of False Atman, while embracing unity in diversity is an attribute of Atman.

Atman bids the truth seeker let go of impossible foundation in separate self. False Atman, which makes itself a god, fears and despises diversity. Like a charging bull, it's determined to stamp out everything through machismo, gender or racial suppression and religious fanaticism, anything that looks or acts differently from its infantile and tribal self.

In truth, both gay victim and basher cling to Thanatos: the refusal to evolve to a higher form. Both erect barricades in the path of Oneness. They fear each other because both have undertaken a radical retreat from the quest for Atman. The gay man withdraws to a royal court of diplomatic immunity, an imagined superiority. The basher flees SPIRIT>Mind to vest himself in the brute force of fists, an admission of failure that also springs from a failed father-son relationship. (The basher, however, stops short of willing the father's nonexistence, but endures his bullying by passing it on.) Both players, chained to Thanatos, fear to give up one iota of Ego-Body. Thus is true brotherhood and reunion with Spirit perpetually deferred.

Since the original father-son rupture occurred in the twilight of the soul (to be replayed in the womb and infancy), any analysis of or "solution" to homosexuality can only be through Spirit. The *a priori* condition of homosexuality can't be uprooted through conscious will. Much less by corrective therapy or religious sorcery. It forever seeps back around the edges. A person can't go inside his own brain and yank out complex wiring, any more than a gay basher can stamp out homosexuality. Least of all will a born-again experience miraculously change a homosexual into a blueprinted heterosexual.

Simply stated, a person can only be reborn into *what he already is*. From this viewpoint, yearning for Lost Father, Mister Right and ultimately God, rather than a multiple Lack, manifests at least partial high density Beingness. For what is homosexuality in its inmost being but the divine drama of Spirit (a la Hegel) losing Itself in order to rediscover Itself in a golden flood of light?

Spiritual promptings speed up at male menopause when a man would normally expect to be not only a father but a grandfather. A lonely sorrow wells up. For the straight man, the "ferocity" of fathering mellows into the "benignity" of proud grandparent, church elder and community pillar. Since the gay man was in many ways always more "benign" than his straight peer, he feels doubly left out. His sexual history doesn't add up to a legacy of value. The yoke of male tension can't be laid on the shoulders of a gung-ho, likeminded progeny. He feels not fulfilled but empty, not at peace but secretly angry. To compensate for his exclusion from the chain of life, he seeks a roundabout, back door—and saving—path to Spirit.

An intensified yearning catalyzes a turnabout from separate body to a reconciliation with Lost Father. His gym-toned physique won't last. To slow or reverse aging with a toupee, trendy retro clothing or a tummy tuck are sadly laughable. Besides, he's lost the will for the feverish search for pleasure that once masked a sense of Lack. The specter of meaninglessness catapults him into self-confrontation.

Can all this be happening, he cerebrates, because in some basic way homosexuality goes against the grain and doesn't work? How and why, beyond obvious anatomical challenges and spurious reasons hammered home by bigots or a church pulpit, he's at a loss to say. He's left no stone unturned in his search for fulfillment as a gay man. Yet the dream didn't quite materialize. He never found Mister Right. Or if he did—and here's one of his greatest fears—he didn't recognize him. Worse, he unwittingly slew (a la Oedipus) the relationship before it ever began. Against a mocking firmament of Lack, he's had to successively lower his expectations in finding partners for sex and romance.

Is unworkability a constant in the gay equation? If so, it should apply not only to lonely singles, but to those in long-term relationships. Being in the arms of another man feels wonderful, exactly right, a gift from the Divine. But how often after perfect lovemaking does a haunting sense of apartness creep back like an uninvited ghost! There arises a subtle intimation of something missing. Even though Lost Father has moved on in his own spiritual journey and, like a waning moon on the tides, exerts less pull, the mid-aged gay man carries forward this Absence in the form of a weighted backlog of longing.

Singles may try to fill this Lack in the company of stable married couples or other "orphans." This too can backfire. How often do gay gatherings, designed to foster group rapport, degenerate into mutual satirizing and veiled contempt! The frustration and affront to the mature gay man on the brink of the Third Ordination seems less a stroll in the park than a forced march down an ill-fated garden path. Propping up False Atman reasserts itself as a last ditch effort to sabotage finding meaning singly or in relationship, as well as blighting universal selfhood and full citizenship in the Cosmos.

This speeds up a stirring of sympathy for Lost Father. Maybe the old man wasn't so callous and cold after all. Didn't he have his own problems? After all, he gave the gift of life. This doesn't mean the Third Ordination dismantles homosexuality. Not even death can do that. It's simply this: It takes the "do or die" out of body idolatry. The mature truth seeker is for once content to be an empathetic bystander rather than an active participant in the meat market or dating game.

Not that he has much choice. Finding partners is ever more difficult short of resorting to hustlers or male prostitutes who, no matter how well paid ("Honey, I take cash, Visa, or Mastercard"—better yet, stocks and bonds, or a house in the country), hold him in veiled contempt. What the Third Ordination achieves is to restore body idolatry to its rightful place in the SPIRIT>Mind>body hierarchy. For deep inside he knows only Spirit can heal the breach of continuity manifested as loneliness, childlessness, grandchildlessness, low self-esteem and lack of honor.

Until the Third Ordination, he tight-walked a narrow ledge between the absence of divine sanction on one side and the impossibility of self-foundation on the other. In-itself, for-itself and being-for-others (as with ego, id and super-ego) were at perpetual odds. These warring factions triggered an escape up a sheer cliff-face of promiscuity, and when that didn't work, the hot air balloon of camp. But alas, being neither Prometheus nor Icarus, he belonged to neither earth nor sky. Can existence be more afflicted with Nothingness, one that makes a farce of divine paternity and yet forbids self-analysis?

Clinging to a precarious cleft in the rock, he puts on that other face of camp: narcissistic mother-love. The father withheld love out of indifference, envy, hidden disgust or outright hostility. The pre-gay infant/child, acting on a primitive morality, rejected all such negative responses as fraudulent. He'd accept love only in its purest form. But didn't mother-love prove an equally unreliable bestowal? If not betrayal? Because of male secondary sex characteristics and body-idolatry, he can only be a caricature of her. He's a fake mother dispensing stylized love. He offers only the love of a great actress: the incongruous gestures of a man mimicking an actress who only imitates a real woman.

"We will be our own outrageous non-foundation," clamors a troupe of grotesquely mascara-ed actors in the early Fellini film, *Variety Lights*.

Atman stagnates in False Atman. Eternal truth degenerates into theatrics, substance into special effects. How well demonstrated in the vicarious identification with faded movie stars! The stars are discarded and perish like scraps of celluloid on the cutting-room floor. The failed past must be constantly replaced with sparkly previews of coming attractions. Yet throughout the masquerade, he never stops believing that life has to be something more than a feverish search for a perfect body, or if failing that, a glittering burlesque act, all leading nowhere.

The gay man, a prototype of mankind, searches for and then demands meaning and foundation for his brief sojourn on Planet Earth. Despite the energy invested in Eros and Thanatos, his true nature seeks long-term healing rather than momentary pleasure with the inevitable pain. Ego-Body prolongs the pain of separation. It perpetuates the myth that flight away from Higher Self and Spirit leads other than to suffering and loss. He eventually exhausts himself with the sheer energy needed to maintain separation. Spiritual growth becomes a matter of survival. Evolve or perish.

But first, a word about Sartre. He had Simone de Bouvier and the adulation of primarily intellectual readers. Even that must've been small compensation for being so brilliantly wrong; for failing to perceive the missing Content of his multiple negations; for not deducing the necessity of a Creator. Or not realizing that his celebrated mental-emotional states, nausea and anguish, arise from fear. Fear, the opposite of love, lends them what shadow existence they do have. Fear is dread of the Void of being alone. It emanates from separation from Source. All negative emotion comes from the loss of God, all positive emotion from regaining His fatherhood.

It finally dawns on the aging seeker that self-interest is best served by shedding the role of lone combatant. A standoff or truce isn't enough. If God is absolutely and eternally good, and all things serve His purposes, then all things serve the Good. If all things serve the good, then they *are* good. A just and sane Creator wouldn't undermine Himself by creating a Satan in league with heaven-storming legions of evil.

In the same way, He wouldn't create deviant freaks endlessly afflicted with futility and pain. Just as He wouldn't bring into being homosexuals without hope of experiencing joy or expressing physical love. Otherwise, we're flung here by a capricious S&M God. If God is all-caring and all-good, one must assume that gay men and women are lovingly produced and beyond that, created for not just an ordinary but an exalted purpose.

Given this brighter prospectus, but in the interest of completeness, I briefly return to our existential sub-theme. Can the for-itself unite with in-itself? Can freedom (existential doing) occupy the same space as predestination (essential being)? More to the point, can the gay man, shot through with evanescence and nonbeing, achieve the spiritual density (meaningfulness) to conjoin with Higher Self and thereby attain Atman and union with Brahman?

Both the Sartrian and Freudian schemata describe not union but perpetual isolation. Sartre posits man as a "useless passion" incapable of holding concourse with God (Who doesn't exist) or fellowman. Happiness is a precarious, chance affair. How can it be otherwise without a Higher Power to confer divine blessing? In-itself, for-itself and being-for-others, as with ego/super-ego/id, correspond to no anatomical or functional areas of the brain. With a coldly cerebral version of Ego-Body as the end-all of existence, Sartre pens a bleak description of man in stark isolation from himself, others and all hope.

The mid-aged gay man (I prefer to call him "gentleman"), prodded by Spirit, seesaws between an old vacuity and a foretaste of fullness. He agonizes in front of a brutally unkind mirror. He sweats a lot in both private and in public. Facing the conflict head-on takes courage, since the fullness bestowed by the Second Ordination now asks to be seen as Lack. The price of passage to a higher plane is the shedding of Eros and Thanatos. Meaning replaces Lack when he leaps free from the futile carousel of earthbound maya. That is, when he transcends the search for foundation in Other-Body-as-Father-Surrogate. Another way of saying when he bids goodbye to salvation in Mister Right, who existed at best as a flawed approximation.

Finally, by accepting himself as a fully credentialed child—and high priest—of the Cosmos.

In summation— Rebirth to a higher plane entails conflict and pain as well as a reordering of values. The reward is an exchange of body tension for spiritual peace, internal disruption for Wholeness. This turnabout coincides with resumed downflow (or inflow) from Spirit. You are meant to be here, you belong, enter into your birthright as your father's son. "I and the Father are one," spoke Christ.

No matter how one weathers the tempests of the three Ordinations, being gay is and always was part of the Grand Scheme. Otherwise there wouldn't be homosexuals. To claim otherwise makes a mockery of logic and is an abuse of power.

The hierarchy of self ceases to be an arena of conflict. Other gay men, rather than a mosaic of body parts or sides of beef at a meat market, are complete wholes that likewise bear the stamp of the infinite. The mortar of Meaning fills in the cracks and fissures of separation.

The alumnus of the Third Ordination at last views the Other as Brother (now as *Loved One*) with neither rampant lust nor fear of attack, because they are One in Spirit. Spirit tames the feral rage of ego separation. Promiscuity and bitchiness are shed as useless garments or armature. Slowly is the tyranny of body conquest and the fear of its loss let go. Ego-body is seen for what it is, a fleeting shadow existence.

It's like those giant high voltage stanchions that march in ghostly columns across the Mohave Desert. Empty, barren, meaningless. Going nowhere but to more desert. Ego-Body (in contrast to homosexuality that has eternal authenticity because it derives from Source) lacks the density of being to endure past a brief dash of color in its evanescent and disruptive mortality.

CHAPTER SEVEN

THE PRE-GAY ON THE SCHOOL GROUND

Three Modes of Escape:
Self-Amputation, Withdrawal and Artist of Masquerade

Simultaneously with the quest for Mister Right, that tends to be social, is an antisocial desire to be alone. This is due to the subconscious flight away from Rejected Father. This flight is also a profound search. The repellent being (genetic father with a small "f", who throws a damper on the fun-loving mother-son duo), must be escaped, rejected and denied existence; in a word, nihilated. This, as we've seen, is the mechanism of the First Ordination. Whereas, birthright Father (with a capital "F")—cosmic, idealized—is the object of a lifelong quest (Second Ordination).

But since the pre-gay is "stuck" with a Lazarus-style imposter, who, despite being willed into nonexistence, stubbornly refuses to stay entombed, the sacred quest for "F" (how quickly it becomes profane!), is reduced to a search for an infinity of surrogate "f's." There it lies shackled and squirming in the deep subconscious until the mid-life awakening or male menopause that draws the curtains on the dispensation of the Second Ordination and heralds the dawning of the Third.

I now return to the First Ordination that begins in the womb or infancy and continues through early childhood, through the pre-adolescent promptings of feeling different and the final plunge into the Second. As the pre-gay "bites into life," he forgets through the amnesia of birth his origin in primal Spirit, that he has pre-chosen himself. Or that he has descended from the essential into the existential, from the divine into the mortal.

I'll now attempt to describe the pre-gay on the school ground. If the home atmosphere is sufficiently unhappy and oppressive, the buried conflict of Father quest/father denial may carry over into school, church and community. In extreme cases, father-flight/search expresses itself in radical withdrawal. This includes flight from the rough-and-tumble of the little boy's Playing Field toward the softer, more congenial world of little girls' Safe Court. Rather than competition-combat, the latter operates on the principle of cooperation-conciliation.

This is much to the pre-gay's liking. It's a welcome chance to lay down the struggle that began with his brutal ejection from the womb into a world of giants, which like Mount Olympus is ruled by the male god, Zeus. This hierarchic Pantheon, filtered through earthly father, he must simultaneously appease, resent, despise, try to respect and pretend to love. In the process, the Safe Court of little girls subtly metamorphoses into "home sex," while the thunder-and-lightning world of Zeus, little boys and fathers into "opposite sex."

If being-for-others (super-ego) is rigidly developed into a "thou shalt and shalt not" dichotomy (little boys must play softball and dislike dolls), the pre-gay will blot out or carefully mask his cross-sex inclinations. This leaves him in a double bind. He flees Father at home only to find his slain avatar on the playground. There's nowhere to hide. An innate desire for acceptance and safety forces the pre-gay into a no-man's-land of masquerade.

Decked out as the boy society expects him to be, he searches for a niche on an outer fringe of the playing field. He dare not heed the seductive summons of the girls' volley ball court. At recess, the boys swarm onto the battlefield; the girls hold polite, orderly, nonconflicted court. He's both "there" and "not there," a simultaneous appearing and disappearing. He braces himself for the carousel existence to come in which he'll both flee from and chase his own tail.

Since home is an emotional battlefield, where he covertly despises the father whom he must nonetheless obey and respect in order to please Mother, another battle is too much. Oh to chummy up with the girls, play at being boy friend, charming little suitor, even husband!—in short, unite with them.

But the disapproval of teachers, even Mother who doesn't want a sissy either, sends an unmistakable signal of a line not to be crossed. He can't act out the little girl he secretly desires to become. Thus he is what he is not; ironically, the nihilated father which he can't help inadvertently resembling and even becoming (shudder!) in a secret part of his brain.

The hard choices he faces can be roughly grouped into three categories. All three bear the mark of the Impossible, which he will come to personify: 1.) self-amputation, 2.) withdrawal and 3.) artist of masquerade.

Self-amputation occurs when the pre-gay rejects and represses his desire for female identity. The little boy tries an exaggerated macho pose. He forces himself onto the playground. He even leads his playmates in catcalls against girls. The chip on his shoulder—an aggressive lashing out at parents, teachers and peers—comes from his debarment from Safe Court. He makes it a hard fast rule not to sample the joys of Wonderland. Unwittingly he traps himself into being a counter-male or impersonator, a Henry Winkler-style Fonz.

He pays a high price, a lifelong resentment, for acceptance into the arena, but he makes it. Father is pleased with his spunky little warrior. His peers find him strange but amusing in his fervent femaphobia. Putting on a surface disgust for girls isn't hard, since he already despises them for being the Girl he can't be. Similarly will he be attracted to other boys across the unbridgeable distance of Safe Court. Forbidden to whisper amorous sentiments in a playmate's ear, he can only send love messages by bouncing a radio signal, as it were, off Mars. He covets what he has placed forever out of reach: the part of himself that longs to be female. Father-rage is transferred onto innocent girls, who he's forbidden to and can't let himself join.

Differently stated: He undertakes the project of paternal severance, only to position himself with secret amorousness toward the boys of the playground as *father surrogates in miniature*. But parents and society (super-ego) tell him they can't be lovers, only neutral playmates. This forces a double denial. The struggle for gender identity and emotional survival propels him into self-amputation. He becomes a sacrificial hero of the Warrior God, but underneath, a fraud shot through with Nonbeing. If the father tends toward violence in reaction to a repressed feminine component of his own, it speeds up the process. The pre-gay forces himself by the scruff of the neck onto the field of combat. He's well on his way to being a make-believe warrior, convincing on the outside but miserable within.

He rides the crest of resentment into adolescence and young adulthood where it settles into a put-down posture toward women. They must be punished, since being disallowed to be one of them costs him the exhausting labor of playing imposter. The vendetta dooms him to carrying on the charade of little warrior long past his time. In romantic conquests and later in marriage he'll be unable to release pent-up anger in coitus. He shakes his fist and over-reacts at sports events, while putting down his wife or women in general. He maintains a rigid rape posture.

Should he manage to liberalize—for instance, run into a former teammate who accepts women's, Black or gay lib—he may discover within himself the heresy of an unsuspected homosexuality. He can't face the fact that he secretly longs for another male. He mustn't endanger his hard-won status as a member of the team. But should a chance arise to express himself in private—on a hunting trip or a public restroom with a total stranger—he's surprised to find himself capable of turning on the spot into one of those "damned queers."

Furthermore, if he allows himself to be fellated or in an off moment actually gets down on his knees to do it to another man, he'll blame it on too many beers. Or on the pretense there were no women around. Shock and shame are suffused with a contradictory anger directed at both himself and his parents, fed by the realization that from earliest childhood he was forced to squelch a forbidden desire to "diddle another boy."

A side effect of the clandestine homosexual fling is a mellowing of rage toward women. But the price is the devastating discovery of an aberrant sexuality. He sweats being a traitor to the team. Given the right opportunity he could actually turn gay! He's thrown back into the limbo of the school ground. Since he can't live without a scapegoat, who to hate or not hate? If he stops hating women, his arrow-straight image and hence his manhood will unravel and allow his suppressed gayness to surface. Damned if he does and damned if he doesn't. The best solution is to hate the homosexual in himself and even more vehemently in others.

But that is to reject a vital part of himself, to play his own judge, jury and hangman. As pointed out, homosexuality precedes sexuality. He must nihilate not only the father, but the totality of himself as a full sentient being. As an adjunct, it can further be stated that desire (essence) precedes pleasure (existence). In other words, desire for the male precedes the inability to derive pleasure from female rape. Desire and pleasure strive for simultaneity—but too late. The schizoid macho adaptation has been set through long, anger-laden reinforcement. Desire and pleasure are permanently at odds. He can't admit that he actively sought the shadowy homosexual fling. He condemns it while hoping for a chance recurrence. Nor must he desire the female. She's just for anger release, a channel or tool for reaching the inaccessible Male as rejected but real opposite sex.

A legacy from the sex-segregated school ground is festering ill-will toward his wife for not being male. At the same time, he hates homosexuals and the homosexual within himself for exposing the roots of two guilts: 1.) maltreatment of the "little woman" and 2.) betrayal of the team. He blames his homosexual coconspirator for his own capitulation, transfers his weakness onto him by holding him responsible and in contempt. Paradoxically, he harbors a nostalgia for that very weakness (on a higher level the Fullness of a yearning for a lost paradise) which is the forbidden allure of Safe Court. Since he can't appropriate to himself the "weakness" he longs for, he must hate it in someone else. This is apt to be fags, Blacks, Jews or homosexuals in general.

He bears a nagging guilt for buying into the world of queers through a cowardly but exciting backdoor rendezvous. "Crack me another beer," he testily commands the little woman, in whom he has instilled a service mentality through fear of his blustering rages, as he returns to the sportscast. Little does he realize the football game or boxing match replay the unresolved conflict of the father-denial of the First Ordination projected onto the grownup arena of the TV screen. Or that he's a homosexual who fucks women.

The adaptation of self-amputation contains a telling lesson. Had this redneck bully been allowed to accommodate and assimilate without fear the forbidden world of little girls into his psychic makeup, he'd be a more complete man, his wife a happier woman and the planet a safer, less violent place.

The adaptation of withdrawal has at one end of the spectrum the anti-social recluse. The competition of the Playing Field is too much for this retiring pre-gay. He's too timid and passive to join the fray. Yet in Safe Court he'd stick out like a sore thumb, appear falsely animated, risk being an object of ridicule. He simply wants *not to exist* on the plane of being-for-others.

Accordingly, he rejects both Playing Field and Safe Court. The whole playground structure is a frame-up. Such precocious logic nevertheless engenders guilt. But isn't guilt itself an unfair burden to be borne, something thrust on him from the outside? Teachers and principle enforce the law that boys must be boys and girls must be girls. Boys must like catcher's mitts and girls, dolls. Shades of color between dirt brown and pretty pink aren't allowed. No matter how democratic the school paints itself, he finds himself in a totalitarian regime.

In rebellion, he attempts to "dispossess" himself of his penis. It's the first part of him to disappear. This tool of differentiation is what caused the problem in the first place. A penis pees, it squirts in a rude arc. He denies this symbol of social differentiation by avoiding urinating with anyone looking. Nor must anyone see his bare behind. The final stage of disappearance is a cell-like privacy. The desire for penis-nonexistence makes it seem smaller than it is; while hiding the buttocks has the opposite effect of making them appear larger, more unwieldy and mysterious, hence more womanly. Penis awareness, moreover, precedes buttocks awareness. Readily visible from the front, the penis commands attention. For the "little thing" to spurt outward into open space would return it to normal size. That would in turn constitute a territorial move, since urinating in a proud arc, as with all sports, is an aggressive claim to territory.

The Playing Field is, appropriately, larger than Safe Court. The uro-genital definition of territory is the culprit behind the despised dichotomy of a world at war with itself. The penis is expeditiously withdrawn into the lower abdomen. The judgmental gaze of the Other causes both this vanishing act and the constriction of water flow. The pre-gay is distressed and confused, since the mandate to withdraw comes from a hidden region of the subconscious over which he has little or no control.

The greater the need to release urine (which would betray the dual projects of female identity and rejection of male territoriality) the more he cannot. His physiology (the shrinking of the penis) replays the primal rejection of Father and Playing Field. Urination succeeds best with a distended flaccidity, a pre-readiness for sex that exists in children. The mandate to withdraw interferes with this readiness and blocks release.

Thus is sexuality, a vital component of being-for-others, posited in denial. The withdrawn pre-gay wants social and sexual differentiation to disappear along with himself-as-Other. He makes the austere choice of solitary confinement.

Fortunately, his fractured world comes back together in the integrated safety of the classroom. Body is reabsorbed into Mind. Status based on aggressiveness and athletic prowess is relegated to the background. The grinding gears between Playing Field and Safe Court are oiled and smoothed, made less grating, in the comfort of identical desks facing a common blackboard and if not a female, at least a sympathetic male teacher. Question and answer sessions don't smack of sexism. He basks in the neutral atmosphere of unbiased thought. But alas, the recess bell. He must resume the feared exile of the bustling sexist corridors.

Worse, he finds himself living out and subtly *becoming* the spurned father with all the fake games of "pretend." A variation of the old saying, "Be careful what you hate, that's what you'll become," aptly applies. The more the pre-gay distances himself from the negatively charged force field of rejected father, the more he inexorably moves toward it, a cosmic law he'd be the first to vehemently deny. The societal demand that he be a little scrapper of the playing field has the acrid taste of a lie. It forces him to betray his true self in order to survive in a totalitarian regime of fraudulent value.

He finally reaches the conclusion that the masquerade isn't worth it. It goes against the grain, wastes energy, stifles growth. A child has an innate sense of destiny and personal rightness. At six or seven years of age it's fairly well set what he will and will not be. This much he knows: His destiny isn't batting balls or picking fistfights. He refuses to be a counterfeit like the nihilated father who committed the unpardonable sin of presuming to judge him in the first place.

With both Playing Field and Safe Court off-limits, he withdraws along with his penis into abdominal exile. The project of retreat calls for the retraction and denial of the organ of "reaching out." He thereby severs connections with classmates and assumes a saintly sexlessness in order to stand alone in an idealized Safe Court of his own creation.

The rejection of social contacts, besides leading to a false sense of security, has the side effect of retarding and distorting sexual development in adolescence. Since the inturned sexual milieu has a flavor of a conspiracy against "all of them," he invents antisocial ways to "get it on and off." He's spent his short life learning concealment. Guilt over masturbation, however, results less from deviation from social norms or defiance of God than from *betrayal of the mandate to withdraw.* Masturbation requires at least the partial awareness of an Other. A shadowy Phantom of the Opera lurks in the wings. The sexual scenario revolves around mutual rejection. You shock me, I'll shock you. I deny your fleeting quasi-existence with my antisocial orgasm . . . .

Despite multiple denials, the Other remains the ground of the onanistic act. The phantom can't be fully exorcised. He seeps back around the edges like smoke trapped behind a locked door. The withdrawn early gay masturbates both contra and via the Other. In order to focus erotic imagery and thereby increase pleasure, he lures the phantom partway on stage. True, this narcissist desires himself. But since pleasure is obtained through orchestrated encroachment by the Other, the release of tension (a violation of the project to withdraw) requires a complicit and likewise devious playmate.

But this only compounds guilt. The contradiction (guilt over withdrawal from society versus the violation of the mandate to withdraw), more than fear of societal or divine retribution, is a primary reason for the perpetual conflict inherent in the project to withdraw.

This leads to another facet or modality of the project to withdraw: sado-masochism. S&M is a specialized but socially retrograde (practitioners will disagree!) means of eroticizing mutual rejection. The gay onanist imagines himself maltreated and forced into submission by a rowdy top. (This may change to self-as-abuser as he gains confidence and through resentment of abuse received, seeks to amass control.) The libidinal milieu evolves with fanatic haste toward debasement of self and the artificial elevation of the Other (or vice versa). He desires himself as victim but must use someone else to achieve it. The Other abuses at his bidding and under his control.

The onanist thereby slyly retains the Seat of Judgment. The Other's performance is either let stand for further elaboration or edited out. It has no absolute weight, no lasting authority; it is illusion and ultimately fraudulent. The puppet performance is used only as a means of achieving orgasm. The onanist temporarily appropriates the Other in an attempt to achieve the fusion of desire and pleasure. He ingests the Playing Field melee, only to regurgitate it after a quick utilization. He uses it in order to reject it; he rejects it in order to use it. The project to withdraw thereby remains intact. He plays lone satyr at a sado-masochistic bacchanal.

A related modality, based on the eroticization of rejection, results from a fascination with the digestive process. Since the withdrawn early gay tends to seek his own company and eat alone, ingesting food is a solitary and intimate event. This fascination comes to focus on defecation, the ultimate antisocial act. The private, outwardly repellent ritual is an amalgam of father rejection, playing field and the oppressive system all rolled into one. Defecation occurs directly below instead of in an expanding territorial arc. Moreover, it's the same for boys and girls. Both sit in isolation behind a discreet partition. Contrarily, urination for boys takes place in open-to-view urinals.

The withdrawn early gay, as shown, regards urination not as a proud sport, but as a threat not just to personal privacy, but to the sanctity of inmost self. Defecation is self-contained and shut off from the gaze of the Other. Girls perform both functions in private, while boys urinate by "unsheathing their sword" of competition and conquest. The pre-gay's stream refuses to arc, which he won't allow, in the mandated territorial manner.

Therefore, to avoid embarrassment and save face, he combines both functions in the sanctuary of the discreet stall. Hence, rebellion against an unjust social structure leads to an elimination fixation. He deposits his stool as both a personal production number and as rejection of the System.

A related adaptation may propel him into obesity. Obesity arises from a reciprocal and confused obsession with food intake and elimination. The obese onanist eats more both to hoard social approval and to expel the gorged banquet before the judging Other has a chance to change face and reject him. The busywork of sitting down to eat and attending to toilet duties gives an illusion of being a step ahead of the dating/mating game.

In reality it's a retreat to an infantile stage in which all his needs, diapers changed, etc., were performed by an accepting parent, usually the mother. The organ of differentiation retreats into rolls of fat. While putting on a jolly social front, his primary goal at the dinner table or school cafeteria is less to socialize than to slip away in guilty grandeur to the self-indulgent rite behind discreet walls, much the way a nicotine addict hurries through his food in order to savor an after-dinner cigarette.

The rolls of fat serve, more profoundly, as a partition to hold the Other at bay and enclose the onanist in a gelatinous embrace of womblike sameness.

The desired undifferentiation manifests in his androgynous Buddha-body. With grand beneficence he unites Playing Field and Safe Court in his ample being by eliminating in a private place, like a monk slipping off to confess at the secret shrine of a patron saint.

By eroticizing the socially unmentionable, he makes himself a secret ambassador for uniting opposites. Through "wiz"-ardry doth he elevate a repugnant act to a hallowed rite. He fails to perceive, however, from the Olympus of Antisocial Decree that the conflict, rather than resolved, has merely shifted. By denying sexual differentiation, he becomes trapped in Body. He is body locked in a self-embrace.

I here shift from psychoanalysis back to ontology. Eclipsed SPIRIT>Mind, aware of entrenched body idolatry, attempts to "shine through." This higher faculty has, however, been used for too long to maintain isolation for it to effect the quick behavior modification needed for social integration. First, let it be noted that moderation is control of the impulse to over- and under-differentiate. It is the consent to civilization. A higher awareness of the need to lose weight, if only for social and health reasons, requires the dismantling of a lifelong defense mechanism and the unhiding of the penis.

Unbiased Mind, highly valued by the pre-gay in the classroom, becomes the unraveler (spiritual downflow) of the asexuality and resultant deviant behavior that he devised (upflow) in his attempt to found himself sans Body. This leads to the surprise realization that sexual suppression espoused by religions is a deterrent to true spirituality, to unimpeded downflow. Spirit tells him to his consternation and amazement, that his penis isn't his exclusive plaything. It belongs to the tribe, to society, to God. Sex is meant to be shared with a symbolic Other who represents all of mankind, but only within prescribed boundaries. Thus his personal pee-pee both is and isn't his. Hidden or on full display, it's a tribal mystery object.

The Playing Field conflict wasn't resolved at all! The school ground, he discovers, is neither good nor evil. Although far from risk-free, neither is it unrelentingly vicious. Basically amoral, it simply *is*. He internalized, mistaken or not, the projected conflict by making himself an infernal eating machine.

What He couldn't face in childhood must now be played out in his rumbling innards. Rather than withdraw, he's forced to acknowledge and confront an encroaching Other. The Playing Field, brought forward in time in the form of the competitive world of business, is still there, but with a less grating edge. It's not the *Lord of the Flies* combat zone remembered from childhood. It includes women with soft dresses and make-up and self-assured, well-spoken men.

While he was stuffing his face, a grown-up integration of Playing Field and Safe Court was taking place. Women's lib, along with the taming and commercializing of the Warrior God, brought about an unforeseen masculine-feminine interpenetration. The competition of business has a surprise cerebral aspect. Unlike the ill-fated "Piggy," brains count for more than hunting wild boars.

While affording a measure of comfort, this reflection fuels an awareness of having spent a major portion of his maladapted life on the outside looking in, of being a pariah couch potato. But no more, it's time to strut a little, show his true colors. Underneath the fat, isn't he as much a man as anyone? But alas, enlightenment always comes too late. For isn't the fragmentation and displacement of time a common factor in all modes of escape? A consequence of not living in the Now?

Thus the playground conflict remains locked in interiority where it began. Yet rationally faced, in order to make business contacts and form meaningful relationships, as well as avoid a heart attack, he must slim down to a reasonable facsimile of a cog in a social machine, a man in society. The project of withdrawal backfires through his ejection out of financial and social necessity onto the Playing Field of the workplace. The beached whale must fight its way back to perilous open seas. Still present but in an altered state, male-female dichotomy forces him, like it or not, into differentiation and identity with his penis-for-others. Sexuality becomes not a choice but a necessity of survival.

Hence, in a universe of Oneness, the project of sexual withdrawal and denial isn't just a delusion but impossible. It's even more true of homosexuality. It exists in order to be expressed. Differentiation, or unity in diversity, leading to Oneness is a condition of Atman; whereas retreat into a safe but static sameness characterizes False Atman.

The phantom of separation fades into the wings because it doesn't really exist. Social and sexual withdrawal contain through the inevitable ascendancy of SPIRIT>Mind, the corrosive elements of its own dissolving. Total sexlessness is impossible. It always seeps back around the edges. A full expression of what one is, and that includes gayness, isn't just condoned but ordained by Spirit. Therefore by God Himself.

I now digress from the broad heading of Withdrawal in order to focus on a prime ingredient of all three sub-modes. The factor of religion. In their zeal to reform and replace outdated tribal customs, taboos and sexual mores, religions actually reinstate them in camouflaged form, just as Christianity incorporated Greek and Roman elements into its mythic dogma. By religion, I refer to those major belief and control systems (Hinduism, Judaism, Christianity, Buddhism, Islam) that present themselves as possessing an exclusive handle on Absolute Truth.

In church, the pre-gay is subjected to another unpalatable dichotomy. That of the Sunday morning sermon. Since the message is couched in authority, disagreement is forbidden. The sacred words direct from God must be swallowed whole or repressed. They contain two opposing theses. 1.) God is Love. Therefore He is also forgiveness, kindness, mercy and tolerance. 2.) God is the Avenger. He won't tolerate sin or a hairbreadth deviation from mandated belief. Blood sacrifice is required, witness the wholesale slaughter of animals in the Old Testament, the crucifixion of Christ and the grisly martyrdom of early Christians in the Roman Coliseum, not to mention the Crusades, the Spanish Inquisition, witch-burning and other horrors. The history of religion, with the possible exception of Buddhism, is a saga of violence and bloodshed. Peace and love that belong to the province of women are swept under a subservient rug.

The Mad Wizard called God is possessed of a vast schizophrenia. He created both the violent Playing Field and peaceful Safe Court. Christ's command, "Let not the left hand know what the right hand doeth," is a barometer of the hypocrisy. The early gay wants justice, good will and acceptance. He desires to be loved for who he is. Yet acceptance for boys depends on being a Little Warrior of the Playing Field. God, the Avenger, controls this domain. The God of Love rules Safe Court.

Should he believe both? The Split Being must be at war with Itself to allow the Great Imposter, Satan, to meddle so disastrously in human affairs. The entire system from Godhead downward is shot through with contradiction. By unloosing a Satan, God perpetuates conflict and warfare. Furthermore, by fanning the flames of violence, suffering and falsehood, He *is* those qualities.

Yet, on proviso of blood sacrifice, God's Son, the gently-beckoning, androgynous Christ (with bleeding heart and heaven-turned face) offers forgiveness to the truly contrite and repentant—the female or effeminate man—for a warrior doesn't give in. (Just as a real man doesn't turn the other cheek or eat quiche). Mother-Goddess is a beatific moonrise over a scarred, bloodied battlefield. What cares She for the noise and stench of war? She bestows her blessings upon whomsoever she willeth, male and female alike.

But wait— The Reign of Peace (eternal Safe Court) is founded on the damnation of a majority of mankind to flaming Hades. Only a part of the Planet's population is Christian and only a fraction of that "washed in the blood." To a Pentecostal Southern Baptist, eternal torment awaits Catholics and other fringe groups like Mormons and Christian Scientists, not to mention heathen Buddhists and Moslems. The skewered theology is projected downward in the form of Hell, the ultimate Playing Field, and upward (Safe Court with pearly gate and streets of gold). Hell is the more menacing for its inaccessibility, somewhere beneath the surface of the earth (near its molten core), and the frightful immediacy of tongues of smoke that, through the minister's doomsday vociferations, practically breathe down one's neck.

The deception starts to come clear. The dark side of creation is shoved down a theological rat hole so that the horror of legions of souls in eternal torment can't be beheld directly by God or man, just as teachers by looking the other way condone the violence and injustice of a fistfight. Beatific Sunday love reverts to the warfare of Monday's Playing Field. This conflicted state of affairs, held in place by a schizoid Deity, retains a vice grip on human affairs, all of which comes to resemble a divine comedy or farce.

No wonder the pre- or early gay adolescent sees God as a Sham Who poses as the Male who dissolves into Mother-Goddess only to turn back into Avenger. Through its brute inconsistency, the male world becomes a stage prop to be erected and taken down at will. It has the transient quality of a sideshow in the horror and thrills section of a carnival. The "reasonable" little-boy viewpoint shaped by the First Ordination attempts to dismantle the male imperative and mystique of combat, while manipulating it to advantage.

The overall stage production is decidedly feminine. Mother-Goddess is behind it all. The Warrior Deity (the seat of authority left vacant by the vanquished Father) comes and goes, male uniforms are donned and shed according to the needs of the drama. A Force so lacking in stability and justice, therefore dangerous, can only be relegated to a subordinate, controllable position.

Thus is born in elemental form the male impersonator or leather man. Like his antithesis, the female impersonator or drag queen, the basic principle is the same. His primary loyalty is to Mother Goddess. Black is the infernal color of the Playing Field. The attack world of playground taunts and fistfights is imitated and exaggerated in order to be made manageable, only to be out-flung in the form of motorcycle gear or a military uniform. The leather man calls forth God's secret underside from the nether world. Clad in diabolic black, he tames the Playing Field by both aping and outdoing it. Through exaggeration (the combat severity of the donned costume) he kneads and molds it like potter's clay. Yet he's never *it*. Hence the incongruity of a butch leatherman who opens his mouth only to sound like Joan Rivers live at Studio One. Without knowing it, he's a walking dichotomy, a microcosm of the school ground he so anxiously seeks to escape.

The male impersonator goes from one pose to another on the sliding scale of Camp. Acutely aware of his inauthenticity, he plays out anxiety over his incapacity for self-foundation by parodying himself and others. "I'll fool them, butch it up, then shock everyone by pulling out the props so they'll see I'm fake. Most of all I fool myself. I exert power by making you think I'm real, only to throw back my head and crow like a great actress." The leather man is more Bette Davis or Judy Garland than Marlon Brando or James Dean. Witness a motorcycle run or beer bust where the club members take hilarious pains to point this out to each other.

In fairness, it's also true that *exclusive* male embodiment exists only on the fringe of gay leather society. A hard-core butch act is expected to reveal a comedic side, to mutate any moment into a joke. A real leather man runs the risk of finding himself ostracized and alone. Contrarily, even for a "sosh" pretender, beneath the party-time camaraderie there lurks a gnawing emptiness. Masked with a toolbox of butch disguises, the male impersonator is secretly alone. He finds himself back in the Corridors of Withdrawal. The adaptation to withdraw into solitude may then give birth to and feed its flamboyant opposite: Master of Masquerade.

We can see how the conflict of pleasure versus desire reflects the "segregated" playground. The leather man, unlike the self-amputee, covertly desires union with the Goddess of Safe Court. But pleasure derives from a furtive encounter with the Midnight Male. Beneath all lurks a fear that the playground tug-of-war is itself *in error*. The temple of the Goddess reveals disturbing cracks. The alabaster Parthenon is in danger of crumbling to the ground. He flees the acrophobia of a chunk of marble pillar poised perilously overhead by seeking refuge in the claustrophobia of a womblike bar.

But first, another reference to ontology—

The mature gay man on the brink of the Third Ordination flees the discomfiting discovery of finding himself not only incomplete and unwhole, but *in irremediable error* (inroads of Nothingness). That may catapult him into joining a self-help or community organization in a search for meaning and self-foundation.

Or attending a Gay Pride parade—

For once his full leather isn't just for cruising. The vesture of communal engagement and belonging substitutes for a suit and tie. It proclaims him one of the elect. He makes his way a bit nervously but with a jaunty bearing to the designated boulevard, by night a heavy cruise area. Daylight lends a sense of propriety like church ushers taking up a collection. Fellow leather men show the courage to come out and be counted. Animated, freshly shaved faces and relaxed poses attest to successful completion of the Second Ordination. Insider jokes spring up. Nightlife is recast in light-hearted party argot. The mingling of masculine and feminine mannerisms, like merging fog banks, isn't a crime calling for condemnation at a Last Judgment, but the guilt-free prerogative of responsible gay men who know who and what they are.

But wait! Someone in the crowd makes an insulting remark about fags. A gay basher breaks ranks from an undifferentiated background. The peaceful Monet changes into the stark cubism of a Guernica. The horror of the Playing Field is juxtaposed upon the civilized city. With the scuffling of boots and the shriek of a police whistle, the leather man is thrust back in time, but never quite all the way, toward the primal breach of the First Ordination. The three modes of adaptation—self-amputation, withdrawal and artist of masquerade—come crashing together in the melee. Little do the principal players—the basher, the leather men and the police—realize they're all looking for Lost Father.

Outraged by the bashing on "his boulevard," the withdrawn victim recedes into the background so that the charged-up activist can be born. Spiritual awakening comes on pain of death; Atman upon the transcendence of False Atman. Suddenly he's not afraid to speak out because he's no longer embroiled in Eros and has shed fear of Thanatos. For once, his main priority isn't dragging home a trick but a wider engagement in life. The donnybrook, originating in radical separation, is a first step, actually a quantum leap, toward reconciliation and Oneness.

Furthermore, and most importantly, fear of the batterer and the policeman's baton pales next to the specter of AIDS. The pandemic is a far more insidious threat than the Playing Field. Besides laying the body waste, it bears the stigma of "queer." To this glaring injustice God the Avenger turns a stone face of indifference, if not outright condemnation. It suddenly dawns: *Condemnation is a confession of failure.*

Would a supreme Creator descend into a petty thirst for revenge? Play a sadistic cat-and-mouse game with his creatures? Wouldn't an all-powerful God possess the grandeur to love all His creation equally, be the quintessence of compassion and forgiveness? To abandon His gay children to the ravages of AIDS is a sign of weakness, that His creation has failed. For Spirit doesn't fail. It knows only peace, light and love. Mother-Goddess and Avenger briefly merge into One.

Surprise! The demand for social justice and a cure for AIDS, driven by an awareness of a Higher Power beyond idol deities, miraculously turn the night prowler into a daytime scrapper. A call to battle summons him from the Corridors of Withdrawal. A readiness for sacrifice leaps to the fore above and beyond mere body gratification.

The sacrifice of short-term pleasure, then, brings about a higher order Desire: Of Doing (the Avenger) to unite with Being (Mother Goddess). Longing for and identity with the Male, not as banished Father but as a vital arm of mankind, flourishes in the rarified air of idealized struggle. Make no mistake, he's still gay and so he will always be. But for once, the secret defector to Safe Court longs not just to play or flirt, but join with a Male of the Playing Field. More profoundly, to merge with Lost Father. Finally, to embody this eternal dyad within himself.

He never dreamed engagement as an activist would have this unexpected outcome. It can come in a flash or take a lifetime of sorting through tricks and lovers. It is simply this: He need search no longer for his perfect male counterpart, for Mister Right. The struggle can be laid down—because he *is* that male. Manliness isn't a pose or invention, something to be usurped or vampirized from someone else. It's the birthright from earthly and Cosmic Father, from Eternal Continuity written into the order of things. The specter of death, especially the premature, disease-ridden and tragic exit of a lover, or even oneself (the omnipresent ghost of AIDS), bestows the courage to reclaim lost Self, to be the Male he never thought he was or could be—yet was all along.

In the third mode of adaptation—artist of masquerade—the pre-gay flees the rejected father into the actual court of women. He's a sissy through maternal indulgence and paternal indifference. The father, not locked into the tension of suppressing a female component, doesn't force the son into the role of little warrior. He feels no obligation to counteract on threat of violence the scandal of the "void" of his wife's vagina. He has the freedom to express some of her softness. In fact, she's more assertive than he. Her femaleness "wears the pants." He's a mere extension of her queenly domain. She feels the definitive emotions; he's their passive recipient.

Nor does he interfere with the son's mother-identification. Male-female relations aren't polarized into rigid "good-ole-boy and good-ole-girl" roles. A society tending toward unisex mutes the struggle to hold the sexes "in extremis." Marriage isn't a combat zone of dominance and submission, of violence and appeasement interspersed with limpid pleas for forgiveness. They're much too civilized. The father-son relationship simply drifts away. Even negative male bonding fails to take place. The relationship is one of neutral coexistence, of sleepwalkers passing in the night. Just as the father gave up trying to dominate his wife, he gives up with the son. He leaves the upbringing to her. Father-son talks are postponed until puberty when the kid will be more grown up. Anyway, the sheepish husband is burned out on mortal combat. The inward eunuch lets Mommy run the show.

Under these lenient conditions, the son's female identification is emboldened to the point of not fearing to be a sissy. Mother will protect him.

She lets him join her at the make-up mirror, be with her as she sorts through her dresses. Her very own little courtesan! She doesn't mind his fascination with her "things," since the husband fails to counterbalance her leonine femininity. She asserts, he obeys. The household is hers, along with the little boy-girl. Though decked out as "boy," he develops into a psychological female in the absence of father-as-warrior, hunter or coach who would nip girlish tendencies in the bud.

In her vanity, she doesn't see him turning soft around the edges. She craves the assertive intimacy she doesn't get from her husband. Any tension in this civil, noncombative family stems from the husband's refusal to fight, from passing the burden of command onto her. She often wishes he'd rape her. She dreams of passionate lovers, of pillagers and plunderers. But she'd never allow such beasts in the boudoir. She'd claw their eyes out. All told, she prefers the predictability and security of her weak husband and adoring little Lord Fountleroy.

Off goes the little fashion plate to school. It doesn't occur to him to avoid the girls' volleyball court. He's naturally one of them. He wouldn't dream of dirtying the crease of his freshly pressed knickers on the Playing Field. He's quickly pegged a sissy. He endures taunts from bullies. The girls snicker behind his back. Teachers regard him as an oddity. Other boys make fun of him in the restroom. He shuns urinating in public; likewise, the foul-smelling stalls. Boys make embarrassing noises in them. He bears the brunt of jokes about panties and bras. Mother never taught him to hide his fascination with dresses and jewelry. She always projected a blatant femaleness: Being what she is whether anyone likes it or not. Rather than hide, the boy-girl ignores the taunts. He goes along with the gag. He too will wear panties, grow breasts, if only in play. Bearing the brunt of off-color jokes is preferable to being forced onto the Playing Field.

The Court of Females, then, is his proper milieu. To secure his place, he exaggerates certain gestures to hilarious effect. Underneath, he longs to be the sweetheart of a hero of the Playing Field. Like Cinderella, he needs a powerful prince and ally. The double burden of sexist taunts and unrequited desire leads to a premature "integrity." He assumes a saintly demeanor to compensate for an impossible situation: Being a psychological little girl with a grafted-on boy's exterior continuously eroded by feminine mannerisms derived from Mother.

Unable to keep up the masquerade, he finally stops trying. Oh for a boyfriend to bring his inner and outer selves into synch, who will let him flirt, make girl-talk, dress up! Male teachers cast censorious glances, but consider him too far gone to reshape into a scrapper boy. Who can imagine him on a softball team or in the Marine Corps? The boy-girl achieves his goal of being left alone by the rough element.

He enters the storybook land of Safe Court. He fantasizes wearing a dress, having a bosom. A hidden part of himself effects a transformation into a woman. To venture onto the Playing Field is as unthinkable as joining the French Foreign Legion or riding a rocket ship to Mars. Instead he invents male personas like cardboard cutouts. The models don't come from the Playing Field, but from the world of make-believe, from the magic of the theater. Persecuted but undaunted, Little Lord Fountleroy is well on his way to becoming an artist of masquerade.

Music and drama classes are a saving grace. Ambiguity is the essence of acting. Anything to do with show business holds the allure of heaven. He takes male parts, knowing he can return to the boudoir. As a dancer, he's an idealized male lifting up the ballerina, a stylized female. Intertwined male-female figurines, together they create art.

His ability to play all parts impresses students and teachers alike. The male roles will later come in handy for use in risky situations. He "puts on" Cary Grant, Leslie Howard, one of the Barrymores. He learns to smoke like them, gets their gestures down pat. Unlike the leather man, he doesn't need to mimic one of the Bettes, Midler or Davis. He avoids being locked into a stereotype. A psychological extension of Mother, he comes complete with his own mystique and show business aspirations. An inbred femininity pervades his being. This allows him to run the gamut of male impersonation.

Finally, he learns to be a male escort in order to escort *himself.* He learns the tango so as to lay himself with a dramatic flourish onto the floor. He's a stable of male courtesans like he is for Mother. The actressy young girls accept and adore him. Even the boys are impressed by his bold pantomimes. He becomes part of a select circle of theater-oriented friends. These future artists and eccentrics share a malcontent that makes them appear other than what they are. His talent is nurtured by an art-promoting teacher who thinks he can go places. He appears in every play and musical production.

Despite his fear and distaste for the Playing Field, he holds a value for the school as a budding star. He cultivates a suave theater voice. The female enshrined inside, his legacy from Mother, is protected by an entourage of courtesans. They form an ensemble group, but like the homeless bird of the for-itself, in the mode of not being any of them; of always being a stage production viewed "from the wings."

A new problem arises. Mother sees only the courtesans who admire and flatter her. She's blind to the competing female unfolding inside her son. She has no idea how accomplished and complete he/she is, how skillfully he emulates in order to surpass her. She's older now, less glamorous. The time has come for him to date eligible young ladies. He appears as much a man as the mealy-mouthed husband who, after all, fathered a son. Yet for him to reveal the full extent of his feminization, including his revulsion at the thought of bedding a member of the opposite sex, risks losing her love and respect.

Father, the family's most dispassionate member, already knows. But he doesn't care enough to intervene. He too stands in awe of Mommy. For once, the gay son finds an ally in this affable nonentity. Both fear her, but for different reasons. The father doesn't want her to see the inadequacy of his love, how he relies on her for "Mommy warmth." The son mustn't let her see the debut of the inner female: Venus rising resplendent in her conch shell. She must always think of him as a charming courtesan full of savoir faire.

To imagine him a competing female would infuriate and crush her. He thereby polishes up "elegant escort" with a studied masculine veneer. He makes it a rule never to "swish" in her presence. The theater teaches concealment and the inspired selection of "vehicles." Mother can be held at bay, plied with princely charms. In the meantime, she can be counted on to protect "her darling baby boy."

When in his mid- or late teens he comes out of the closet as openly gay, a worse problem arises, precisely because he never expected it to be a problem. The production of testosterone and secondary male sex characteristics. He's too assertive at critical moments in his love life. A romantic embrace he dreamed of for years proves impossibly clumsy. Two faces with day-old stubble scrape together. Knees bump. Throwing his legs in the air to facilitate entry, he relinquishes grace for the gymnastically grotesque. The sweaty animal posture triggers an unplanned surge of maleness. The refined actress must change on the spot into a wrestler-contortionist.

Stung by the betrayal of not being allowed to live out his inner female, he assumes an imperious attitude— The rutting wench is after all a queen! My authority isn't to be questioned. You exist for me and because of me. Don't forget it, big boy. You're an ornament in my crown. "Oh do it again, harder!" The repressed male comes booming through, to be quickly replaced by the actress. I really must bridle my tongue! I can be such a beast, I mean bitch. Oh yes, the tits. Massage those little gems.

Giving in, paradoxically, makes him acutely aware of his male potential. Broad shoulders, strong arms, deeply resonant vocal chords, a lordly demeanor. In a crisis he could easily thrust his sex partner onto the floor. Like Mother, he wants to be simultaneously worshipped and raped, pampered and abused. He's a male-female poseur, a wildly revolving jack/queen playing card. He's caught in the rip tide of a feminine need to submit and the cresting wave of a male will to command. The contradiction drives him inexorably into camp, into being what he is not and not being what he is. He'll spend the rest of his life, on stage and in gay lounge bars, fleeing that anathema of show business (which he already is by virtue of his forays into Nonbeing): a nobody.

Bitchiness and sexual excess produce a deep-seated guilt that most fully reveals itself in the force field of Lost Father. Now that Mother suspects, although she won't admit it, her aloofness doesn't bother him all that much. Cunning and selfish, she got about what was coming to her. Dad's the Mona Lisa of the equation. He scarcely knows him. Not that he wants to. Rather, he desires to unveil the totality hidden behind the pose; to uncover the truth of this maddeningly passive nonentity. Where did his unassertive, anonymous nature lead *him*? Into being a ghost in Mother's shadow.

But isn't that better than the son's degeneration into a bar queen? Little Lord Fountleroy has become a forked-tongued virtuoso of ready impersonations. He hurls back insults faster than anybody. At his best, he gives himself to the creation of good theater. He's polite and charming, generously withholds the barbed retort. At his worst, obnoxious to the point of loathing. Both poles reveal the range of his theatrical possibilities. Beneath all is a searing emptiness. He has no male role model to look up to, no comfortable self to settle into.

Father wasn't a sufficient force to chip out even a counter-male. The man neither criticized nor smothered. He simply wasn't there. And now, with nowhere to turn, there's no one to be but the shifting constellation of courtesans orbiting a fading, absent star. He feels the vertigo of trying to catch a comet by the tail. Never did he dream the attempt to father himself, to create his own paternity, would be such utter hell. He mugs shamelessly for any crumbs of adulation the public will throw him. He doesn't realize that the pursuit of fame conceals a deep-seated deathwish; rather, the longing to end the death that is his life.

Now late mid-aged, he takes stock. Like the late Paul Linde, whom he admired and identified with, he's played mainly character parts. He appears in back street drag shows. Heaven help him if his serious theater patrons find out! Somewhere along the way crow's-feet appeared at the corners of his eyes, his lithe dancer's body turned pear-shaped. An identity crisis precipitates a return nostalgia for Lost Father. The man didn't go around in circles. Wasn't he always there, steady and reliable, behind Mother's voracious appetite for attention? Too bad father and son never found the time to kick back and talk. How nice to just be *boy* without pretense or alibi. To be with Dad in the garage with his tools, a dusky place with a grease smell the little courtesan never deigned to go. Mainly because Mother wouldn't approve, or so he thought.

He suddenly realizes that, rather than to escape or deny, it was to *attract* this gentle but stalwart being that he dared to try on Mother's dresses and assume her airs. In his childish way, he wanted to bring them together so he could be loved by both. Father was the only one who really saw him. The mother-son duet was too vain to see past itself. Now at the threshold of the Third Ordination, he feels like the tattooed lady in the circus, an obscene mass of bartered flesh. It would take another lifetime to shake off his myriad cocktail poses and the flurried gestures of the theater.

Yet the tragicomedy has a surprise ending—

After a pedestrian bit of dinner theater, he's seized by a sudden pounding in the heart. Uncharacteristically, he ignores the applause upon which he's come to depend. The Absence-Who-Wants-To-Be-a-Star abruptly exits stage left. With a queasy feeling he falls into the arms of the Void . . . for waiting in the wings is his greatest fan, the hidden Link to the Eternal he didn't know was there, yet who was there all along. They know each other the way one recognizes oneself in a mirror.

They're about to embrace when the phantasm vanishes in midair. Not even a facial contour or outline remains. Only a sandbag, a barren fold of stage curtain and a control panel for regulating the lights . . . .

The character actor gives in to momentary panic. Muffled clapping tells him to get back out there. The play isn't over. Something propels him back into the bright lights. A resurgence of applause. Despite his devastation over the baffling disappearance, he knows he'll somehow have the courage and stamina to make the last curtain call. He owes it to the Mystery Guest, the vanquished Father, whom he's spent a lifetime blotting into nonexistence, but whom he can never fully resurrect.

Yet the masquerade isn't over. Someday they'll meet again in an unlikely setting. A farm in the Midwest. A marketplace in old Algiers. The mouth of a Cro-Magnon cave after the last Ice Age. Whether tilling the soil, forging objects of handmade brass or spearing wild game, the emergent outline possesses timeless validity and wisdom. And he knows he's come home, that he didn't have to play all those character parts, be that flaming queen. *Boy* was enough. Just as *man* works perfectly now. He catches a glimpse of Wholeness. That moment marks the Rite of Return, launches the escape chariot of the Third Ordination.

The Great All, he knows without knowing, is steady and unchanging with no need of role-playing or costume changes. Neither does Spirit value him any less for the theatric Purgatory he went through in order to arrive, with an expelled breath of infinite relief, at this sacred moment, for Spirit has unlimited patience and loves unconditionally and eternally . . . like the backstage Visitor's ghostly cameo in the wings.

The ancient rupture at last finds healing. The heavens open with a flourish. And there, Eternal Father (Who unites Warrior of the Playing Field and Mother Goddess of Safe Court) welcomes him into his birthright—a sudden exhilaration which the actor, moustache and eyebrows whitened with chalk to enhance the effect, passes on to the audience in one of those rare, assured performances when everything miraculously comes together.

CHAPTER EIGHT

———— ❧ ❧ ————

The Myth of Christ's Physical Resurrection

D uring a Sunday morning sermon Troy Perry aptly pointed out that Jesus Christ said *nothing* about homosexuality. Actually, Jesus said very little about sex, period. A rare exception were His words to the Samaritan woman caught in adultery: "Neither do I condemn you. Go your way and sin no more." This compassionate bending of Judaic law saved her from death by stoning. It likewise stood in dramatic contrast to the brutal political system of the Roman empire. For a Man, Jesus demonstrated a caring—a situational ethic that shows the unconditional love of Mother-Goddess—eons ahead of His time.

Neither did He conceal that John was the apostle He "loved." According to the gospel narrative, this devoted and sensitive young follower laid his head on the Master's breast at the Last Supper. The Leonardo di Vinci masterwork suggests a wedding banquet. Although the subject of homosexuality, so far as we know, wasn't breathed out loud, was even taboo, close bonding between Christ and his chosen disciples is strongly implied, while romantic ties with the opposite sex are conspicuously absent.

Jesus was martyred at age 33 at the peak of His physical prowess, but before He had to "face" a commitment to Mary Magdalene. The demands of a healthy young body were perpetually deferred in the service of Spirit. The relationship with the sisters, Mary and Martha, has the quality of a menage a trois. Jesus keeps them both guessing while committing romantically to neither. An amorous overture to one would offend, even crush, the other. The rejected sister would resent the honored Guest bestowing divine passion upon her earthly rival.

A gay man typically carries on such intrigues. He fascinates a lonely, unattached woman by doing nothing to discourage the fantasy that she's the sole exception to his exclusive homosexuality. Both parties receive an ego boost, followed by the inevitable letdown and disillusionment. On a higher level, she's relieved, even flattered, that he limits the relationship to the Platonic. It's her vivacious personality, keen intellect, rich spiritual aura, etc., that keep her highly individualistic lover coming back for more. She dreams of being divinely singled out, of being romanced by a demigod who rewards her "sacrifice" by lifting her to sublime heights. This special lover realigns static body>mind>spirit into dynamic SPIRIT>Mind>body. For once here's a man who's not the slave of his hormones. Thereby is she elevated above body idolatry. The relationship rises from the ashes of the mundane to the stratosphere of Ideal Love.

Platonic or agape love transcends male-female dichotomy toward spiritual Oneness. Lower order, sweaty, animalistic sex recedes into a collective memory of the race. The pesky problem of carnal thoughts, illicit sex and masturbation are left far behind on a retreating pinpoint of dust dimly remembered as the mother planet, it being one in millions, even billions.

Picture two soul beings merging into each other like nebulous, pristine clouds. Or cherubim and seraphim cavorting with playful innocence. Obvious exaggerations. Still it's relatively safe to say that only love rooted in timeless Spirit, rather than body fixation, outlives this realm of dust.

How persistent yet transitory is the phallus! What hullabaloo over its preeminence in human affairs! One can go so far as to say that its misuse or abuse has sent countless innocent souls into poverty and death. The most conspicuous abuse is the usurpation of power. Case in point: The all-male Vatican not only dictates the one approved means of salvation, it sanctions over-breeding by refusing to endorse birth control.

The harm perpetrated by this power grab is incalculable. The Vatican is a "penal institution" in that a primary goal is to seize and hoard male power. As previously noted, male supremacy is by nature and on principle sublimated homosexuality. "Penis power" is demonstrated in the troublesome fact that ten percent of the population consistently turns out gay—a "problem" that not only must remain unspoken but relegated to nonexistence (collective double nihilation of the First Ordination).

Axiom Number One: All power grabs are *self*-denial in that they are denial of Higher Self.

Axiom Number Two: Banishment to the subconscious of the "scandal" of male power-grabbing (the Father's unfair, exclusive claim to the Mother), far from denying homosexuality, actually creates it.

Corollary "a": Homophobia engenders homosexuality.

Corollary "b": Homophobia, by virtue of being a "not," is concealed homophilia.

What is a battle with swords or rifles held to the ready but a collective erection? In other words, sublimated homosexuality, since the objects of conquest are other males. Impalement by a sword or penetration by a bullet transforms the enemy into a ritual love object. Is this so different from the love/hate "miracle" of coitus? The warrior's covert homosexuality is consummated in death, in killing or being killed. By going to war he obeys the summons of a repressed homosexuality.

One can say that Donald Rumsfield or George Bush has a hard-on for war. This expresses a collective desire for a warrior-king. What are rifles and howitzers if not erections; guided missiles with nuclear warheads the phalluses of the Space Age? So long as male sexuality is linked to power, along with fear of its loss, mankind will remain trapped in Wilber's Mythic Membership phase, stay constipated in the early Mental-Egoic (better but not best) and barred from the higher, less combative and compassionate Psychic-Intuitional in the Great Chain of Life. And continue to exhibit a constant ten percent incidence of homosexuality! (This figure will likely increase with the large scale emergence of the Psychic Intuitional or Era of Oneness.)

Axiom Number Three: Homosexuality is procreated by the same forces that try to annihilate it, in that it is substantiated and validated by its attacker.

Corollary "a": Taken solely as the outcome of a double nihilation, homosexuality (like its hidden progenitor: machismo) evinces low spiritual density. The mutually-produced/producing dyad of macho/gay rises and falls together.

Corollary "b": This reciprocal negation is powerless to harm, yet alone destroy individual Soul, which is timeless and indestructible.

Axiom Number Four: The direction of spiritual growth (after a brief detour into sexual differentiation) is toward androgyny and Oneness.

Corollary "a": Cross fertilization between homosexuality and religion *leads the way* in androgynizing the human race.

Corollary "b": Androgyny which homosexuality prefigures and embodies, is, paradoxically, the latter's dismantling and dissolution into a higher form. That doesn't mean this higher form doesn't bear homosexual traces, but it's certain to be quite different from its earthly manifestation.

In this chapter and throughout the book, I attempt to show, while integrating the other main theses, that religious mythology, like machismo, "procreates" homosexuality. Contrary to what Christianity or Islam would have us believe, spiritual authority or Godhead doesn't wear pants, have a long beard or hoist a spear. Spirit doesn't compromise itself by descending into the war of the sexes (homosexuality wisely opts out of the struggle, witness Jesus' silence on the subject). To the degree, therefore, that mythology is linked to earth body it exerts a causal relationship with homosexuality in the existential now. Fundamentalist religion and the fanaticism it foments, no matter how fervently the opposite is claimed, are breeding grounds for sexual deviation and expression. One produces the other.

Christ's bodily resurrection is an example of a carry-over present-day myth. I'll go so far as to claim that this lingering superstition facilitates homosexuality and that homosexuality, like the Marines of Iwo Jima (with a gay flourish), despite machismo's every denial, hoists aloft the banner of this potent and enduring myth. I take similar—I hope not blasphemous; rather, reverent—liberties with the teachings of the Apostle Paul, including the "blood and flesh" of the Eucharist.

But first, a return to the phallus and its historical (sometimes hysterical) role in the spawning of religious mythology.

Since, as previously pointed out, lower forms symbolize higher, one might ask free of campiness: Does the phallus reflect a higher spiritual reality? Or failing that, reflect what that higher reality "is not?" Necessarily both. Like the birth canal, the penis is a tube or chute of passage. It leads to a space or reality greater than itself. It is finitude in the service of the infinite. It's analogous to the disposable first stage of a guided missile. It signifies the rapacious rather than the restorative, the primitive rather than the evolved, the transient rather than the eternal. It's a mortality symbol in the way that a sword or rifle symbolizes death. Genetic reproduction as we know it, and probably the genitals as well, cease in the spiritual hereafter.

But first, a brief digression to Sartre, who together with my homosexuality, helped motivate this book. To that self-proclaimed heterosexual atheist, the goal of lovemaking is the pressing together of the maximum surface area. The genitals are just a symbol of that wider desire. How telling and true from the viewpoint of timeless Spirit! A fascinating little book, *Private Dowding*, about channeling an entity from the other side, suggests that sex *over there* is a merging of two essences in which both parties completely penetrate the other unhindered by blood, bones and the barrier of skin.

In Isaac Asimov's *The Gods Themselves* "melting" occurs in a para-universe between three cloudlike beings of varying densities; in other words, between *three* sexes, one being a motherly, nurturing male. One can surmise with some ontologic accuracy that in a non-corporeal afterlife the phallus is as superfluous as gills on a land mammal. Like the physical body that it "adorns" and is erotically but superficially attached to, with which it marches into war and makes love, the phallus is "not." It is neutralized and rendered an absence, like the dotted outline the imprisoned Genet at the end of *Our Lady of the Flowers* uses to describe his dreamed-of lover, Darling's, endowment . . . that in turn like all of Genet disintegrates into nonbeing.

Analogously, Christ on the cross is a discomfiting display of a physical body about to exit earthly existence. The grieving disciples and Mary Magdalene quite certainly saw no more of it via the five senses after the entombment and "resurrection." To see Him roaming in the flesh about the Galilean Hills would contradict and dilute, indeed make horrific, transcendent holiness. The garment worn on the cross—ripped, sweat-stained, blood-drenched along with the winding sheet of death—would hardly undergo the same trans-biological metamorphosis as a body, if even that.

Rather was the risen Christ arrayed in the "raiment of angels." Artists of the Middle Ages and Renaissance covered up or omitted anatomical details such as chest hair or genitalia to avoid giving a spiritual event a jarring connection with dust. Yet Mary Magdalene and the disciples reputedly saw the stigmata and sword gash in their Lord's side. How would a glorified body, freed from blemish and imperfection, retain destroyed cells, lacerated skin and the gross imperfection of a sword gash? Obviously it would not, unless the beholder sees them *transcendentally* through the eyes of Spirit. These soul-stirring visions blaze forth with high density Beingness (meaningfulness) invisible to brute (evanescent) body.

However, these observations, no matter how soaring and grand, offer scant hope to soldiers blown apart in battle, martyrs with mutilated limbs, etc. Heaven would be a hall of grotesqueries, a supernatural freak show. What the disciples and Mary Magdalene saw were visions of the essential Jesus. In other words, what moved them deeply, compelled them spiritually.

The existential Lord of the flesh taught and exhorted, celebrated life, suffered and died, all to enlighten a backward mankind—not to leave the believers mired in a morbid cult of body worship. Such lurid details as surviving stigmata are signs of body fixation, emotional naivety and mental myopia that Christ urged his followers to surmount toward eternal Spirit. For the risen Lord to exhibit such remnants of human mortality as a mutilated body furthermore presents an absurd theological dilemma. He didn't triumph over the human condition at all! Rather is He permanently nailed to a cross of body limitation.

To return to a prior thesis—

Body supremacy and Thanatos immortality that permeate and mold the homosexual psyche arise, with roots in Egyptian and Greek mythology, from the misconstruing of Christ's resurrection and ascension as a geo-physical event. A major problem: The universe of infinite galaxies has no up or down, no in or out. A literal ascension is like a rocket ship, while attempting to penetrate and conquer the Cosmos, in other words, to go somewhere, is more accurately absorbed.

For a heterosexual, the penis has as a goal a kind of mutilation magically redeemed by its fecund result. It gores, thrusts and slashes. The female receptacle neutralizes the "harm" by transforming the assault into physical pleasure and procreation. Swords are beaten into plowshares, the battlefield becomes a fertile oasis. Coitus repeats the age-old drama of destruction and redemption. The fixed border between Playing Field and Safe Court is momentarily blurred. By extension, the "permanence" of Christ's wounds is a projection of phallic plunder, a denial of the feminine (Mother Goddess) function of reconciliation and redemption—as though Christ were being kept on tap for endless torment by Roman soldiers.

I here interject a theme already presented. That of sadism/masochism. Sadism plots its own perpetuation, seeks a false immortality through violence.

In other words (witness its origin in the "thrill" of injustice) it revels in the impossible. It courts, mimics and replays death. As such, it's an exercise in nonbeing. This blind alley constitutes the outer limit, draws the curtain, on the unaided body attempt to transcend the barrier of death, to lift oneself by the bootstraps out of the prison of space/time. It's reasonable to assume that Christ no more took stigmata to Heaven than He did testicles undergoing spermatogenesis. Rather did the ascension release Him from the earthbound prison of corporeal existence or maya.

The sex act, then, apart from a declaration of love (a symbol of Spirit), is a confession of separation that culminates in the symbolic death of orgasm. Its raw physicality proclaims it to be of the nonessential. Spiritual concourse, on the other hand, based on Platonic or agape love, shows forth Oneness. Instead of one partner conquering or usurping the other, essence merges freely with essence without thought of conquest. (No doubt present to such ethereal coupling is an Edenic memory of such dualistic earthbound states as pleasure-pain, kindness-cruelty, happiness-unhappiness.) Such low order maya, then, shot through with nothingness, is no longer sought or even desired.

Through and in spite of the apparent contradiction, or interplay, between predestination and free will, lower physical *existence* builds toward, contributes to and is finally absorbed into the *essence* of Trans-Existence. Though fleshly coupling be no more, its effects linger like ripples on a pond. This follows from the principle that in a Universe of Oneness (limitless meaningfulness) the essential is never lost; but neither is the non-essential, like gills on a land mammal, retained. Excess baggage is discarded—for what is death but the molting of the armature of superfluous skin—so that the journey toward Spirit can continue unabated.

Given the spiritual redundancy of the sex organs and sexuality itself, can a gay man be faulted for finding another male physically attractive in the fleeting arena of the here and now? First let me reiterate that the longing for Missing Father, concealed in the quest for Universal Male, is set in pre-reflective freedom before the advent of the analytic faculty. This is tantamount to saying prior to incarnation on Earth, even, transcendentally speaking, before the creation of the planet. The infant pre-gay "decides" in the way the fetus reacts to bumps and changes in the womb. It likes, it dislikes. It feels its needs met; it feels deprived. It moves instinctively away from pain toward pleasure. At the same time, it responds to a Force that transcends bio-chemistry. On a primordial soul level, it has pre-chosen itself.

The instinctive movement away from pain toward pleasure constitutes a primitive code of ethics. A direct, vital response to stimuli operates in the womb, infancy and early childhood. A higher, more sublime code, honed and refined by the Second and Third Ordinations, will later guide the gay man in a soul return to Source. While innocent of his gayness, he is simultaneously its author. His gayness is a lantern in the dark that guides his spiritual journey. GAY is what he decided to be before he ever set foot on the Planet. The Oedipal mechanism and moral/sociological forces thus far described simply enable this higher process and truth.

The First Ordination is—now well known to the reader—Oedipus Complex taken a final step into the willed nonbeing of being fathered and continuance through fatherhood. To escape a guilty conscience, Oedipus, in a further nihilation, wills the act of patricide *itself* into nonbeing. As a result, the gay man unwittingly posits this double negation or Absence as an Eternal Value. Infant Oedipus commits regicide, never dreaming that in the process he unlooses across the firmament a spreading negation like ink on a blotter.

An unsuspected consequence, then, of casting the father's murder into the sea of God's forgetfulness is that the gay man toys with and tempts, only to cast himself, into the same perilous waters. To flee guilt and move toward the tranquility of a clear conscience, he refuses to face, let alone analyze, the reason he rejects (why his infant self grasped the sides of the playpen with such vehement displeasure) the imposter's every appearance. He's made a lifetime project not to be in every respect what the Fraud-Posing-as-Father is not and not be everything he is.

The reciprocal nihilation obscures the transparency of true Self by making it an opacity. To cope with and flee the Unknown, which looms as a fearful Absence, he reinvents himself as Other-than-Self. This in turn fosters the narcissism of unrequited self-longing. This is the dusky and darkened boot camp the gay man has pre-chosen in order to advance, if haltingly, toward Higher Self.

In the mad swirl of both denying and desiring higher Selfhood, a boundary is erected between existential self and Eternal Male, which he longs to conjoin and finally become. In a last desperate stab at False Atman, he may try to anchor his fractioned, floundering being in Mother, who he thinks he can trust. In so doing, he creates a counterfeit world in which he can only reach the Male from the illusory reef of Mother Identification; in other words, through Nonbeing-as-a-Male. He condemns himself to being the "not" he has made of himself.

Thus he lives out a tenuous Foundation-in-Mother who may at any moment wean and cast him overboard in favor of the vanquished father—a dread event glimpsed only in the mad carnival of dreams. Eternal Male, forfeited through patricide, lies across an unspannable chasm. That is one reason the gay rights movement appears to lack the cohesion of Black, female or religious lib. (That's not to say these admirable social movements haven't their own glaring pockets of nothingness.) Strive though gay liberation may to achieve a solid ontologic footing, it undermines itself on the Ego-Body level by playing out a collective, self-vanishing project of Nihilated Father.

I return to a gay float in a holiday parade. I'll show the counter, passive, feminine aspect of the Ascension by comparing the apocalyptic upward movement (ethereal rather than thrusting) of Christ into space with the surreal, dreamy passing of a float in a gay pride parade.

Although its movement is horizontal rather than vertical, the float's "groundlessness" makes it appear to "ascend." To a homophobic bystander it's an intolerable *absence*. It is disappearance masquerading as appearance; absence posing as plenitude of being. The mannequins on display, blowing stylized kisses, are present to themselves primarily as Other. They have the scandalous appearance of borrowed being. The in-vogue poses reflect the encasement of the tableau in nonbeing.

Homophobia arises from precisely this infuriating absence. The Male is expected to be there *in toto,* to be fully the being that he is—since the simultaneity of male existence and essence forms the backbone of tribal solidarity.

A "tres gay" Robin Hood, for instance, planted in a leafy spray of faux Ficus branches isn't one with his bow and arrow. It's not there for function but for effect. Surrealism, among other things, is the juxtaposition of incongruous images. The float proclaims incongruity rather than integration. It lacks solidarity with the ground of the world. Mother-identification is on display together with the impossible reach for the Male through blatant impersonation. The archer holds the bow in "anguished caprice." No one wants to see the Male in the position of not being able to be himself; as failure.

The parade, besides entertain, is expected to confirm a reliable world. The gay float erodes the reliability of appearance. Homosexuality is nonbeing externalized which the outraged redneck bystander carries within himself like a negative pregnancy. The scandalous display is a scary demonstration of freedom gone amok; rather, the perversion of a freedom that was free before it knew itself to be free. It is freedom calcified in the monstrousness of a sideshow exhibit; that is, in nonfreedom.

The float both curtails and explodes the boundaries the greater society places on freedom. Too much freedom can backfire into a vigilante lynching or repressive Third Reich. Or a disgusting gay matriarchy. Freedom must be stifled and controlled, just as predestination is cemented in such Biblical injunctions as "Spare the rod and spoil the child"; in a word, fear of the primal, explosive freedom of children. Or Wipe out those damn queers.

What haunts the redneck/skinhead most deeply is that the gays couldn't leave the float (or Christ the cross) even if they wanted to. Even at their most audacious, the float members are prisoners of merciless space-time. It forces the redneck bystander to confront his own inner Void, to recognize his complicity with the hated gays. And that, if I may say so, really pisses him off.

The same forces—squelched freedom along with rigid boyhood conditioning that produced the redneck or skinhead in the first place—could under different conditions take an unexpected turn. His early macho training could short-circuit—shudder!—into a distaste for softball mitts and toy trucks. The revolt of the inner "little girl" could germinate and spread like the slime thing in the Alien(s) movies to a state midway between a disgrace and a noxious disease. Homophobia is felt in the solar plexus as a threat to male freedom that in turn depends and flourishes on the enslavement of others.

The redneck homophobe fails to perceive the extent of his own brainwashing at the hands of parents and the jousting field of social competition. He imagines himself in godlike control of his destiny. He could slip unawares—heaven forbid!—before the authenticating stamp of identity with the Male kicks in, into the sick farce of the gay float that has the indecency to proclaim itself independent of God, male superiority and the honor of going to war! He simultaneously feels the confirmation of solid maleness and an urge to wipe out its antithesis gliding with swanlike arrogance out of reach of his macho outrage. He thinks of forming a vigilante squad—just as orthodox religion feels a self-righteous impulse to stamp out heresy.

Axiom Five: "Heresy" is an anger (Thanatos) response to a spiritual event or vision denigrated into a sexist, bodily act. Rather it's a male supremacist or False Atman revolt against the androgynization required for progress toward Atman.

Corollary "a": The artistic/historical rendering of Christ as an androgynous being with long flowing hair and a pure white robe generates in lower order heterosexuals a secret aversion to similar qualities in effeminate gay men or homosexuals in general—precisely because gays are a misunderstood, reviled but accurate bellwether of mankind's present stage of spiritual development or lack. The face of Jesus unwittingly and unnervingly reflects the face of countless gay men.

The internal negations of the gay and macho male (strange bedfellows!) exhibit an opposite yet similar response to the pain-pleasure principle, in turn refracted into pleasure/desire. Since both are searching for Lost Father, each exhibits a desire for the male, which is only differently pleasured. The macho man reaches the Male through the passing distraction of women, while the posing archer reaches it through impersonation.

Additionally, suffice it to say, the pre-reflective choice of the posturing float mates to be gay is morally neutral, certainly not a sin, since it replays a prior destiny. It prefigures mankind's androgynous future among the stars. By definition, sin is the choice of a cognitive existent to commit harm against itself. Since man is SPIRIT>Mind>body, sin is that which willfully subverts the downward (or outer to inner) flow of divine energy.

Coming out of the closet in the Second Ordination feels right because it *is* right. It's a vital and courageous move toward internal integration. Only when it later dawns, with a whole new set of values, that the choice was based on Absence-to-Self founded on original father nihilation, does a new imperative loom on the horizon: The return to Cosmic Father and Wholeness. The brave embrace of the Second Ordination, once an act of high spiritual density, now reveals a contradictory evanescence, an alarming glimpse into the Void. The road to Atman falls into False Atman. It seems the battle must be fought and won all over again! And on even more stringent terms!

But that's only a ground floor of the edifice of gay being and becoming. Another loftier floor is qualitatively different. The High Order, Androgynous Beings who come to Earth as Messengers, Saviors and Messiahs can appear sexless, bisexual or even gay. These advanced Souls reveal a transcendent knowledge and integrity that demonstrate a powerful link with and immersion in Spirit.

As a higher awareness grows, the gay man is increasingly perplexed and outraged by the injustice dealt him by an oppressive society and the yoke of organized religion. At the same time, he realizes that his reach past integration (the Second Ordination) toward integrity (the Third Ordination) reveals a profound Lack. He's found wanting and betrayed all over again!

Can he be rejected by God only to be deluded by self! Where is eternal justice and truth? Worse than God and religion proving to be a sham is for that sham to turn out to be himself. But what is this cruel reversal but an impetus to reach past Ego-Body toward Higher Self? Despite the confusion swirling around him, he feels the stirring of a love affair with the Cosmos. What appears as betrayal is actually a summons to embrace his native *godness*.

An inner voice tells him that his reach from integration (Second Ordination) toward Integrity (Third) is an act and attribute of indwelling Spirit. This discovery saves him. No priest, moral code, theology or government can take it away. Just as homosexuality precedes sexuality, so does Integrity precede and enfold his homosexuality. Likewise does inner Integrity inform and color his relationships—happy, lukewarm or intolerable—with family, friends, the greater society and even his vision of what God may be like. Thus essence (integrity) precedes existence (homosexuality). This umbilical cord with the Cosmos is what gives an AIDS patient the courage to face death when society, family, friends and even a lover all turn away.

We're now in a position to define Integrity in Sartrian, ontologic terms. The in-itself, before being nihilated and recast in freedom by the for-itself, bears the imprint of Original Being. For-itself is the "irritant" or growth mechanism (the "anguish" of freedom) that goads the in-itself (complacent, unchanging) toward a higher destiny. In-itself, or original constitutive Being, is prior to for-itself. Innate integrity corrects (for-itself) errors and detours away from primal beingness (in-itself). The lower pain/pleasure ethic evolves into the higher: Integrity fosters long term (rather than short term) pleasure.

Integrity is written in the cells. It fights disease, instills a will to survive, implants a desire for self-realization, undertakes a quest for Meaning and finally a return to Source. The integration of body>mind>Spirit (Second Ordination) presages the Integrity of SPIRIT>Mind>body (Third Ordination). But to the degree that all three Ordinations are undergirded by Integrity, they are One. Just as all roads lead to Spirit. Integrity pervades the beingness and becomingness of man, just as it propels the gay man, at the cost of dismantling Ego-Body, toward spiritual Wholeness.

The Third Ordination, as seen, can unloose a temporary crisis worse than its two predecessors. It decrees the death of non-essential being, the condition of all growth. The move away from pain seems to lead only to greater pain, like a salmon battling fierce, crashing waterfalls. The vision of peaceful spawning waters plummets into a fearsome nightmare, leaving only blind faith. The Seeker of Truth walks the Valley of the Shadow of Death.

He may opt out of the struggle by yielding to the hedonist dictum: Thou shalt have a good time. False Atman again holds sway. He outfits himself in flashy fashions, is seen at all the "in" places, attends the White Party, avoids self-analysis, denies Spirit, all to shore up the myth of Eternal Body. Meanwhile, a subtle disintegration takes the helm. It doesn't take long for body-in-isolation, lived for quick thrills, to show the Void at its most hideous. The unveiling of the Adonis of Pleasure reveals a wrinkle room troll. To take a wild leap and further tempt heaven—doesn't this evoke Christ ascending skyward with stigmata and sword gash intact? What is this disturbingly incongruous image but a Thanatos clinging to the shell of mortal body?

Both homosexuality and Christ's physical resurrection founder on a reef of body immortality. Belief in a literal resurrection—like the alumnus of the Second Ordination fearing to move to the Third—shows a lack of mental acuity and spiritual insight needed for attaining Atman. Body primacy, held in place by mythologies swallowed whole, delays union with Spirit. The cross-bound Christ and the gay man enslaved to body are imbedded in existence and blocked from essence. Body is both too much and too little, both a lead weight and a vanishing into ether. "Evil" has less to do with this heavy/light burden than with a refusal to outgrow it—like a future dragonfly clinging to its existence as a grub at the muddy bottom of a shimmering pond.

Axiom Number Six: The myths of Eternal Body and Christ's physical resurrection are mutually causal.

Corollary "a": The downgrade of transcendent spiritual visions or insight into gross body imagery expresses False rather than True Atman.

Corollary "b": The First and Second Ordinations culminating in the Third all presage and lead to Atman. As such, they transcend mythologies promulgated by organized religion as absolute truth—in turn used to exclude gay men and women from the ranks of the faithful.

Feeling as though he's drowning, the mid- to late-age gay truth-seeker cries out for help. He goes to a psychiatrist, attends a rap group, even darkens the door of a church. Yet something is missing. The old support systems no longer hold up. He considers suicide. Right at crisis point, when least expected, there dawns a summons to be whole. He realizes he bears the imprint of the Divine. Ego-body had its day, but is in fast decline toward old age, senility and death. Spiritual growth exacts sacrifice. Progress toward Atman, though painful and frightening, brings a foretaste of a higher joy. It overshadows, while rendering less compelling and unneeded, the endless cycle of pain-filled maya.

To conclude: All mankind, heterosexual and homosexual, is immersed and participates in this process. *Spirit Is.* Regaining primal Integrity brings to an end the pain of separation, just as it ushers in the joy of Reunion.

Realigned SPIRIT>Mind>body—elevated to: BEING-IN-SPIRIT>Union of In-Itself with For-Itself>Being for Fellowman—is the goal of all religions from Buddhism to Baha'i. All roads lead to the Light. For the gay man that Light is mirrored in a predestined gayness. It is the lantern or lighthouse that must be trusted to lead him safely to his birthright and home in the Cosmic Beyond.

CHAPTER NINE

THE MACHO AND THE FEM

The Sacrament of the Touch

In the throes of giving birth to this book, I thought of Being and Nothingness as polar or approximate opposites—therefore equals. I believed by taking an open-minded, uncensored approach, I'd arrive at, if not higher truth, at least a workable and enlightened synthesis. This would be an unsentimental truth gained through the integrity of pure thought (hopefully unmuddied) with a sardonic, earthy touch. What I didn't factor in was the possibility that by giving Nothingness equal-but-opposite status, I might be unwittingly discrediting homosexuality; turning it, too, into a negative—in much the same way that society and the church savaged me.

Might I secretly blame homosexuality for failing me as a homosexual? It didn't occur to me I might on my part fail homosexuality by refusing to accept myself and my gay brothers as God's children, as full-fledged citizens of the Universe. Might what I intended as an exercise in unbiased thought instead be hidden revenge for an undeserved and cruel visitation I didn't want? I felt the underlying justification for the book slipping away like a Malibu hillside in torrents of El Nino rain.

Concealed resentment, I cogitated, drove much of Sartre's vast literary and philosophic output. I considered omitting this chapter for that reason alone, because of its obsessive courting of Nothingness—just as I had a dangerous but brilliant chapter titled The Metaphysics of Anal Intercourse. Enough already! Upon rereading the original version of the present chapter, I discovered in its outward depravity and blasphemy an admirable nostalgia for Higher Self. After much soul-searching, I decided to leave it in, while omitting its presumptively outrageous brother.

I'd opened the original with a chart of "ontological relationships," which I still find helpful, even indispensable. I deemed it advisable, two-thirds of the way through the review, to clarify in the reader's and my own mind the nettlesome contradiction between "evanescent" and "opaque." And: "high density" and "transparent." These are soul states easily misconstrued and distorted when applied to the phenomenal world of heavy matter. From the myopic viewpoint of Ego-Body, they collide like butting rams.

In the interest of clarity then and now, I decided to include the aforementioned diagram, which I preface with a few brief remarks:

"Density" in its present usage isn't a measure of physical properties (those possessed by a rock or oak) but of Meaning. A moving experience or work of art is dense or "pregnant" with meaning. Transparency refers to access to Meaning. In and of itself the physical body is meaningless and opaque. Mind, the mediator between Spirit and body, is Meaning-in-the-making, or Being attempting to unite with Spirit. Spirit is utter MEANINGFULNESS. On the spiritual plane, Meaning (density) and Light (transparency) aren't opposites but mutual reflections. *Over there* they intersect and blend without contradiction into a higher Oneness.

Meaningfulness, then, is Spirit's highest goal and its reason for being. High density signifies replete or flush with Meaning. Raw sexual mating with its male-female polarities, straight or gay, is a blindly lopsided and unequal quest (low density) for Meaning. Spiritual conjoining, on the other hand, is balanced and equal. Such ethereal union under the auspices of Oneness transcends separate body. It is ontologically transparent (of high spiritual density).

Here is my indispensable chart:

	SPIRIT	Mind	body
Mortality–Immortality	High density (Meaningful–ness)	(Meaning in the making)	Evanescence (meaningless–ness)
Accessibility	Transparent	"Through a Glass Darkly"	Opaque
Ontological State	Essence (Being)	Existence (Becoming)	Nonexistence (Nonbeing or nothingness)
Conjugality (Mating–sexuality)	Immediate	Mediate	Illusory or impossible

It will help to bear these relationships in mind as I describe a truck stop encounter and then a worship service at Metropolitan Community Church, concluding with the Sacrament of the Touch. I continue to employ the thesis-antithesis (Being/Nothingness) approach with which I started. That should enable us to arrive at the synthesis (maybe glorious) toward which this investigation was then and is still inexorably moving.

I here repeat a truism with which this book abounds: Without contradiction and the struggle it unleashes there can be no growth or progress toward higher truth or Atman. To understand homosexuality in any kind of depth is to see it as an ongoing oscillation between affirmation and negation, as a cogwheel in the grinding zone between Somethingness and Nothingness, another way of saying in a meat grinder. It's like a washing machine set simultaneously on agitation and spin that due to its high speed, gives the impression of standing still.

Such a furious whirligig I present in the form of a covert encounter between a macho man and a fem—

A big rig driver from Georgia (he wears Dickies trousers and cowboy boots and was raised Southern Baptist) stops to relieve himself at a truckers' rest stop. Having sat for hours and with time to kill, he picks his nose, recombs his hair and then steps into a stall to stretch and loudly blow away any remaining boogers. He realizes he's being watched by someone he quickly pegs as a fag. Blow-dried designer hairdo, effeminate scent of cologne, clog platform shoes. Despite the imposter's efforts to blend in, his movements are both too angular and too fluid. He's a fish out of water.

The truck driver is at once angry and threatened by the poseur's amorous glances. He wills this heresy into nonbeing. Or tries. (This parallels the First Ordination in that it replays the trucker's infantile and boyhood struggle against a latent homosexuality.) He attempts a long-postponed, latter-day apotheosis into a "gay" in the mode of *not being it;* that is, in denial of both his feminine self and his hated admirer.

To the fem (he's not there to relieve himself; he took care of that in a private stall), the macho man comes across as a gorgeous hunk or opaque fullness. The contemptuous curl of the lip only increases the allure or inaccessibility of his deification into Eternal Male. For the trucker, on the other hand, to be placed on a pedestal like a male Venus de Milo is both a compliment and an insult. He's filled with contempt for his fem admirer. He has an impulse to wipe him out.

The impasse sets up a conflict in which both members of the unlikely duo are both miserable and secretly exhilarated. Each is the first to deny the potency of these primal emotions. Inbred pride (Ego-Body) prevents them from facing their true feelings or even speaking. Both are seized by fear of the unknown. The macho man thinks of decking the fem. Not understanding why (a miasma of negation rising from a swamp of Nonbeing) prods him toward the quasi-solution of violence. The fem, conversely, fears making a scene, of being an object of ridicule. He fears having his pretty face rearranged by a planted fist. More to the point, he fears being exposed as the internal negation *that he is*.

In his zeal to worship an adonis of the Playing Field, and flee the sanctuary of Safe Court, the fem fails to realize that this aloof god suffered his own painful and probably traumatic extraction of a female component in boyhood. He was forced onto the operating table by a team of unsmiling adult surgeons.

Acting for the tribe, the father, under the guise of having the boy's best interests at heart, demanded he not be passive and gentle, that he shun dolls and little girl things. The graphed-on taboo created a shell or fence of negation around all girlish attitudes, gestures and pockets of the mind like barbed wire around danger zones. Any softness in the little boy/warrior must fall to the knife. The classic Amputee, or negative homosexual.

The taboo now manifests in a refusal to be admired or even looked at by this grown sissy whom he can't let himself be even if he wants to. The fem presents the disturbing specter of his own squashed, male alter-self, a "possible" petrified into an impossibility. The hungry side glances have an insulting, satirical cast. The macho man's hands form fists. He places himself on guard alert. He's both angry and inwardly flattered; one feeds the other. Like his fem counterpart, he bears the burden of a radical self-reduction. He perceives his slain alter-self in the mirror of this despised Other. He catches a fleeting glimpse of himself as a fraction; a detotalized totality.

As an adult, to deal with frustration and anger over this boyhood lobotomy, this man/boy joins an all male organization. He goes hunting. Or starts a barroom brawl. He's a foot soldier picking his way through a minefield, never knowing where danger lies. Bonding with other Warriors in like danger provides an illusion of safety and false Completion. For the hunter (a retreat to the Corridor of Withdrawal), untamed Nature—its surfeit of beingness allows the guilty pleasure of gratuitous death—gives an impression of fraternal protection. A score is being settled, an old wound healed. However, so long as the nihilated pockets of the squelched female remain unfaced and unexposed, wild animals will continue to die. The score is temporarily settled from kill to kill, just as for the fem the wound of desire is momentarily bandaged by each act of fellatio.

The macho man's love life, as shown, plays out an angry incompletion. The female is eroticized in terms of subjugation. He wears himself out, may die prematurely of cancer or a heart attack, from punishing her for embodying his multiple negations. He's both pleased and outraged that she enjoys, or pretends to enjoy, his sculpted masculinity. She must pay in perpetuity for the pained being that he is as a result of the tense vigil he's been forced to set for himself. The Marine wife or motorcycle chick is the beneficiary of a unique privilege when the self-made (amputated) man makes his special brand of love-war. He's the end result of vigilante camps set up all over his brain.

This festering battle, moreover, creates a psychosis of "us" versus "them." The world is split into enemy camps. Likewise are wild animals the enemy. They exist only to be shot and mounted as trophies on the den wall. For the good ole boy, a barroom brawl is the logical outcome of the ritual consumption of copious amounts of beer. Most country and western songs are a concealed lament at the network of prohibitions or female notness *that he is*. The words and music appeal for sympathy but never repeal of his welded-on machismo. They reinstate and sentimentalize the perpetual conflict while refusing the possibility of transcendence to a higher plane. The good ole girl must bend to him. She must revel in his unhappiness which she must convince herself is happiness after all. She's been brainwashed, like racial and other minorities, into believing this man-child is a demigod not to be questioned. In his matrix of incompletion *he is*. Her lover/abuser is, after all, the warrior unit of the Western World.

The fem admirer, conversely, is a threat and an insult because he/she gives scandalous shape to the missing content of these pockets of nothingness. The fem wasn't forced or refused to be manipulated by the male power structure into setting up a tense vigil against sissyhood or nonmaleness. Rather the opposite. He violated the code of the Playing Field by waltzing nonchalantly into Safe Court where warriors fear to tread. In the process he slew the dragon of a latent maleness. The fem, a projection of the macho man's nihilated alter-self, is the latter's greatest fear. It is the possibility of Christ yielding to Satan's temptation. The fem must be vigorously willed into nonexistence, wiped out with a blow of the fist or a rifle bullet. The world isn't big enough for them both. Just as it isn't big enough for contented, freely roaming animals. Or fleshily dressed, undisciplined minorities.

A hitchhiker from West Virginia, whom I had the faulty judgment to pick up and invite into my home, came unhinged upon seeing Jesse Jackson wearing a tuxedo on TV. For the then presidential candidate to be beamed into red-blooded households doing anything but munching a banana in a jungle was an outrage. With a gun handy he might have blasted the TV to smithereens like Elvis Presley is reputed to have done with anything that displeased him.

The fem, then, who is the nihilation of a denied, embryonic male component, eyes with greedy longing the macho man who is the amputation of his female component. The fem secretly longs to graft on his Missing Male.

The macho man, conversely, desires union with his Missing Woman. The fem aspirant to this privilege, however, is a fake man. He hasn't the balls to stand up and be counted. He cowers in dark corners like a hunted animal. Worse, he has the gall to project salacious designs upon the macho man's sacrosanct male person. Admiration comes across as presumption or insult, even though the fem is in a better position than most women, through the harsh boot camp of social ostracism, to admire this achievement of sculpted maleness. Since such an exalted state is for himself unthinkable, he must beg, borrow or steal, usurp ownership, of this impossibility. It is just this unspannable oppositeness that makes the fem the macho trucker's most adoring and proper congregation.

Yet this worship fails to attain its goal. It short-circuits on the ground of its impossibility. By holding his idol up to naked display, the fem exposes him in his bald incompletion. The fem thereby reduces his quarry to a sex object, the great no-no of the feminist movement. True, the macho man wants to be idolized, but by a worthy Other, by a woman, not a travesty of a female. Worship by this swishy imposter is an affront because it mirrors with deadly clarity the reciprocal nonbeing of this antagonistic duo. In their depth of need, both members are a cry for healing and wholeness. Yet each is the refusal to take on and rescue the other's (hence his own) impossibility. Neither will sacrifice his martyrdom. Neither, on pain of death, will allow the other to reverse the stern terms of his self-inflicted imprisonment.

Instead, the macho man wills the fem into nonexistence as did the pre-gay fem the father in the First Ordination. Yet this stifled aggression falls short of its goal; rather, like all psychosis, it succeeds in failing. A reverberating circuit of fascination/repulsion is set up between the truckers' nihilated female self and the fem who has the nerve to flaunt himself against the "obsidian glow of the Void." In a reckless mood and with a six-pack under his belt, the trucker might display himself at the urinals or be sucked off in a stall, but only if it serves to release pent-up anger and bolster male vanity. The "victor," for whom feelings are forbidden, is left with a pared-down range of emotion—from indifference to contempt—for the vanquished. For him to experience pleasure from a queer equals the death of desire. After shooting his load, he never wants to see the lowlife again. He zips up and clears out. So he got his rocks off humiliating a fag. Serves the creep right.

His swaggering disdain soon, however, gives way to a deep disturbance. It takes *someone* to feel humiliation. That someone stole a vital part of himself.

His inmost being commingled for several minutes with a slime-ball homo. They came together in a forbidden rite. It starts to look like a mistake, even a sin. Yet the trucker refuses to be angry or ashamed. He'll have no part of regret. Isn't that a sign of feminine weakness? Of sexual complicity? In a heterosexual parallel of the First Ordination he wrestles the shadowy event like Jacob and the angel into nonbeing.

Such *en bloc* suppression, however, is easier said than done. The fem seducer haunts the back of his mind as a mocking absence. An inroad was made into the forbidden zone. He must either redouble his defenses or risk setting the stage, through the corrosive power of imagination, for another foray into the minefields of the Unknown. Putting down a faggot was a kick. Next time he'll call him a few choice names, rough him up. Problem is, it isn't a woman, but some kind of freak, a tart in a man's body. But isn't that a twisted sort of turn-on? Who doesn't enjoy a little imposture? Like running a job for the Mafia. At the same time, the imposter must remain faceless and formless so no hint of feminine weakness taints the sacred domain of male superiority.

Yet on pain of death the conflict mustn't find resolution in the androgynization of either combatant. The macho man refuses to climb a single rung up Jacob's ladder into the Psychic-Intuitional. Rather he chooses to remain in the grinding zone between the Mythic-Membership and Mental-Egoic. Father-son tension, resurrected in the form of male-female warfare, may erupt any moment into fisticuffs. The creative, nurturing world of Safe Court and gay men—which he fails to realize pervades religion, the arts, commercial advertising, even the packaging of the food he eats—is wiped out with another slain deer or belch of the Harley.

The detested fem, on his part, feels a mixture of elation and despair. Through a kind of sorcery he extracted his quarry's vital substance. On a deeper level, he brought about a merging of subjectivities. But isn't that mere wishful thinking? Actually all they did was cast shadow images across the blank screens of each other's nonbeing. Every precaution was taken that the images be as transitory and insubstantial as possible. No words spoken, minimal eye contact. A handshake or hug: forget it.

Despite the fem's superhuman endurance in hanging around the truck stop for hours, his quarry remains stubbornly Other. The macho man is gone and probably won't be seen again. The screen returns to blank. All the macho man left behind was his semen swathed in a penumbra of contempt. The glaring absence amounts to rejection of the fem's carefully cultivated femaleness along with an obliterated male component. Most devastatingly, rejection as a total person in the world.

In retrospect, the failure arises from the fact that for subjectivities to merge a rudimentary bonding must take place. This requires a degree of mutual acceptance and respect. The restroom playing out is an obscene scandal because it takes place outside the aegis of Male Continuity. Performed in the Void, it partakes of the Illusory; which is to say, the Satanic. That is, like Hamlet, at the core of the fem's anguish: *To be or not to be*—an outcast refugee from the sanctuary of Safe Court. He/she failed to capture the Male on even a small corner of the screen. Empty-handed and alone, the fem is suddenly an *is not* who's only future is that of a *has been*.

The truck stop seduction thus dissolves into a garbled and farcical bad dream. The fem realizes (like Monica Lewinsky?) that sperm isn't the man. The readily bio-degradable substance is less than a memory. Success is thus failure. Since the fem sacrificed pleasure in his eagerness to usurp the Other's being through giving pleasure, desire goes on unabated. The Other's inaccessibility reflects his own inaccessible core of banished maleness. Desire is never quenched in a desperate bid to appropriate the impossible. The fem comes away from the encounter with a surfeit of nonbeing. That is, with nothing.

The macho man didn't fare much better. He both took and gave in a conflicted state that subtly eroded the fortress of male impregnability. Henceforth he'll be hounded by phantasms of weakness and sexual ambiguity, which he'll hide under a disguise of male chauvinism. In an unguarded moment he might—shudder!—even imagine himself one of them, actually drop to his knees in a penitential position . . . .

Despite the cloistered drama and bravado, both parties stagnate in incompletion. The mutual reduction has the heady feel of a vice, of taking the dumbwaiter to oblivion. In the last analysis, failure (encroaching fingers of the Sea of Nothingness) is what is forbidden by the universe. In physics, matter is neither created nor destroyed. Correlatively, Being isn't free to turn into Nonbeing. There's no escape from Wilber's Great Wheel of Life. Suicide would only condemn one to come back (assuming one believes in reincarnation) in an even more debased and conflicted form.

To give the truck stop encounter a religious or mythic cast, I here change macho man to "donor" and fem to "supplicant." This will further dramatize the mutual causality of homosexuality and religion. In other words, gayness invokes religious imagery, just as the ritual magic of those myths in turn engenders homosexuality—a wafer heterosexuals and homosexuals alike may find hard to swallow.

At the risk of incurring across-the-board discomfort, even wrath, I return to the "sacred" act of fellatio—

Both donor (macho man) and supplicant (the fem) play God. The former dispenses the Divine substance, the latter appropriates It; each incarnates the other's guilt and shame. Contempt generates a decadent fascination. They fill each other with a violent tender anger. In the enclosed confessional of a toilet stall the co-celebrants seek a divine transubstantiation; if one wills, auto-deification. To simultaneously break and reinstate the laws of Godhead, while defying a host of social traditions and taboos, produces a quick thrill. Encased in separate solitudes, they enact the clandestine rite of fellatio.

Furthermore—

The supplicant, kneeling before the donor, believes himself both born of and arrayed against God; or in the deep subconscious, against earthly father. In a rite both sacred and profane, he makes a last ditch effort at self-invention. In his willed notness will he yet *be*. The donor must be skillfully evoked, appeased, manipulated and reduced to a mere contingency. The supplicant accepts abasement in return for the pumping up of his being. He makes the donor a channel for the delivery of Fullness. The pirated substance that floods his palate unites him with Eternal Male. Yet the attempted apotheosis is fraught with illusion, for alas, sperm isn't the man.

The reader will recognize another infernal whirligig. To take the furious impasse a further step—

Fellatio is an updated cannibalism repackaged for Twenty-First Century consumption. Human flesh and blood refracted into semen are re-spun and made instantly available in an erotically tingled cyber world. The female principle which derives from Mother Goddess, a constant from the dawn of time or Garden of Eden, is determinative. She decides all. With Her authority the supplicant plucks the apple of Completion and relays it tantalizingly upward. He exerts control; the donor like Adam merely follows his animal instincts. The subjectivity of each player thus remains opaque and unknowable (low spiritual density) to the other.

If they could read each other's thoughts—like a policeman's flashlight bursting upon a dark tea room—the game would fall apart. Their desires would be revealed as not only out of synch but in direct conflict. The donor usurps the fallen divinity of the supplicant by assuming a godlike stance. The supplicant, on his part, preempts divinity (attempts to capture the donor's subjectivity) through a transfer of shame—by exchanging abasement for martyrdom, martyrdom for sainthood, then effecting the donor's downfall to criminal status and finally to inmate of hell.

He insists that the donor, whom he suspects in anguish cares nothing about him, at least be made to feel guilty; in short, to be fallible, the opposite of the god he trumps him up to be. He simultaneously inflates and deflates this untrustworthy stand-in for The Male. He must therefore appropriate divinity through robbery and betrayal. For the undercover game to work, each player must remain locked in body, which as seen, always betrays. The supplicant, as both thief and saint, deludes himself into thinking he receives a divine bestowal, a gratis grant from the universe.

The failure to assimilate and possess the divine elixir fuels a frantic search for an infinity of partners. His dedication to the hedonist credo, "So many men, so little time," arises from the fact that each donor, no matter how virile, lacks the density-of-being of Eternal Male. Each surrogate is as transient as his life substance. The arrogant indifference that follows orgasm decrees that the fem once again walk the gangplank into the Sea of Nothingness. A new avatar must be found for the missing Colossus of Rhodes or Saint John's Passion—a shifting collage of body parts, hollow gestures, blurs and absences. A sweaty brow here, a hairy chest and rippled, contracting abdomen there, an anonymous animal grunt that fades in the night . . . .

In a world of radical separation—that of Ego-Body—no appearance of being manifests Being. All being is encased in a stubborn otherness. Motives and actions lack organic cohesion. Individual body parts are warring factions. This results in moodiness, irritability, migraines, insomnia and other psychosomatic disorders. "Why do I do these things?" agonizes the fem/supplicant. "This queen needs her head examined."

Ironically, he's his own Other, but as an Absence. He hasn't a clue what drives him to seek completion in abasement. He dare not defascinate himself with himself, see himself as he is, lest the cresting wave he rides like a flower-strewn motorcade dump him unceremoniously in the sand. The living error that he is requires that he remain a stranger to inmost Self. He weaves a tapestry of silken dreams. The term, dizzy queen, refers to the irrational and impossible attempt to appropriate the riches of the universe (remember the Evil Shoe Fairy, Imelda Marcos?) on the QT.

The secret project to replace God with imperial self finally leads to such sordid excess, backbiting, despair, even madness, that the seeker of truth, whether butch or fem, finds himself as a last resort at of all places—Metropolitan Community Church. (MCC here is a metaphor for the mutual causality of homosexuality and religion. Catholic "Dignity" or a Ramakrishna monastic order would also serve.)

Sunday morning. An American Gothic, wood frame church (soon to be burned to the ground by hate-filled vandals) sits a few blocks off Hollywood Boulevard. Two ushers man the flower-bedecked vestibule. In the main sanctuary, piano and organ play in rhapsodic unison. Troy Perry is a phenomenon that couldn't happen. Collective gay bravado tends to disintegrate, to break down in self-parody. Through a freak fissure in the male power structure, Troy's brainchild shows remarkable staying power. The Sunday morning service has the flavor of a Broadway musical production. Or a seriocomic opera. It flaunts its inherent theatricality to the max.

For the individual seeker—beyond the spectacle of deacons in white robes, emotion-charged hymn singing and ecstatic handholding—a miracle is conjured up. That of divine ordination. God the Father gathers unto Himself these lost ones, who can't help who and what they are, through the intercession of the Shaman-Founder, who displays the density-of-being of a prophet. Troy's male solidity, buoyed by the line of deacons, galvanizes the gathering of sexual outlaws and flighty queens into a cohesive whole. More importantly, it transforms them into a congress of ethical beings capable of taking responsibility for their individual actions.

A product of the Southern tradition of fiery evangelical preachers, Troy bestows upon his congregation the authority of the Absolute. He empowers them to take a quantum leap from frivolous (low density) camping to solid choir member, usher, lighting man or deacon (high density)—all performed with the gravity of The Male. His heaven-sent leadership solidifies and masculinizes the congregation. That doesn't mean instantly turning butch; rather, the freedom to attain through his mediation a secure ground of being.

Rather than a jellyfish passivity, his listeners get a taste of command. The goal of the magic transformation isn't just a surface happiness. Troy's magnetic persona cuts through the neon-flashing city lights and blaring disco bars to the timeless domain of Spirit. He confers inner worth upon the drag queen, alcoholic and leather man. No matter to what debased behavior his rapt listener fell the night before, he's elevated to a full humanity that reflects the divine.

Thus the maxim: "The more forgiven, the greater the gratitude." Emotions run high at MCC. A robed choir exults to the rafters. A foretaste of Fullness transforms the compulsive need for a man into choice. One has the option of not pursuing the false completion of: "I must be married in a dress and then forcibly violated, the only way I can attain my fabricated divinity." Or: "I must don my own nothingness in order to uphold the man." Troy's down-home preaching proclaims that the compulsion can be surrendered without sacrificing true Self.

More important than pursuing idle dreams, furthermore, is the procurement of dignity. No one is going to knock your fantasy. Go ahead and attend the mad tea party of bar life. Or a quilting bee of the Lavender Ladies. But you have the power to put such things in second or third place. Differently put: Cling to your committed femaleness or trumped-up maleness—or climb a rung up Jacob's ladder toward authentic selfhood. The butch is mellowed, the fem solidified. Boundaries are broken down; opposites flow into each other.

The fem, as for the butch, long since forgot how free he is. His self-invention isn't irreversible—although the more acted-upon, the more second nature; just as possibles not acted on tend to atrophy and die, so too do the range of possibles decrease with aging and locked-in boundaries of self-image—but nonetheless free to divest himself, if he wants it bad enough, from the stranglehold of outworn and calcified dreams. Without judging, Shaman Troy tells his rapt audience they may cling to opaque (low spiritual density) phantasms of the past, or opt for the joyful transparency (high density) of rebirth onto a higher plane.

The Battle Hymn of the Republic is sung in ever ascending keys of triumphant optimism. The stained glass windows refuse to shatter in deference to such unbridled joy. Yet more important than donning patriotic camaraderie is the appropriation of its causal power. The seeker takes charge of his destiny. He need not return to a glory hole or confessional stall to found his being. Instead he receives an injection of self-worth. Troy promises a special blessing:

You. You can be liberated from enslavement to dead-end desires and find *you*. You can still drain the cup of a hundred phalluses, only a few, or none. Saint Troy offers the choice wine of ethical selection. The spirit of the risen Christ (heroic with a decidedly androgynous edge) appears in the fervent hymn singing. Incarnate in His prophet, the Son grants the male prerogative of rightness before the Father. The broken chain of Continuity is magically reforged.

Hence the unspoken writ of a new dispensation: The Eucharist replaces the urinal. Addiction to the mediate warrior substance is exchanged for the immediacy of partaking directly from Source. The old cycle of slavery and guilt: rescinded. The forgiveness the seeker couldn't grant himself shimmers palpably above the communion table, there for the asking. The most sordid sins, the bitchiness and backstabbing, the self-loathing—lifted! Behold the prophet, robed arms lifted to heaven. A miracle: The seeker is released from body-time into timeless eternity. The slate is wiped clean, the door opened for even the most jaded sinner to a bright future complete with the priceless gift of foundation in Spirit.

Pax Saint Troy.

On the wings of mystic angels—or a wide-angle camera mounted on a boom that through the miracle of computer graphics changes into an ascending helicopter—we leave MCC with its rhythmic handclapping and soar over smog-bound billboards and the Capitol Records Building high above billowing cumulus clouds where lo and behold, dwarfing the giant letters H-O-L-L-Y-W-O-O-D, is herewith proclaimed

THE SACRAMENT OF THE TOUCH

Sent down from a Kingdom of Light, its transforming power replaces all that went before. It renders obsolete centuries of religious ritual, from bowing before stone idols to fingering rosary beads. It marks the convergence of the physical and the spiritual, the lower and the higher. A little touching by the earthly father would save the need for so much touching later—blind groping in baths, parks and public restrooms, cloistering in monasteries and quite possibly the Crusades and the Spanish Inquisition.

Advice to fathers: Spare the touch and condemn the child to body idolatry and loneliness, which amount to the same thing. If you want to save your son the radical reduction of an alienated sexuality, touch him, embrace him, confirm him as a whole person. If you love him, straight or gay is beside the point. Too late anyway. It's well established by the American Psychological Association that homosexuality is set in infancy or early childhood, usually by age five. It's now regarded—such generosity overwhelms me!—as a valid alternate lifestyle.

The Touch can at a crucial stage of development even turn the tide of the First Ordination (not that this is desired) into the open waters of simple heterosexuality, if that be his destiny. Yes, I know—viva the complicated! Whatever the son's sexual kismet, it gives him a better chance of accepting himself along with his fellow gay men, lover, family, society and the Cosmos. A little roughing up, even spanking or use of the strap in a spirit of parental guidance, is better than withholding the touch. This wisely administered sacrament will help him become an appearing, an upsurge, rather than a disappearing in the heart of the world.

The body ages and dies. Its nature is to break down, suffer death and disappear. The touch is a vital instrument of father-son continuance and immortality. It transforms terminal Ego-Body into eternal SPIRIT>Mind>body. Heterosexual, bisexual, homosexual, transsexual . . . what does it matter? From the lofty viewpoint of Spirit they're just outer garments. The touch, by calming the rage for an infinity of debasing encounters, shortens the cosmic distance to Atman.

Michelangelo's painting on the ceiling of the Sistine Chapel depicts God's finger lightly grazing Adam's. Divinity vouchsafes wholeness, bestows the gift of continuity. At the Third Ordination, by reversing the primal choice of self as irremediably Other, which is to say, fatherless, the gay man regains his birthright as a citizen of the Universe. Not that he ever lost it. He merely contrived to hide it from himself for a while.

Spiritual energy flows psychically and electrically from the fingertips. The sacrament of The Touch confers healing and wholeness. To withhold it from a child is to refuse to pass on health and light, to deny continuity. It also shows an incapacity to enjoy the divine gift of sex. Such denial is the first stage in a revolt against the corroding fortress of a rigid heterosexuality, which in a few generations, like an avalanche gaining speed, will result in a full-blown gay. Or a prospective high priest. Talk about procreation! The Universe does look after itself!

The touch preplays the caresses of adult intimacy. If the father finds hugging a sissy son embarrassing or repellent, chances are he feels the same way about the mother, as well as himself. Withholding the touch signals shame. Shame arises from faking it. It's precisely an intimation of fakery, with the resulting insecurity and sense of danger, that triggers the First Ordination. The father's self-presentation as a protective being rings false. He's secretly engaged in undermining himself and his family, while pretending the opposite. And the pre-gay infant/child knows it.

More profoundly, homosexuality is a brave attempt, a cosmic corrective measure, to bring the hidden to light, to change fraudulence into honesty, apathy into passion. For as a weak cousin of failure, apathy is a second thing the universe won't allow, at least not for long. The generational slide into homosexuality—one can almost hear an ancestral sigh of relief—is a vital component of mankind's upreach to Spirit. By bringing falseness out of the shadows, homosexuality takes, paradoxically, such falseness upon itself. It shoulders that falseness the way a soldier leaps onto a live grenade to save his buddies. Or Jesus accepts the horror of the cross. It facilitates a hyper-jump back to Source.

Can this be, I asked myself, the uncensored SOMETHINGNESS this investigation has been searching for! I felt the blessing and heat of being a great deal closer.

Just as at its most depraved (or deprived) homosexuality is vilified by pundits and fire-and-brimstone preachers as the epitome of decadence—that is to say, *change*—so at its finest is it a barometer of planetary survival and continuance. Without the negative, or a scary dip into the inky backwaters of nonbeing, there can be no soaring positive. Are the poles of the sacred and the profane so far apart? In a universe of Oneness, don't they interpenetrate, flow into each other?

Thus the daring of this chapter, what it does and doesn't say, and the entire book. Tiers of ascending and descending angels help me! I still feel glints and swatches of their nonjudging light.

I've portrayed the macho and fem as clandestine lovers. Like the intertwining double helix of a DNA molecule. Or an infinity of galaxies curving back on itself. Or finally: The three Marys reaching up from their bleak patch of earth to embrace their divinely suffering Lord.

By the same token, loving another man, if done with honor and from the heart, is the same as worshipping God.

The gay man attempts against great odds to unite his male and female components, to merge into One. In itself a heroic act, it is also the embrace of Diversity leading to a final home in Completion. Isn't androgyny a common goal of human striving? Of history and religion? Of civilization? Homosexuality precisely mirrors this evolutionary process.

That is why—despite what first seemed (upon rereading this chancy chapter) a possible downer, obscene to some, blasphemous to others—gay men (nor do I exclude Lesbians), through their bold daring and originality, are Jacob's special ladder to the stars.

CHAPTER TEN

THE PATH FROM TRINITY TO ANDROGYNY
DESCENT INTO OEDIPUS

"The unexamined life isn't worth living."
—Socrates

The basic mechanism of homosexuality, as shown, resembles but is not identical with what is popularly known as Oedipus Complex. It goes a step farther into nonbeing. Instead of sleeping with the mother and murdering the father, nothing quite so simple, the pre-gay plots not only to be part of her, but *to be her*. This is concomitant with willing the father's nonexistence. Simple murder is a move *toward* the victim to consciously do him in; in a sense, it confirms the victim's existence. I call this the Courting Dance of the Warrior.

In being aggressed (an unsuspecting King Laius by his own son, Oedipus), the father is *confirmed* as an opposing male, an equal in battle. Overt aggression with the aim of murder is a sign of defeat, a loss of control, an admission of weakness. On a deeper level, it's a failed or stalled attempt by Incompletion to remedy and fill Itself. The Complete isn't threatened by other existents. In its plenitude it can afford to forgive and be generous.

Forgiveness (mutual conferring of Beingness) is the quintessence of Completion. The unforgiving young assassin makes himself non-exist in order to inflict nonbeing on the father. By the same stroke that he makes himself not be, he wipes out his forebear. The price of eliminating the adversary is to make oneself an Absence. This brings about a defection from Playing Field to Safe Court. He accomplishes the prodigious fete of making himself a double nihilation. The pre-gay achieves his sovereign goal of incarnating the Impossible.

Guilt over this quietistic murder may be temporarily assuaged through a pose of self-righteous hauteur. Hence the tendency of some gay men, especially an Artist of Masquerade, to display a monarchial arrogance. A post-patricidal "innocence is bliss" doesn't quite come off. The horror of the hangman lingers on. Repressed guilt must then be diverted into surrogate guilts.

For instance, an overly sensitive gay man (Corridor of Withdrawal) may transfer guilt onto a physical defect like acne, a receding chin or premature balding to the point of thinking it more unattractive than it really is and go to great lengths to conceal it. Or he may be unable to urinate in public because he imagines his endowment to be hopelessly small, dysfunctional or nonexistent. Yet despite these surrogates, guilt over Guilt remains.

The entire complex harks back not only to the original father-son split, but the spiritual fall of mankind. Adam and Eve realize they are naked against a changeable, often violent earth and sky; that is, before God. Defenselessness (radical alienation) is a prime source of guilt. Instead of arising from innocent body, guilt is a SPIRIT>Mind imbalance that results from a feeling of cosmic helplessness.

Oedipus, heterosexual or homosexual—all males to some degree resent or hate their father—feels guilty not only from committing patricide, but because he stands defenseless before an indestructible Adversary. Patricide doesn't erase the father's stubborn immortality as a cosmic survivor. Rather, it imprints his memory and continuing influence with greater indelibility. It feeds the realization that Oedipus failed to act from a position of strength. He can't found himself on a corpse. By dint of this failure, the victor is perpetually defeated by the victim. Earth father "wins" qua his station as an avatar of Eternal Father.

The female world to which the pre-gay defects and tries to claim as his own is infused with a central myopia. Since the fanciful kingdom is enshrouded in a negation brought forward from an abhorrence of the Playing Field—"You can't go there because you're a boy" or "You mustn't be a sissy"—the defection proliferates a host of secondary denials. Anger, resentment, fear of being different, concealment of true self—a notness—spread like a noxious vapor over the storybook landscape.

In a Rene Magritte painting a stone castle or lion is typically about to fracture into an hourglass pile of tiny pieces. The feminine world—to choose it generates guilt over betrayal—fragments into a mosaic of disjointed mannerisms, posturing, non-sequiturs and cutting remarks; a choice of form over content; of symbol over meaning. Rather than images integrated into a reliable background, they loom in bas relief against an Absence. This is because the gay man, through the pre-choice of not being his father's son, is impelled into radical self-invention. He's both an empty canvas and the hand that holds the brush. Strive as he may to conform to social demands in order to survive, compulsive commands from the core Nothingness haunt these norms and crack them into a million pieces.

The attempt to fit in (Thanatos false completion) backfires into self-conscious caricature. The prototypal gay man throws up invisible barriers in his path. He must constantly reinvent himself through flight from the nerve center of dank Nothingness toward a Never-Never Land in which he must mason the bricks, erect the walls and *"Raise High the Roof Beam, Carpenter!"* (courtesy J.D. Salinger), not to mention embroider the linen, engrave the silverware and grandly roll out a trousseau. Everything appears as cubist art because all is displaced within shifting, alien boundaries. Each compartmentalized event is the internal negation of every other. An alter-self is formed in response to the female world of Safe Court and the father's presence in the form of an irremediable Absence.

This impossible or very difficult dilemma may catapult the gay man, as often happens in human history, into genius.

We now return to Oedipus Rex and its relevance to homosexuality. I will demonstrate the pivotal role of gayness in the spiritual evolution of mankind. I'll further show how it redirects a fundamentalist and erring Christianity back on course. A telling example is the doctrine of Trinity. To compare Oedipus Complex to this flawed mythic schema, I list principal similarities and differences.

Similarities:

1.) God the Father and God the Son (King Laius and Oedipus) impregnate the same woman, Mary (Jocasta).
2.) Christ (as a full Member of Godhead) mates with His own mother like Oedipus with Jocasta.
3.) Both the Father and Laius cause the mutilation of the son (Christ crucified, a spike driven through Oedipus' feet.)
4.) Both Christ and Oedipus appear in the world fatherless. (Christ stands free of procreation by Joseph; the infant, Oedipus, is found abandoned on Mount Cithaeron).
5.) Both Christ and Oedipus shun and struggle against the nothingness (freedom) of a homosexual component.

Differences:

1.) Oedipus retaliates (subconsciously) against the father; Christ does not.
2.) Laius and Oedipus seek physical (Ego-body) conquest of the earth. Christ the Son, acting for God the Father, seeks a spiritual dominion.
3.) Jocasta commits suicide. Mary surrenders to the holy "martyrdom" of virginity. (Her sacrifice, however, is temporary since she and Joseph have other children.)
4.) Oedipus stops short of the Second Ordination; he remains a Self-Amputee. Christ as divinity traverses all Three Ordinations in a timeless instant.
5.) Oedipus *expresses his latent homosexuality as territoriality;* Christ, as a heavenly kingdom.

Corollary a: Androgyny reduces territoriality.

Corollary b: The sacrifice of physical territory exponentially increases spiritual maneuvering space on the order of Einstein's $E=mc^2$.

Corollary c: the Third Ordination facilitates body-transcendence to a higher spiritual plane.

6.) Patricide, or Theocide, is Christ's impossibility; Oedipus carries it out, although against his awareness. (It's for the pre-gay—Narcissus expanded into Socrates—to expose and surmount the dual nihilation of patricide, take it a transcendent step out of willed Nonbeing.)

At this point in our discussion it's appropriate and necessary to re-pose the age-old question of freedom versus determinism. How can Oedipus, as an allegory of fatality, show progress in the unfolding drama of human freedom? First, freedom is a *means* of seeking foundation in solid Fullness. Merely a desire, it has no existence in and of itself. Both Laius and Oedipus are sexually driven, that is, driven by fear. Fear of what? Fear of unconstrained freedom; of formless Nothingness. Rampant freedom, as both sadly realize, has a tragic finale.

To further dissect the paradox— Freedom is like trying to pin down a drop of mercury with a metal probe. The drop continuously escapes. Yet try we must, even if it means using interpolation, metaphor and blind punting to coax freedom "out of hiding." Freedom is the air in the mortar mix that holds together the building blocks of Edifice (Oedipus) transcended, excuse the pun. Or again: Unconstrained freedom is a roaring brushfire that devours everything in its path. Or finally: A black hole that sucks bricks, roof beams and trousseau into its voracious, obliterating mouth. Total freedom terrifies because of the diabolic unpredictability of its results.

Laius fears being conquered or killed by a younger warrior (Oedipus). Such is his absorption in Ego-Body that he refuses any challenge to political power. He attempts to usurp any potential son's freedom by adding it to his own the way the victor takes spoils in battle. Gross body freedom always sees the Other as a threat. The sex act (like murder) is a fear-based acting-out and propitiation over Incompletion. For both Laius and Oedipus it manifests as greed.

The Oedipal myth, then, is an allegory of greed. Both Laius and Oedipus ("a chip off the old block") want sons, but sufficiently emasculated in order to make them incapable of encroaching upon the sacrosanct court of the harem.

Fear arises from greed fanned by runaway freedom; from being naked and defenseless against an unpredictable and violent sky.

Christian Trinity solves the problem of greed among the Members of Godhead by removing unilateral freedom. But the price of Unity is the locking in of male dominion and the creation of male-female inequality. How strange for the way out of sexist superiority (via a descent into Oedipus and climb back up through Narcissus/Socrates) to be a reenactment of greed! Through the fatal head-on clash, Oedipus realizes too late that he and Laius are bound into *One*. Had both discovered inherent Oneness (too advanced for the Mythic-Membership Phase), there wouldn't have been a tragic confrontation on the road to Corinth.

Father-son greed also drives Jocasta to suicide. As an object of conquest, womankind is debased rather than fulfilled. It's her tragedy as well. Lopsided male supremacy and female inferiority result in greater unfreedom for both. Beingness, however, "protects itself"; it both eludes and prevails against the nefarious threat of Nonbeing. It shuns the midnight horror. Satanic fancy, which is love of the impossible, refers to Nonbeing's inability to capture and lay claim to Being. But since Nonbeing is ultimate icy indifference, full robust Beingness, even though triumphant, lives in mortal dread of a Rorschach ink monster lurking in its midmost heart.

Oedipus, marooned in the Mythic-Membership, is simultaneously engaged in an inner battle on the brink of the Mental-Egoic. Advancement into the Psychic-Intuitional depends on the dismantling of male-female dichotomy and global integration of androgyny. And this requires that *mankind pass through a homosexual phase.*

The following diagram of a descending (on the left) and re-ascending (on the right) arc will help make this clear.

God "Reinventing" Himself
(through the expansion and appropriation of freedom)

I. Man's
Spiritual
Level: MYTHIC / MEMBERSHIP <<MENTAL / EGOIC
         <<PSYCHIC / INTUITIONAL

II. Man's
Perception of God:

TRINITY	DIVINE ONENESS
(sexism)	(androgyny)

CHRIST	NARCISSUS/SOCRATES
(partial acceptance of androgyny, but denial of homosexuality)	(homo-sexuality) *

OEDIPUS

(sexism with the freedom to express radical incompletion and its consequences)

(*Note: Homosexuality dismantles male sexism, but replaces it with an Ego-Body fixation of its own. This is neutralized and transcended in the Third Ordination.)

To further clarify this important principle:

Homosexuality is heterosexual sexism (shored up by Trinity) reaching toward androgyny. It's a means of redefining God (God rediscovering Himself). The Third Ordination is a limiting of earth freedom (a white flag truce with Nothingness) vital to attaining Wholeness. The refraction of sexism into component parts reveals homosexuality to be a prime ingredient. Both Laius and Oedipus, fearing the heady freedom of homosexuality, overcompensate in male territoriality. Acceptance of their inner woman, personified by Jocasta, would have prevented her abuse as a double negation, a sexist edict she carries out in suicide.

Picture the Cosmos as a giant wheel or a computer file simultaneously rewinding and fast-forwarding in time in the evolving/unraveling myth of Trinity—

Here is a schema in which Mary is astonishingly *both* wife and mother of God. According to the Biblical account, the Holy Spirit comes upon her like a vapor in the night and impregnates her with the germ of Christ, a full member of Godhead. A chaste peasant woman is elevated to the exalted station of incestuous mother-wife of Ultimate Deity. Since competition and in-heaven strife are by definition absent within the unified Will of Godhead, Mary remains a virgin and still is a party to incest only through sex in the abstract, in a mythic dream state. Thus Being manifests itself through its own disappearance.

However, that's not the only chink in the theological armor. Consider this: Since Christ has a fallible, human side, He must wrestle with Himself against Himself. He is finally abandoned by God (although He is God) to flounder in earthbound maya. Satan, with whom He has a lateral confrontation, tempts Him with ego exploits like throwing Himself off the temple to be spectacularly rescued by angels. Christ wisely spurns such a flashy PR stunt.

He later cries from the cross, "My God, My God, why hast Thou forsaken me?" Cut off from Godhead (which would have catastrophic consequences for the entire Cosmos), He must invent off the top of His head, appeal for help, beg for a drink. He is suffering, contingent humanity severed from its divine Birthright. Christ becomes existential man. Yet He remains loyal to his Sonship despite the trauma of temporal separation.

Rebellion is thereby left to His alter-ego, Satan, as it is for Oedipus and the self gazer, Narcissus, merged into a self-examining Socrates. Because of Christ's loyalty to the Father, ego ambition remains buried beneath the threshold of actualization. Yet by being a *possible*, the ideation of Satan achieves a certain beingness. To assume the fantastic form of Lucifer, green robes unfurling in fiery blasts of brimstone (think of a boa and sequins at a drag show or a Mister Leather contest—may a lenient Higher Power, that both bridles and drives me on, forgive me . . . !), Christ is in the untenable position of willing the nonbeing of both the Father and Himself. It would be the triple nihilation of Godhead, since the catastrophic apostasy would take with it the Holy Spirit, hence the totality of Creation.

If Christ did have homosexual urges, orthodox theology, to retain its hold on the heterosexual masses, assumes He didn't act on them. But didn't He teach, "He who lusts after a woman has already committed adultery in his heart"? Wouldn't the same hold true for homosexual promptings? To consider for even a split second a homosexual act is to commit it, to *be* it. With infinite possibilities capable of turning in a flash into damning truths—the human Christ couldn't escape the intrusion of a sexual thought somewhere—the only safe course outside marriage for a Member of Godhead isn't only celibacy but *suppression of all illicit thought.*

He thereby retains divinity by refusing to improvise or free-associate, by renouncing or severely limiting freedom. He refuses to reinvent Himself contra the blueprint handed down by the Father. His foundation of being as Son of the omnipotent, life-giving Creator thereby remains intact. But the price of such solidarity is acquiescence to a subordinate state, like the relationship of a five star general to a private. Although both serve in the same army, it's for the former to obey and the latter to command.

What of the Holy Spirit, the Third Member of Godhead Who carries out the incestuous will of Father and Son, Who are Both sanctified above earthly mating in spite of being the Two anthropomorphic Members of Godhead? The Third, the One most likely to be without a human body and phallus, carries out the immaculate conception. This Surrogate allows the Father-Son relationship to remain stainless and pure. The mysterious Third is the bonding agent of the First Two jointly carrying out divine procreation.

For fundamentalist Christians, the Divine Impregnation, Salvation-Bringing Crucifixion and Resurrection are a sacred sequence of events never to be repeated through eons of geologic time including the Ice Ages and clear back to the Big Bang. The mystery of mysteries, forever and ever, amen . . . The Son wills and participates, not just once but over and over again, in His own conception. Only in this way can He be His own foundation; still be Eternal God. Such vagaries of logic are excluded from religious discourse, if not summarily stamped out.

Likewise is the earthbound Mary's role stretched to the metaphysical limit. To her is given the breathtaking task of not only incarnating as Earth Mother Goddess but exemplifying perfect chastity. Despite her "voluptuous past," she must match, even surpass Male Trinity in purity. What seduces, revels and enjoys, is wounded, bleeds and suffers, is tainted by Earth maya. She mustn't invite amorous approach or appear a temptress. She must be inviolate, must incarnate the ephemeral, as well as the Impossible.

Although Conception occurs in the mist of a dream, the ethereal coupling retains the earth flavor of male domination and female submission. The Holy Spirit, a virile but beneficent Fog, hovers over, possesses and impregnates an awe-struck but willing peasant virgin. The fantastic event conjoins stainless Male Divinity with corruptible female flesh. Absolute Diffuseness (transparency) mates with contingent particularity (opacity). The result is a God-man.

And a seriously flawed theology.

In psychoanalytic terms, the Holy Spirit is the Father-Son will to Continuity. This invisible Force carries out the time-honored tradition for the Other Two. The Son (Oedipus) is the Father (Laius); the Father is the Son. They are interchangeable in their single-minded purpose of insuring mankind's future among the stars. Or in Nietzschian terms, Each Other's eternal recurrence. The Holy Spirit is the unified will to procreate in the form of the world. But a world, religious pundits arrogantly overlook, that excludes homosexuals—at the highest level of the arts, politics and religion where they most creatively and invaluably abound!

Fast-forward to the revolutionary advance of freedom as seen in an adolescent, self-adoring Narcissus matured into a reflecting Socrates. I use the blended self-gazer and adult analyzer as a symbol both selfish and altruistic of the gay man. (Myths are meant to be bent even if it leads to sacrilege.) The father-son breach (First Ordination) is tantamount to Christ refusing to bond with God the Father and instead dancing off in the alter-ego of Satan. In this scandalous schema Christ isn't obligated to conform to the paternal blueprint. He's free to deviate and invent. He can carry out his attraction to the beloved disciple John, consummate an out of wedlock affair with Mary Magdalene or take time out to go pleasure boating on the Sea of Galilee—blissfully free of His mission to ailing mankind. He can choose hedonism. He can pursue Eros. He can go gay.

But the price is the forfeiture of divinity, which for the Son, if He be God, is unthinkable. The role of loyal Son then falls into a truncated determinism. Christ isn't free not to be Himself, which orthodox Christianity insists must include celibacy. But since freedom is both a frightful, nihilating synapse and an enabling vacuum—the tentacles of Nothingness—isn't such limitation mere body illusion?

The astute reader will detect another swirling contradiction. What need has celestial Fullness of hit-and-miss earth maya? Of mindless, animalistic sex? Doesn't divinity transcend base desire, sin, guilt, struggle and death? "I am that I am," spoke Christ. Freedom is a nostalgic longing (for-itself) for Being (in-itself). His Holiness achieved the prodigious fete of welding the at-odds factions into a noncombative and harmonious Whole.

This is vividly seen in the 1960's sexual revolution, dramatized by flower children, where the heady experience of pitting oneself against an outdated and oppressive White Male establishment, more deeply meant dramatizing who and what one *is not*. For instance, a San Francisco Easter parade, spoofed by the Sisters of Perpetual Indulgence and Dykes on Bikes, wherein both defy the heavens as if to ask, "Who and what are we?"

With Oedipus, the father/son mating drive with the same mother/lover demonstrates the psychoanalytic function of Holy Spirit. In this sense, Mary is Jocasta is Mary, etc. Bear in mind that in a universe of Oneness, myths, folklore, parables and allegories with widespread indelibility and potency derive their staying power from a Higher Energy Source. In the Kingdom (or Queendom) of Light, Holy Spirit is the love bond between Creator and created, a bond of eternal Oneness.

On this earth plane of heavy matter, "imposed incompletion" (propped up by Trinity) is fated to descend into the arid isolation of Oedipus in order to re-ascend via the auto-love-turned-self-analysis of Narcissus/Socrates back into Completion. This downward/upward spiral (like the DNA molecule) posits man *and* God in radical incompletion. This is reflected in rigid religious dogma and male-female dichotomy. Androgyny, on the other hand, shows forth divine lenience in the form of Redemption and Return, Healing and Wholeness.

Trinity therefore denies both the androgyny of God and the possibility of His being a woman. But doesn't God—as Primal Essence, as First Cause, as Creator—gather all Being into Himself? Doesn't all creation reflect His Will? Oedipus is a step that God, split into three parts, takes to heal Himself and regain Totality of Being. Descent and ascent through Jesus, Oedipus and Narcissus/Socrates mirror both limitation (denial of diversity) and unlimited freedom (plenitude in diversity) needed to regain Cosmic Wholeness.

Similarly, the alienation of the Second Ordination is requisite to achieving the reunion of the Third. In regard to the vacuum of absolute freedom, it can be said that, like the atoms that make up a steel girder, "the strength is in the spaces."

But all is not well in the heavens. A ground-up reshuffling of Godhead is in the works. A fatal crack in Trinity is revealed when the Father unilaterally orders the Son's execution. For the Son, there is no court of appeal; His role is utter resignation. He has no choice but to drain dry the cup of martyrdom. After a cruel death, He is miraculously resurrected to rejoin, not in revenge but in joyful gratitude, the Father Whose authority isn't to be questioned. Christ, in a dramatic display of divine obedience (like Abraham about to sacrifice Isaac), survives the "murder attempt." It was all a test, a top level drama, a celestial acting out—in order to reaffirm male dominion. During His sojourn on Earth, Christ refused to defy the Father by defecting to Satan, since such betrayal would mean separation and death.

His Holiness Christ consequently refused the downward "advance" into Oedipus. The descent into a homosexual fling would mortify and "murder" the Father by breaching divine Continuity. At the same time, it would allow the freedom to think and invent. The denial and mutilation of the analytic faculty is at the core, is the corrosion of, Trinity-as-False-Completion. Free-wheeling thought might tempt Christ to switch allegiance to Mother-Goddess. He might come down from the cross and join the three Mary's as a Fourth Grace. Rather than betray Trinity, He upholds it. Not until later will homosexuality in the form of a self-enamored Narcissus grown into a mature, reflecting Socrates play a vital role in elevating sexism into androgyny.

Christ-as-Mohammed (the Divine Messengers serve an interchangeable, world-educating purpose) crossed into the Court of Women by taking 17 wives. Divinity thus runs the gamut from celibacy to polygamy. Both poles are revered by a major religion. Such whimsical yet ordained variety shows not only the infinite face of God, but the interpenetration of sex and religion. There is no one true religion any more than there is one true sexuality. The interplay of sex and religion demonstrate (to shout it out would threaten civilization which tends to be fragile) male sexism's suppressed homosexual component. Androgyny, on the other hand, incorporates homosexuality without being threatened. For what is Oneness leading to Completion but tacit admission of the inevitable fact of homosexuality?

Oneness, then, is only achieved through the assimilation of its homosexual component. Spirit "relies upon" homosexuality as a dismantler of sexism. Homosexuality serves both a temporal and eternal, existential and essential, role in the Great Wheel of Being. It's the nature of Existence (for-itself) to self-immolate and merge with Essence (in-itself). The advent of Narcissus grown into Socrates (transformation of over-indulgence into a philosophic mellowing and flowering) is a final stage of God rediscovering Himself. Homosexuality, despite its roots in the ink blotter of Nothingness, is a luminous alter-face of God, at once serious and playful.

Which brings one to ask: Did Christ, assuming He had homosexual urges, undergo the First Ordination? Since according to the Bible, Joseph isn't His genetic father, the question appears at once redundant and automatic. Christ doesn't invent His lack of earthly paternity; it comes ready-made. As Divinity, He can speed through all Three Ordinations in a flash. Or rather, defuse and demote homosexuality from imperious command into optional indulgence. Or most probably, live out a perpetual postponement.

Sexuality wasn't even a side issue of His mission. It's as if sex doesn't exist. He transcends Ego-Body at the Satanic temptations, via Self-enforced celibacy and finally the bloodletting horror of the crucifixion. Homosexuality, symbolized by the scattered, frightened disciples, hadn't yet crystallized into a world-transforming role. If Christ did transcend homosexuality in the batting of an eyelid, it doesn't mean He didn't experience earth maya as keenly as any other in-the-flesh mortal.

Christ, lifted up to heaven, chose not to descend into androgyny by joining the three Marys. Through this refusal He remains Eternal Son. But He thereby fails to attain parity with the Father. This furious whirligig has the effect of freezing in the human consciousness the myth of Trinity. Collective False Atman bears witness (Christ taught neither homosexuality nor androgyny) that heterosexuality isn't morally superior to homosexuality. Rather is it a pragmatic matter, a situational ethic that changes from culture to culture, age to age. By a similar logic, the life of Mohammed illustrates that monogamy isn't superior to polygamy. Both poles are irrelevant to true spirituality and the unfolding of Divine Will.

A brief return to Mohammed. The Warrior-Prophet withdrew from the battlefield into the Court of Women. Historical narratives claim His relationship with multiple wives was primarily protective. He's a charismatic but nurturing Father Figure. Like Christ, He probably sped through all Three Ordinations without allowing murderous thoughts toward an earthly father or their crystallization in homosexuality. By presiding over a harem, He moved mankind, despite Islam's dark history of suppressing women, closer to androgyny.

Through the vibrational energies of the coming Psychic-Intuitional Era, all humans experience some variant of the Three Ordinations. The eternal cycle of "descent and ascent," "alienation and return," can take place in seconds or be spread over a lifetime. Christ's maxim—to think something is to both do and *be it*—admits the possibility of homosexuality not only for Himself, but for followers of Krishna, Moses, Buddha, Mohammed and all races and kindreds of mankind. Gay is here to stay. The Golden Age of Oneness can't arrive without it.

The human psyche is a gyroscope, at once wildly free-wheeling and finely balanced, centrifugal and centripetal. Man's limitless possibilities, within the bounds of space-time, are in a constant state of flux. A wise and inspired use of freedom demands that this oscillation include homosexuality. In a future utopia gayness won't be engraved in the human psyche as "aberration" or "sin"; it will simply *be*.

As in the saying, "The more forgiven, the more grateful," so does Reunion consist of the range of "aberrations" it assimilates. Forgiveness embraces without reservation the Whole. Homosexuality is a gauge of Oneness, a radio beam from Spirit. As such, it had to exist in Christ's and Mohammed's awareness. It can scarcely be denied that the suppression/sublimation of homosexuality was present in the Warrior Courting Dance of the Crusades. Just as it underlay the tragic uprisings in Yugoslavia, Iraq, Afghanistan, the Arab Spring and now the horrific slaughter in Syria.

It's not surprising that the outed gay man finds himself at loggerheads with organized religion. Particularly when it fails to fulfill its primary mission of moving mankind from the Mythic-Membership into the Mental-Egoic, and from there into the Psychic-Intuitional and beyond. He knows with the quickened eye of Spirit that the guilt he's made to feel, as an unclean variant of his sacrosanct heterosexual peer, is patently false.

When a straight man performs in the sack, his thoughts are no purer than his; probably more selfish and ruthless in taking a woman than the gay man is with a lover. Is a beer-guzzling football fan more spiritual than a cultured gay man listening to Mozart because he thrusts his unit into a vagina, enters by the approved vestibule—while the connoisseur of great music must enter or be entered through the rear baptistry of hell's back door? The gay man rightly perceives his sexuality as a valid, innocent and moral choice, a facticity, in the great Chain of Being.

What he fails to perceive, however, together with his straight peers, is that sexuality isn't an end in itself, but a measure of spiritual longing. Just as homosexuality precedes sexuality, so does spirituality precede homosexuality. True, the gay man's desire for another male plays out a longing for forfeited earth father. But on the deepest level, it's a yearning for Eternal Father. The gay man isn't guilty of desiring a man, but of being a spiritual Lack.

Heterosexuals, like all contingent being, all that isn't God, suffer their own "incompletion syndrome," but of a less nettlesome kind. Theirs is an "ordained" incompletion, while the gay man's is that of a pariah. The straight believer has the gall, while laying claim to purity amidst the most prurient lust, to expect an eternal reward in heaven. While the gay man is required to hang his head in shame as a sexual outcast.

No matter how tempting the loaf and wine offered by a church, mosque or synagogue, the gay man has difficulty, may even gag, trying to swallow it whole. As well he should. If religion blights or poisons the inborn integrity that underlies true spirituality, it should be unceremoniously spat out. That's his prerogative and duty as a fully credentialed child of the Universe, which deep inside he always knew himself to be.

The behavior of straight men shows the father-son "conspiracy to coitus" to be a Pandora's box of lustful conquest, like two criminals pulling off a job. Religion is a conspiracy of the elect to sanctify the unsanctionable. Or a trick to make heterosexuality the exclusive plaything of a Warrior God. How strange that the Creator of All-That-Is can't tolerate an iota of sexual variety. Such is His outrage at the sight of two gay men beating off behind a park bush that He must not only look the other way but cast the brazen sinners into flaming hell—while the heterosexual couple who lustily went "around the world" after smoking dope, guzzling copious amounts of alcohol and beating their children, receive His unqualified blessing.

Orthodox religion, in an attempt to horde the God substance like chips at a poker table, posits homosexuality as a threat to the trumped-up Casino of Divine Roulette. In truth, what's under siege is its own fraudulence. The fullness of integrity can't be threatened. To divert attention from religious imposture, the church devises Hell for Satan and his followers, especially those evil gays. The flames are conveniently out of sight and mind like a furnace below the basement.

Strange indeed for a God Who transcends Space-Time, for Whom there is no distance! The flames are Other. The suffering of countless infidels is Other. Thus does a fire-and-brimstone Hades give the lie to Oneness. Oneness, not Otherness, is the essence of truly *spiritual* religion. Simple justice would compel a caring Creator, unless He be a depraved sadist, to intervene on behalf of tormented multitudes, loveless and hopeless in flaming Hades.

Official religion takes random circumstance—a chance ability to become aroused under set conditions—to supercede justice and love. To coddle and protect the fragile sensitivity of the elect, the flames are confined to caverns too deep below the earth to melt the glue that holds together, like a framework of bailing wire and plaster, Holy Trinity—

I here pose the axiom: *Homosexuality is the path or detour that God takes to traverse the distance from Trinity (sexism) back to Full Beingness (Androgyny).*

In regard to the regressive nature of Trinity:

1.) It is fear of nonconformity to maleness; that God might be sexless, a eunuch, a hermaphrodite or a woman.
2.) It reinstates the eternal legacy of the male. Or: perpetration of the myth that castration (loss of male dominance) is synonymous with death.
3.) It's an attempt by the Male to portray his contingent being as absolute; in other words, to replace God. (That's why a sexist evangelist like Jerry Faldwell is offended by a statue of the Virgin Mary in a church sanctuary with the darkly suffering Christ shunted off to one side.)
4.) Trinity is an Oedipal configuration in which none of the Players turn traitor. It is a loyalty whose fate, however, is to remain sexist and deprived of reflective freedom.

Christ skirts the brink of Patricide (like the foetal or infant pre-gay at the First Ordination) by refusing to entertain for even a second yielding to His Satanic alter-self. The female camp to which He would defect is maya love of the material world. Like Graeco-Roman deities, He could indolently peel grapes and couple freely with Earth-Mother-Goddess. But her vastness would absorb Him, make Him a tiny contingency, like a twig carried on the crest of a surging tsunami. Divinity would fall into the earth-tainted realm of Safe Court.

Rest easy: Christ doesn't defect to the boudoir, revel in the dresses, jeweled tiaras or engage in make-believe. Or the pomp and pageantry of the Vatican.

But neither does He condemn it. Indeed why should He? What need has resplendent Fullness of fleeting particularity? Rather does Eternal Son remain loyal to divine Continuity. He remains a cornerstone of Trinity. Yet such unswerving loyalty, like a foot soldier to his regiment, perpetuates a male chauvinist mindset of subjugation of the female half of Creation.

In fairness, Christ *did* demonstrate androgyny. Mankind's tribal, male-supremist past rose up to stamp out what His Holiness intended as a message of love and reconciliation. Christ, touted by retributive, even-the-score religion as a Warrior-Conqueror, instead taught planetary survival as a *passivism*: Stop fighting and love one another. He was martyred, not only for claiming divinity, but for challenging male supremacy.

His refusal, however, to directly advocate androgyny is later corrected by Oedipus and Narcissus transfigured into Socrates. They take the quest for the divine into the uncharted terrain of the human psyche where Christ, given the warrior-chauvinist climate of the Roman empire, had the wisdom not to go. Oedipus and later Narcissus/Socrates—unlikely bedfellows—will take the final steps in wedding Warrior and Mother Goddess back into One.

Trinity will unravel in direct ratio to male-female reconciliation, just as Male-as-Warrior will lose its grip in the human solar plexus and brain. Homosexuality—in all its anguish, joy, confusion and *innocence*—is a world player as a harbinger of change. By overcoming guilt over being gay—celebrating the pre-choice of oneself, existing one's essence—comes the dismantling of Oedipus and father-guilt. And eventually the need to be gay. Not that a gay man should be other than what he is. He should be himself to the hilt; moreover, be grateful and proud. Otherwise he limits God, which is the profoundest kind of atheism.

As mankind moves into the Psychic-Intuitional and beyond, homosexuality, rather than a pre-choice that turns into an ingrained command, will be a conscious choice, renewable or revocable at any time. At the present juncture of human affairs such godlike, causal freedom is science fiction, mere fantasy. But several centuries hence, maybe sooner, humankind will be libidinally rewired and spiritually liberated to select sex roles the way one buys a new Easter hat, a set of golf clubs or chooses a video. Anyone can choose any sex role at any time!

So long as the human psyche remains opaque and unknown to itself, father-guilt will be projected on the blank screen of the heavens in the sexist form of Trinity. For what is Trinity but a three-way split masquerading as Wholeness?

The most telling evidence of hetero incompletion is fear of homosexuality. Homosexuality is Trinity's unraveling and hidden truth. When maleness no longer fears its possibility as a homosexual alter-self, Trinity will pass into obsolescence, be a discarded relic of the past. The unreflective command to be homosexual will recede and become a choice. Then will the mutilation of male-female inequality take a final step toward Androgyny and Planetary Healing.

If one truly thinks about it, that is the goal of all true religion and of all Being—and the goal of homosexuality itself. What I boldly and unguiltily proclaim as a High Priesthood.

CHAPTER ELEVEN

THE CRISIS OF NONBEING FOR OTHERS;
ABSENCE OF THE GAZE OR GHOST COMPLEX;
DECLARATION OF A HIGH PRIESTHOOD

Sartre makes a great, I believe obsessive and therefore erroneous, case for *the look* in determining being-for-others. He also uses it to create a rigid subject/object dualism. The corrosive effect of the look must be regarded as symbolic, even theatrical, since the imperious attitude of a blind person or a demanding voice over the telephone (minus a pair of accusing eyes) can "freeze" one into a naked object.

On the brighter Somethingness side, the look is the "tie that binds" of MCC (or any church or public gathering). Through the common gaze, the congregation sees itself not as a ragtag assortment of hustlers and queens, but as whole individuals unafraid to step into the light. This mutual look transforms the lost souls and creatures of night into "the chosen few, "the elect," etc. The side glances and nods of recognition, freed of apology, sarcasm and shame belong to and arise from a collective and protective consciousness of the race.

The basic structure of organized religion, rather than theological, is psycho-social. Church attendance is an exercise in being-for-others. To be alone without foundation is the origin of guilt. As the saying goes, "One starts to imagine all sorts of things." The best defense against original sin and guilt is doing things in concert, as a member of the tribe.

Religion, then, is *a posteriori* to sociology, to the need to belong, to shedding the guilt of separation. The gay church attendee waiting to receive communion from a line of robed, likewise gay deacons feels caught in profile as by a roving camera. It beats preening in the bathroom mirror! For a magic moment he's a star with an adoring public. In ontologic terms, he's a perfect fusion of in-itself, for-itself and being-for-others. Thrust into public view, he's a reconstituted totality. The communal gaze welds his fragmented self back into a unified Whole.

I further take exception to Sartre's claim that the Other's penetrating stare transmutes subjective self into hapless object, turns an autonomous master into a groveling slave. And that by staring back until the Other is shamed into looking away one regains autonomy and enslaves the Other as an object. This harsh either/or schema overlooks the fact that one can interpolate, more than that, *interpenetrate* the SPIRIT>Mind>body electric field or aura of a fellow being by commingling it with one's own.

Interpenetration, then, takes place in the flow of common experience, language and the psychic faculty. Empathy is to feel what the other feels or thinks, not through a clinical projection of mathematical probabilities, but through transcendent soul-intermingling. Sartre's gazing/gazed-at dyad—more accurately, duel—is for automatons (or master-slave duos!) with intuition, interpenetration and soul exchange edited out. The Mental-Egoic is blocked from attaining the Psychic-Intuitional. His is a barren, de-spirited system. Haunted and threatened by the Other, one can little more than haunt and in turn threaten like Halloween trick-or-treaters.

In the 1960's movie, The Tenth Victim, each thrill-hungry player must elegantly and ingeniously kill ten times without being killed. The winner, who executes the tenth kill (either Marcello Mastroianni or Ursula Andress), gets a ten million dollar prize. (Unfortunately for the game, they fall in love.) Sartre's mode of being-for-others is conflict and betrayal, a perpetual one-upmanship that masks a deeper, entrenched desire for separation and death. Winning merely forestalls deathwish. Envy, malice and the desire to wipe out an imaginary enemy are the norms of human existence. This is the bleak result of blocked interpenetration. Rather, it's the projection of self-generated fear and hatred upon an innocent Other. Most deeply: Failure to see the Oneness of mankind.

Degraded into an object by a mental sleight of hand, as well as a bid for survival, the victim transfers envy or outrage over the "self-I-might-have-been" onto the Other, whom he believes has robbed him of that coveted state.

Consequently he conscripts Self-as-Other to aggress or kill the wily, distrusted competitor. Rather than multiple killers and victims, there is really only one player: Myself. I'm not angry so much at my rival's strutting arrogance as at myself for not stealing his confidence and making it my own. To hide my failure, I make him into a thief, petty tyrant or frightful boor for having what I want and don't have.

The dehumanizing power of the look thus begins and ends at home. There's only myself to blame. It's an old trick to project inner resentment or rage upon a trumped-up pair of Alter-Self versus an imagined Enemy. It's not the Other, who in the illusory realm of separate body is an Absence, but my lack of self-love and esteem that makes me easily reducible to an object.

An icy stare, however disarming, can be ignored or tuned out. A distracted shopper, staring through a passing pedestrian, may regard him not as an object (something tangible) but as a mere insect, a nonentity, less than nothing. Neither member of the stared-at/through dyad, however, is under any obligation to accept the dehumanizing verdict. One has the option of resisting detotalization into a debased fraction; into a stripped-bare corpse of nonbeing.

It would seem Sartre never got past the haggard look of men in war in which every glance is that of a potential traitor. (Body always betrays.) Childhood isolation from peers and the German occupation of France predisposed him to the primacy of negative emotion. He hurls out a world devoid of Spirit. Small wonder that love is an impossible enterprise. Unwittingly this brilliant heterosexual (sometimes I have my doubts) described the underside of gay life with an uncanny accuracy he never achieved with the greater society.

Let's return to The Look. I have felt its *absence* more acutely than any actual paralyzing presence. I call this the "non-look," the basis for my theory and depiction of Ghost Complex. This descent into nothingness is far more devastating than mere reduction to object status. At critical junctures in my life—stranded past midnight beside a deserted train track in east Los Angeles or a "no exit" San Francisco bathhouse at a hungover, sweating dawn—I was reduced not just to an object, which would have been a saving "something," but to the zombie-like nullity of the walking dead. The reason, I intuited, was because the trauma of radical separation tripped a deep-rooted deathwish.

Case in point.

In an attempt to bridge alienated SPIRIT-Mind-body and lift myself a few notches out of the pursuit of an increasingly degenerate bar life (a constant struggle!), I attended a discussion group sponsored by the Baha'i Faith. (I was a borderline believer.) It took place at a Community Center in Denver's Washington Park. About thirty people were gathered on metal chairs arranged in a circle. The subject was "The Morning After," a TV epic about a nuclear attack on the U.S.A. by the then U.S.S.R. Everyone faced everyone else, so no one could escape the group gaze.

I was late. The discussion, led by a Black man who I knew was gay (but not by those in attendance), was underway. To reach the last empty chair, I had to circumscribe the entire circle. I had the harrowing sensation, although out in plain view, of not being seen (even in Levi's, red-checkered flannel shirt and engineer boots). Therefore of not being there. Or anywhere. Perhaps my cruisy appearance offended or shocked those present, who were there for purely social, intellectual or religious reasons. Or maybe it embarrassed me against my awareness not to fit in like an ordinary Joe, a cog in the machine of straight, at least neutral, human society.

The Baha'i faith, as previously noted, disallows or strongly discourages homosexuality. (I believed I could live out, actually *be*, this glaring contradiction!) My Black acquaintance was pulling off a charade by virtue of his blackness and having fathered two children by a White woman. He, too, (perhaps also out of embarrassment) pretended not to see me. I was an imposter effaced by a multiple negation—his gayness, his shadow being as a Black, his religious imposture and the group's refusal to acknowledge my presence without so much as a wink or nod. Even a disapproving grimace would have been a saving grace.

I felt like I was drowning. To get back to the door through which I'd entered was suddenly a matter of life and death. A wall with the escape hatch of the door was the surface of a churning, ink-black sea and I was a diver thirty feet under whose oxygen tank has failed. In a near panic I arose from the chair and reinscribed the same arc like a frightened marionette. I somehow found the door, entered a hall and exited, more like exploded, into the saving embrace of green sycamores and gently rustling pines against a pulsing, steel-blue sky.

I'd narrowly averted disaster! I felt reunited with a self I'd come perilously close to losing. It was like surviving a firing squad. The sense of relief, however, didn't last. The narrow escape unearthed a deeper sense of failure. The park trees, vivid the previous moment, paled against a bleached sky. Manicured flowerbeds and hedges faded into ghostly nonexistence. I'd not exchanged a nod or spoken a word to anyone! If I was seen, it was as a passer in the night, a ghost who floats past and vanishes for no earthly reason; certainly not the sort of person one takes seriously. It gave me the burlesque quasi-existence of one of those white-faced clowns that show up in European art films, juggling balls or oranges with mimed seriousness—a gratuitous being with no umbilical cord to the social or mystical life of the community. I wasn't even a meat-on-display, raw facticity.

Rather than confer a sense of belonging, the skirmish with the Baha'is echoed my worst fear: Nonbeing. Instead of present in the Now, I was stretched across time. I'd failed utterly to integrate SPIRIT>Mind>body. The meeting instead recast me as a specter of night. The fullness of Nature, which rescued and welcomed me moments before, issued a hideous disclaimer. The hierarchal arrangement of formal gardens, lawns and artificial forests referred me back to "them." My "ejection" from the discussion group revealed an uneasy rupture between in-itself and for-itself. I was denied not only being-for-others, but Being itself. The session, chaired by a gay Black man, hadn't the basic decency or largesse to reduce me to even an object. How welcome that would have been, no matter how dehumanizing!

Most tellingly, it blazoned across time the double murder of the First Ordination. At this late date I was still acting out that ancient rite with zealous dedication! My reaction to the discussion group replayed Oedipus. The welcoming forest was a temporary stage prop. I was stranded somewhere between the First and Second Ordinations with only a hazy notion of the huge amount of work needed to attain the Third. I felt racked inside and out. And more than a little scared.

To escape the site of disaster, I drove two miles from Washington Park to its sister, the always cruisy Cheesman Park. A Gay Pride float, of which I had no foreknowledge, was about to depart for a rally on the steps of the downtown Capitol building. The headless horseman of Nothingness was gaining speed! Might I find the confirming gaze withheld by the Baha'is (which I'd failed to find in a tableau of spaced leathermen in last night's smoky bar)? Such deliverance, amounting to salvation, wasn't to be. The float shimmered in a time warp. The bikini-clad models (an in-vogue assortment of lean young

Whites, Chicanos, and Blacks) might as well have dropped in from an alien planet.

Just as the discussion group possessed a higher spiritual density than my own, the bodies-on-display evanesced in and out of existence. The departing spectacle had the not-quite-there quality of a waking bad dream. Did the young beauties (I was then in my mid-forties) mistake me for a pine tree or moss-covered boulder? As someone's nihilated and invisible father? The float glided from sight in a nimbus of trendy poses. The staged waves were an Absence, since they were intended not for me but a cheering crowd on the steps of the gold-domed Capitol.

I struggled for belief, any kind of raw faith. Something deeply disturbing but of primal importance was taking place. Perhaps Sartre's *la nausee*? No, something altogether different. Thoughts of suicide raced through my mind. At the same time, I was too curious to know what lay around the next pine trunk or manicured hedge to end it all just yet. Self-annihilation, I cogitated, is too messy. There's the next bar fling or trick to look forward to. I took refuge on an empty park bench. An expanse of grass merged into a planted woods that fragmented a miniature playground in front of high-rise apartment buildings. And in the far distance, the bluish Rocky Mountains.

The discussion group, I thought, precipitated a claustrophobia that made me long for wide-open spaces. At the same time, the float tripped an agoraphobia that made me seek the opposite, a closed-in, tomblike place. It confirmed my ghost status: Someone who eats, walks, reads and retreats to a basement apartment in a robotic preplay of death. I was attracted to the float—through Pavlovian, disco-pulsing, bar conditioning—at the same time that it repelled me. And so soon after my ejection from the Baha'i event, which something inside me keenly wanted to participate in, but which another, censoring, baleful part (an avatar of earth father) wouldn't let me have. Hell, I thought, isn't other people, but the realization of being one's own worst enemy.

The denied group gaze froze my subjectivity not so much into hapless object, but into a nullity. I felt the chill horror of being absent to park benches, a foraging squirrel, a candy wrapper skittering in a gust of wind. Both organized religion *and* gay society were powerless to help me. Oh to be reduced to a raw object by that dozing wino with a newspaper tented over his head for protection against Denver's sudden weather changes! To be lashed to a crosstree of Being! It was as though the Christian Rapture had taken place, the believers pulled to heaven like so many metal filings by a powerful magnet, leaving me alone on a hideously depopulated planet.

The pulsing solitude, I ruminated with the crazed insight of a madman, didn't start with the Other. He stands stubbornly apart from the drama. The tragicomedy begins and ends with *me*. Yet isn't being absent to the Other the death of a vital part of Universal Self, namely Being-for-Others? To unilaterally erase one side of the triangle can't long stand. I desperately needed *him, it, or whatever,* while replaying the ritual murder of the First Ordination. Since to be a totality in the world isn't possible without the assistance of the shadowy phantom of the Long Ago Murder, more than that, without His active participation . . . .

I was going around in circles. If I started with self, I was led to the Other. If I started with the Other, I was referred back to self. Both the Baha'i Faith and the gay float eluded me in the worst kind of failure. I'd wandered into, blindly embraced, a bleak universe that doesn't love in return. I was a diaspora incapable of piecing itself back together; let alone self-love. I longed for the inner fragmenting to cease, to conjoin in-itself, for-itself and being for others into a coherent, functioning Whole. I'd failed utterly both as a Baha'i fence-sitter and guilt-ridden gay man. One exacerbated and wiped out the other.

Near madness gave way to an unexpected glimmer of hope. It was the first glow of dawn after a long, feverish, suicide-tinged night. *I desired Lost Father in the form of the Missing Male.* More to the point, I wanted to be recognized as someone who has this need and is *right* to have it. Homosexuality at the Second Ordination attempts to replace Lost Father with a worthy substitute (Mister Right). I was simultaneously looking for Spirit and the Male. Can both be found at the same time and place, in the same church? Troy Perry passionately so preached. However, reconciliation with the ghost of Lost Father isn't so easy. It requires rending the veils of Ego-Body. Eternal Father is inaccessible until Earth Father is called forth from his sepulcher, ushered into the light of day and openly forgiven.

Similarly, androgyny (a common goal of homosexuality and true spirituality) depends upon reunion with Eternal Father. For the heterosexual, androgyny requires the acceptance of a homosexual component. *The homosexual will always be at odds looking for Spirit without also looking for the Male.* To look for one without the other leads to a hollow church rite or a vain bar. The two quests overlap, are mutually causal, just as homosexuality and religion are intimately bound. To purge religion of homosexuality is to degut religion. Just as de-sexed religion falls into a barren formality. I was finally getting somewhere! There was hope, God help me, beyond any alleged blasphemy!

When I abruptly exited the discussion group, I thought I'd gotten back a stolen part of myself. The lush pines, however, only mimicked Fullness. What is the outward abundance of nature but a projected nostalgia for Wholeness? I'd only succeeded in hiding an inner Lack; chose False Atman over Atman. Deep-seated anger (at being excluded and apart) lowered my spiritual density and made external objects similarly evanesce. Co-existents, animate and inanimate, withdrew to shield themselves from the fury of one scorned. The pines faded into a shuddering outline. The sycamores cowered in fear. Festive flowers paled in gray mourning. Yet it was more than that. I'd come face-to-face with Nonbeing. Did it enter through the orifice of homosexuality? Through the chopping block of the First Ordination? Thank God, I thought, for the Second and Third Ordinations!—solid fortresses against the black tide of Nothingness.

However, these temporary assurances failed to console me. I'd begun to evanesce into a chalk-white effigy. I needed a vital Other—Mister Right, Eternal Male, God Himself—to catch my fall and snatch me back into the realm of the living. I'd falsely pursued Him through separate body. How often had I made Him a sex tool with rope and handcuffs! Ego-Body is a dog-(or corpse)-in-the-manger to rejoining the concourse of souls. A master's doled pain is a means of holding the slave's beingness at bay. Or apropos this discussion, enslaving his subjectivity while leaving my own arrogantly intact.

SPIRIT>Mind>body works to break down barriers. Similarly, the Other, instead of the baleful owner of the look, seeks to waft through my being like an ordaining breeze. If barred from doing so as a Fullness, He will do so as a *Lack*—as I did Him by fleeing into the phantom embrace of park trees (or tying him up). Perceiving me as a hostile Absence, He shrewdly left me alone and went about His business.

Yet another glimpse of the Nothingness that pervades Being! But with a proviso: This Anti-Womb of Nonbeing becomes ferocious and frightful through the incantatory power of human freedom. Nothingness and Free Choice, facets of each other, become mutually destructive and self-prolonging.

Homosexuality, I continued my Icarus ascent into the perilous stratosphere of abstract reason, exists as a "not" in order to be re-chosen as a Fullness. Passage from the First through the Second and Third Ordinations is a journey of spiritual discovery. More rightly, an odyssey of Spirit finding Itself. Or the Creator making tantric Self-Love. I gleaned that from my study of Eastern religions, primarily Hinduism, and most recently, the sexually ambivalent, cross-dressing Ramakrishna.

At least one of the myriad faces of God, I ruminated, has to be gay. The Deity, moreover, will be fully present in that poignant and luminous face. For the homosexual, it's not just self-affirming but necessary that God be *tres gay*. Gay all the way! From my precarious perch on a hard metal bench, I was squirming and brimming with joy! At the same time, I was angry that this obvious truth was for so long suppressed by society and religion. I'd been maneuvered into being a ghost that haunts basement apartments and dark bars, that finds basic human concourse, even the pristine embrace of flowers and trees, precarious and filled with distrust, even fraught with peril . . . and tainted with deathwish.

If gay isn't of God and God isn't gay, I decided, in any of His infinite faces, why go on? If the psychic split within can't be bridged, I choose death. But I was being offered life! The self-affirming God within is a gay Self. I somehow knew this better than any church dogma. I'd denied God a unique mode of Being by blocking His expression of gayness in me! To be a face of God may be too blasphemous for a Baptist, too ludicrous for an existential atheist or presumptuous for a Baha'i—but it was right for me. How well I knew, for I'd drained dry the cup of all three modes of False Atman!

Before I reaffirm the cosmic imperative of a High Priesthood, I'll further analyze "the look," for I believe this distorted and simplistic premise muddies the path to true self-discovery and healing.

Interpenetration (a profoundly sexual idea), not conflict and denial, should be and is the primary mode of being-for-others. Just as a cold stare can capture and slay my subjectivity (if I let it), so does an affirming look reconstitute me as SPIRIT>Mind>body. Isn't that what I craved but wouldn't allow at the Baha'i event—because I refused to let the Other give it? Spirit renders denial of my being-for-him and his denial of me, unless either party be a total hermit, impossible for more than a brief instant. I insisted on being what I am not (Ego-Body) while refusing to be what I am (Spirit). I didn't "exist" for the Baha'is or they for me because I'd murdered them in advance as a dangerous avatar of earth father.

That the gay float might be a like carryover sent chills down my spine. Precisely that ancient murder gave the trees and float their funereal cast! Made me vanish out in plain view! Can I blame fellow humans for respecting, for following orders, in my will to patricide? In my simultaneous suicide? For what is the desire for separation and the subjugation of others but prolonged guilt over patricide? And outrage over the crushing burden of self-foundation? Just as it is impossible for Spirit to nonexist, so is it impossible in a universe of Oneness—and fathers—to be alone. Solitude is the most "idol" of fancies.

Empathic merging will increase, I'm convinced, as old prejudices break down and the world becomes one place. Gays and straights will flow into each other psychically and spiritually; each will be the other's reflection. Ego-body blockage of spiritual interconnection triggered an identity crisis, that of having a foot in both camps while belonging to neither. I was hurled back into the realm of boundaries, separation and Nonbeing. Rather than share a common subjectivity, I was Object-to-Self through what I later perceived as a conspiracy to deny my fundamental right to belong, of my rightness as a gay man. The discussion attendees "helped" me imprint body opaqueness on transparent Spirit. I let them darken my being. The seeker of truth came for salvation but left as one lost. Burdened with seeing too much (of self), I was "seen too little."

I fled the discussion group (Corridor of Withdrawal) with the squandered vessel of my violated subjectivity grasped tightly underarm. I felt ravaged by an unknown assailant. (I did the same to bar tricks.) Attending the Baha'i function was a belated attempt to reforge the broken chain of Continuity, as well as stare death in the face by making up for, redeeming and atoning, the withheld touch.

To be touched by another man, as shown, is a *spiritual imperative*. Sacred or profane doesn't matter. How ironic to go to the bar in search of Spirit and to a religious function in search of body! Talk about interpenetration! Or embedded dualism! All because homosexuality can't be brought into the full light of day. Society and religion made this terrible darkness fall upon the earth.

To return to the question: Should a gay man (myself included) join a church, synagogue, mosque or Baha'i discussion group—since it will involve self-denial and mutilation? Should he seek Spirit in solitude, only with other gay men or abandon the quest altogether? First, the body-separation society foists on homosexuals compounds their vulnerability to being a scorned object, to ridicule and pain.

On that downer but breakthrough Sunday, as I'd later write, I couldn't immerse myself in a religious rite or function no matter how intensely I desired it. Since I "moved and had my being" in an incubus of separation, in my hour of need there was no ready channel for its effectuation. The hoped-for link-up with the Bahai's had the character of a late fix. It left a bitter, curdled taste in my mouth.

Soon thereafter in seeming tandem, an opposite, irreligious reach for camaraderie via a "pagan" float likewise evanesced. There I fared even worse. It was real and I was the bad dream. It was moving on and I was mired in quicksand. Both seeming failures, for Spirit does not fail, came via the negation that is separate body.

But herein lies coiled the serpent of contradiction. Through the suppression of gay body function by a judging society arises a larger and worse disconnect that makes *all* sexuality appear as a mutual reduction or "disease." The ostracism and persecution of homosexuals is a glaring dysfunction and failure of human history. All prejudice, which is fear of the unknown, hinders world peace and retards human advancement.

Homophobia can't coexist in the same time and place with Spirit. Homophobia and hate crimes against gays signify spiritual dysfunction and failure. At the Second Ordination, the gay man finds and accepts himself *contra the Other*. At the Third, selfhood is rejoined to the world process that governs the stars. "Variant" sexual identity finally receives its just due of cosmic confirmation. Apart from what anyone may think or feel, the gay man simply *is*—in the most profound and spiritual sense of the word.

How then is homosexuality a "not"? The answer lies in the First Ordination and its transcendence in the Third. On its underside, homosexuality is the "not" of the will to patricide. On a deeper level, it's an attempt to father oneself, an audacious ploy to supplant God. Yet sexual adaptation, reinforced by several thousand orgasms and millions of nerve endings, can't be disconnected like a caboose at the last station. It persists in all its complex neural circuitry. Such facticity must be dealt with squarely, scientifically and compassionately, even though Higher Self view terminal earth body as a temporary "not" transcended into a "becoming."

This multiple denial—suppression of a subgroup of mankind—*to the degree attacked*, is an acid corroding the bastion of heterosexuality. There is no such thing as a morally or religiously superior segment of society. Or correct sexual orientation. That is to deny transcendent Oneness.

The larger society condemns homosexuality because *it too is embedded in Ego-Body*. To the denial of its homosexual component add the crime of defaming and smashing its mirror image in the world. It thereby makes itself a villain and elevates homosexuality to sainthood. Sexist heterosexuality likewise exists as a Lack, therefore as a Guilt. It raises the spiritual density of its victim while lowering its own. The persecutor evanesces while solidifying its prey. When all is said and done, heterosexuality and homosexuality rise or fall together. One doesn't exist as a Fullness without the participation of the other.

But how, one asks, is a double negation (homosexuality) a preordained fact? I'll more carefully describe facticity. It refers to gross body, to the purely phenomenal; not the essential or eternal. Only mental states and images are nihilated, while both matter (according to quantum physics) and Spirit are indestructible, neither created nor destroyed. Freedom, as the mechanism and enabler of change, is the leap-in-the dark synapse across which the reflective mental faculty comes into being. In a film strip, fast cessation of the preceding frame creates an illusion of motion. Spirit is unbounded Fullness. It's source is Eternal Light. It doesn't require disruptive stops and starts. Nor does it need to leap across a nihilating chasm or wrestle with Nothingness in order to evolve to a higher form.

The body's fate is aging, decay and death. Nihilation refers not to physical death but the "absenting" of states of mind. Homosexuality, as the willed nonbeing of the father and simultaneous slaying of self, is at the same time survival erasure of that dual aggression. Facticity describes simple biology or brute body. Spirit transcends earth-bound facticity. Mind is a mediating tug-of-war lodged somewhere between. Homosexuality, in its brave search for God, is forged in the primordial dawn of Spirit. Earth relations with mortal father, including the vagaries of Oedipus, merely provide a lower order setting for a higher, more exalted purpose.

Before attempting a conclusion, I'll address a final paradox. How is matter neither created nor destroyed and the body still be a nothingness? The answer isn't as prickly as it sounds. Cut off from SPIRIT>Mind, matter swiftly degenerates into the chaotic disorder (entropy) of "flesh to flesh" and "dirt to dirt." Spirit catalyzes upreach toward greater complexity. Spirit holds complexity in place while transmuting it into a still higher synthesis. Body is a "not" in that it winds up six feet under; the end result is death and decomposition. According to quantum physics, that doesn't apply to the atoms and molecules of which this mortal frame of dust is composed, any more than it poses a threat to Eternal Meaning (spiritual density).

As a corollary:

SPIRIT in its Fullness and body in its notness both stand clear of subject-object duality. Dualism, expressed in male-female tension, tribal warfare and religious persecution, originates with Mind. Like all chosen states, it's slated for change and transcendence. Sartre's tyranny of the gaze is an Ego-Body phantasm without spiritual relevance or longevity. The First Ordination, in an impulsive split and cover-up, attempts, impossibly, to surpass subject-object duality and plunge directly into the court of the Divine. It is for the Second Ordination to reinstate duality ("us against them"). Just as it is for the Third to repeal it and finish the soul work of spiritual fusion begun in the First.

Can we assume that organized religion as a system of sexual oppression is, if not anathema, at least unworkable? First realize religion rarely functions as pure SPIRIT>Mind. Between the lines of holy writ it reinstates exclusive hetero-body service: The Cult of the Missionary Position, all else be damned. To enter God's sanctuary, a gay man is expected to leave the excess baggage of his defiled body, if not at the last station, at least in the vestibule. He enters the sanctuary as a SPIRIT>Mind amputee (or ghost) to there encounter a gathering of bodies engaged in rites of mutual body-confirmation.

"We are bodies in Body under God." My crisis with the Baha'is arose from finding myself a disembodied essence in search of a torso who realizes too late he's come to a manufacturer who uses the wrong plastics.

Instead of a celebration of SPIRIT>Mind, he finds himself in a body glut. He's a scale grafted onto a prehistoric reptile basking in its bodiness. The heterosexual couples, married at that same altar, still feel the effects of last night's coitus against the pews. Their glands are God-sanctioned. The itch for the next intimacy is swathed in divine blessing. Salivary glands secrete in anticipation of the roast in the oven (once stripped and bleeding wild game), soon to be outspread as Sunday dinner. Elegant pillbox hats and jewels for the ladies, tweed suits and fine Swiss watches for the men proclaim body-body-body. With all meditating and thinking done for it, the Body of the Elect will soon be free to eat, joke and relax in front of a wide-screen murder/romance or sportscast.

After the benediction and sermon replete with body-identification with the risen Savior—carried to extremis in communion in which Body dispenses Itself as simulated blood and fragments of torn flesh, along with the smug knowledge that those gays are conveniently burning out of sight and out of mind—the cumbersome dinosaur reverses itself in the cramped space and drags itself out through the vestibule, down the steps and into a multiplicity of showy BMW's and Cadillac's.

Should a questing gay man buy into the charade? Hetero- and homosexuality, both parts of the totality of mankind, manifest or else dim the spiritual Light. Spirit animates all walks of life. Until organized religion can speak the word "gay" and not choke in revulsion, it will remain sub-spiritual. It will be out of synch with the Great Chain of Being. It inwardly seeks the rebirth and completion only the incorporation of its gay component can bring.

As previously stated, homosexuality is heterosexuality's underlying truth and secret undoing. The latter can't evolve to a higher form without assimilating the former. The family of man will remain subhuman until homosexuals and all minorities—women, races and creeds—are given not just equal status, but equal Isness.

Since homosexuality is a spiritual pre-choice, and secondarily a response to genetic and environmental stimuli, how can it be unnatural? Spirit, which shepherds all mankind, knows its lost sheep. It won't allow Its special child and future high priest to go on being battered and abused. Although homosexuality be a negation formed in a primal Void, as with all creation, it's evil only to the degree it clings to Ego-Body and stifles SPIRIT>Mind. But since *all* sexuality plays out a Lack, isn't the same true of heterosexuality? Every participant in lovemaking is a fraction striving to be Whole. Why single out the gay man for criminal prosecution? Such hypocrisy but adds to his martyrdom, unveils his heroism and assures his ultimate glory.

I here propose the following: *Homosexuality is female sexism (Earth Mother fixation) welded to male body idolatry.* Well and good, as far as it goes. As we know, heterosexuality exhibits its *own* "germs" (thanks to the former L.A. mayor Bradley and in so many words to those pillars of hypocrisy, Anita Bryant and Wayne Newton) in the mode of duplicity, fraudulence and incompleteness. To the degree it refuses to androgynize, heterosex falls into male sexism (Trinity fixation).

To reiterate, besides the dubious contribution of making too many babies in an overcrowded world, straight is in no way superior to gay. The two camps differ only in their pre-chosen, pre-cognitive state of spiritual evolution; and only later in heredity and environment. A gay gene or undersized hypothalamus, along with the earthbound dust, sweat and blood of Oedipus, are secondary to the spiritual reasons for being on the planet.

The heterosexual male fetus or child dimly opts *not to be* the mother, but stops short of nihilating her, unless she be a vile witch or murderous Lillith. The redneck/Marine (Self-Amputee) considers murdering the father, but falls short in his mission. Father and father identification survive. The nihilation goes only this far: "I hate his guts" or "I'd like to murder the S.O.B." Continuity, albeit of a strained or hostile variety, remains. The Amputee, instead of nihilating the father, murders surrogate males in war and symbolically in sports. Nevertheless, these existential, day-to-day, knee-jerk choices, for both straight and gay, serve a hidden Higher Destiny.

The homosexual, however, *is* morally *superior* in rejecting warfare. Gayness ushers in the Golden Age by transcending Male-as-Warrior. It presides over the smashing of the golden calf of prejudice and power-mongering. By both being and not being (transcending) itself, gayness teaches mankind, like Rodney King, how to "get along." Homophile worship of the male body, rather than violation of a religious taboo, invokes the primal beauty of God. Just as all roads lead to Rome, the gay man reaches out to the Male to find God. It's his special task, no matter how Herculean, to throw off centuries of accumulated guilt and realign the quest as sacred.

Reunion with Eternal Father is a step homosexuality must take to achieve true androgyny—just as heterosexuality, to advance spiritually, must incorporate its homosexual component. However, Earth-Mother (the female principle) doesn't unilaterally bestow androgyny. A balancing act of merging with Eternal Father is required. Otherwise creation stagnates in a murky, dispirited mother-swamp. Troy Perry frees his flock, like water fowl caught in an oil slick, from obsessive female identity. Androgyny is the healing balm that defuses sexual tension and renders warfare obsolete. Both male and female camps, every truly spiritual gathering, and angels applauding in Heaven, heave a sigh of relief at the dismantling of sexism.

To repeat: Should a gay man, as God's ordained child, have anything to do with organized religion? Should he, rather, shun it like the plague?

Unless religion shows generosity of Spirit—a capacity to transcend Ego-body and move into the Psychic-Intuitional—he risks regression to a worse alienation and schizophrenia. He's seen enough ostracism and denial, and with AIDS, sickness and death. To hell with further martyrdom! Worship is meant to celebrate unity in diversity, to promote love and reconciliation. How often does a church reflect undiluted SPIRIT>Mind>body? True Oneness? Nonetheless, to counter heterosexual bigotry, he should try—it takes courage and grandeur—to commingle with the religious mainstream. Until the heterosexual majority recognizes and heals its own notness—its suppressed gay alter-self that it is and isn't free not to be—it will remain a spiritual amputee, a drowsing dinosaur of the elect.

Inborn integrity, free of the guilt religion stamps on his forehead like a scarlet letter, guides the gay man to reunion and communion with Spirit. In or outside a church, a Western or Eastern religion, since at their core the major religions (Hinduism, Judaism, Buddhism, Christianity, Islam and Baha'i), are One in original intent and content, what does it matter? They all teach, until perverted by their practitioners, brotherly love and planetary survival and advancement. Their outer trappings, their schisms and holy wars—their homophobia—are illusory projections of separate body. In their arrogant and vicious tininess, like those who crucified Christ, "They know not what they do."

To progress toward Atman, the gay man must connect and merge, aided by the Other as Brother, with Higher Self. How preferable true spiritual awakening to membership in a church or church building (not so different from a "pagan" casino or snobbish country club!). He has but to burst through the shell of allegiance to Ego-Body, which he mistakes for the Eternal, to discover an embryonic priest enshrined within.

Above all, he mustn't buy into the myth that he has less spiritual worth than a heterosexual peer. By daring to diverge from the norm, he catalyzes human progress. Through the refining flames of the three Ordinations, he earns the rank of High Priest. As such, he's invisibly present at every *spiritual* observance on the planet. In transcending lower self, he is the "not" (the leaven) that shapes and ennobles the loaf of Being. His notness is transmuted into a luminous Fullness. He reflects and expresses, if outrageously, the Divine. Who can say that at least some of the infinite faces of God aren't playful or celebratory? Or that a fine madness isn't an ingredient of holiness?

Lastly, one may object, how can a "not" complete Being? Sartre himself provides the answer. Existence passes into essence (nonbeing into beingness, experience into knowledge) through the interweaving of freedom (Nothingness) into the fabric of Being. Just as the nucleus of every human body cell contains 46 spiral strands of DNA, a complementary set from each parent, so does Nothingness intertwine and "haunt" Being. Freedom is the chasm across which what-is-no-longer passes into what-is-not-yet. It is the heady vacuum that ejects a fledgling bird from the nest in order to soar free in limitless space. Without a danger-fraught plunge, there can be no evolution to a higher form.

Perfection, it can be said, has meaning insofar as it informs the struggle out of imperfection back toward itself. Similarly, by breaking with Continuity, homosexuality, through its own kind of procreation (or germs), shows a unique Continuity in being not only perfect and beautiful but of the quintessence of Being.

Homosexuality is the calling-into-question of heterosexuality that forces the latter to examine itself in the glaring spotlight of self- and soul-analysis. Free thought provides the basis for Hegel's thesis/antithesis=synthesis (which I attempt to employ in this document). Homosexuality is the freedom of angels to cavort in far-off galaxies or remain in Safe Court, to join the Warrior God in a cosmic safari or stay home and attend to Mother Goddess. All are spiritually valid options.

In conclusion, freedom makes love possible. Love is the highest expression and badge of divinity. Love unites being and becoming, essence and existence; turns emptiness into joyful meaningfulness. Freedom is requisite to forming love bonds. Just as these bonds must be continually renewed, reshaped and transcended, so lower body fixation must ever die to higher forms of Love. Spirit inspires, only to limit and remold, an adolescent need to deviate and rebel. (All sexuality expresses rebellion, that is to say, participates in death, even while interwoven with and integral to life.)

Low order freedom is progressively chiseled, ground and polished into a gem worthy of sacrifice at a higher altar. This is the altar of Spirit and Higher Self, which exactly coincide. The search for Mister Right is let go because *you are that male*. The reward is a reborn, breathtaking Meaningfulness.

A final word. Passage from the Formative (macho-sexist) phase into the Golden Age depends upon wide-scale androgynization. The assimilation of a root but severed homosexuality (First Ordination), ordained (Second Ordination) and assimilated (Third Ordination) into the world process pays a huge dividend for both the individual and society. For nothing worth having, not an iota of earthly or heavenly Meaning, is ever lost.

Long-term happiness is the litmus test of the rightness of being gay. To the degree the gay man embraces and takes responsibility for his station as High Priest, so will Meaning exponentially increase. That is what is meant by "Love knows no bounds." And what is Love but the animus behind the eternal cycle of separation and return, common to all religions.

And the gay man's appreciation of the image of God in a priestly co-celebrant or lover.

The quest for Gay Self (Being for Others expanded into Universal Self) reflects this process. Homosexuality is the High Priesthood of man's becoming, of his upreach and inreach toward God. And finally, of *God's reach for Himself*. Like the shaman he inherently is, the gay man mirrors the Divine for his fellow man. He shows them *Who God Is*.

I therefore affirm that homosexuality, despite its origin in the rebellious miasma of multiple denial (Nothingness), partakes of and fully expresses the most profound and elegant Somethingness—that is, the Divine.

GLOSSARY

Atman In Hinduism Ultimate Wholeness or Brahman. Nirvana is the blissful state of the attainment of Brahman.

Atman Project Maya (earth-embeddedness) that prevents attaining Atman (after Ken Wilber).

Baha'u'llah Prophet-Founder of the Baha'i faith, 1817-1892. Translated, it means "The Glory of God" in Farsi (formerly Persian).

Albert Camus Algerian/French existentialist author, 1913-1960. Known for the concept of absurdity in the human condition.

A Course in Miracles Published anonymously by "Foundation for Inner Peace," Tiburon, California. In a nutshell: "Nothing real can be threatened, Nothing unreal exists, Herein lies the peace of God."

Sigmund Freud Austrian-Jewish psychoanalyst, 1856-1939. Famous for subconscious motivation and the terms, Id, Ego and Super-Ego. His ideas, together with those of Sartre, form the basis for my own theory of Oedipus Complex as it applies to homosexuality.

Jean Genet French novelist and playwright, 1910-1986. Most famous for "Our Lady of the Flowers." The subject of Sartre's biography, "Saint Genet: Actor and Martyr."

Hegel German philosopher, 1770-1841. Author of "Phenomenology of the Spirit." Along with Heidegger, a major influence on the atheist Sartre.

Jean Paul Sartre French existentialist and author of "Being and Nothingness," 1905-1980. Due to his importance in formulating "The High Priesthood of Being Gay," I list three of his more difficult but basic concepts in regard to the human psyche.

Being-In-Itself Non-conscious Being. It is the Being of the phenomenon and overflows the knowledge which we have of it. It is a plenitude and we can say of it only that it is.

Being-For-Itself The nihilation of Being-in-itself; consciousness conceived as a lack of Being, a desire for Being, a relation to Being. By bringing Nothingness into the world the For-itself can stand out from Being and judge other beings by knowing what it is not.

Being-For-Others There arises a new dimension of Being in which my Self exists outside as an object for others. The For-others involves a perpetual conflict as each For-itself seeks to recover its own Being by making an object of the other.

Sri Ramakrishna A Hindu "Godman," 1836-1886. A reincarnation of both Rama and Krishna, combining their mystical, austere and sacred qualities. The subject of a biography by the gay writer, Christopher Isherwood, entitled "Ramakrishna and His Disciples."

The Three Ordinations The author's idea of homosexual evolution divided into three parts: 1.) The nihilation of earth father, 2.) coming out and 3.) rejoining earth and celestial father in the reattainment of Atman.

Ken Wilber 1949- Author of "Up From Eden." I'm indebted to him for the concept of the Great Chain of Being, especially its three most relevant phases in present-day man: Mythic Membership, Mental Egoic and Psychic Intuitional.

(And from the Bible, the utterances of His Holiness, Christ, especially as reinterpreted by the Great Apostle Paul.)

www.ingramcontent.com/pod-product-compliance
Lightning Source LLC
Chambersburg PA
CBHW022247290526
45785CB00015B/372